THE GREAT GO MISSION

The Great Position

G.D. Dowey

RIGHTEOUS ACTS PUBLISHING
2020

Copyright © 2020 Gregory Dowey
All rights reserved.

Unless otherwise indicated, all Scripture quotations are from the ESV® Bible (The Holy Bible, English Standard Version®), copyright © 2001 by Crossway, a publishing ministry of Good News Publishers. Used by permission. All rights reserved.

Scripture taken from *The Message*. Copyright © 1993, 1994, 1995, 1996, 2000, 2001, 2002. Used by permission of NavPress Publishing Group.

Scripture quotations marked (NLT) are taken from the Holy Bible, New Living Translation copyright © 1996, 2004, 2007 by Tyndale House Foundation. Used by permission of Tyndale House Publishers, Inc. Carol Stream, IL 60188. All Rights Reserved.

Quotes taken from The Holy Bible, King James Version (KJV), are in the public domain.

Excerpts from *Going GLOCAL: Networking Local Churches for Worldwide Impact*, copyright © 2006 by Gene Wood. Used by permission of the author.

Quotes taken from *Striking the Match: How God is Using Ordinary People to Change the World through Short-Term Missions* by George G. Robinson, copyright © 2008 by e3 Resources. Used by permission of the author.

Quotes taken from all other works cited are in the public domain or adhere to the guidelines of fair-use.

ISBN 978-1-7359876-1-3
Library of Congress Control Number: 2020923617

Righteous Acts Publishing
Irmo, South Carolina

This work is dedicated
to the one who "goes" near and far
to make disciples baptizing them
in the name of the
Father, the Son, and the Holy Spirit.

TABLE OF CONTENTS

FOREWORD	VII
PREFACE	IX
INTRODUCTION	XIII
A RISKY BUSINESS	1
UPSIDE-DOWN WORLD	21
FANATICS & ZEAL	41
A CASUAL THEOLOGY = A CASUAL PLAN	63
YOUR CALL	85
HOMOGENEITY MISSION	107
STR	127
MISSION PLANNING	145
STP	159
BUCKING THE SYSTEM	175
DIRECTION	193
BIBLIOGRAPHY	211
ACKNOWLEDGEMENTS	215
ABOUT THE COVER PHOTO	217
ABOUT THE AUTHOR	219
OTHER BOOKS BY GD DOWEY	221

FOREWORD

What can an author possibly add to the library of work on missions? I believe Pastor Greg Dowey is making a needed contribution to the body of work available.

When I wrote my book <u>Going Glocal, impacting local churches for worldwide impact</u> in 2006 I searched the internet to find "glocal." The only reference I was able to locate at that time was a phone service provider in South America.

Today, it is popular. A couple years back a group from International Management Consultants invited me to join a "Glocal" group of IMC. Our world has changed and how we do work in this world must change or become irrelevant.

There are several reasons you should take time to read what Greg Dowey has written:

1. He is a local church pastor who is DOING what he writes about. I have known Greg for close to 15 years and traveled with him extensively. He lives what he speaks of. It is time local churches recapture their centrality in God's Great Commission. The personal stories and experiences he shares illustrate his heart for what he writes of.
2. He pastors a NORMAL SIZE congregation. Of course mega churches have their signature international ministries. Greg proves all churches can be involved in what he labels STP (short-term projects). Size of your congregation does not prohibit you having a Glocal ministry.

3. He is not attempting to disparage traditional long-term missions or mission organizations. He is advocating all churches consider ADDING GLOCAL to their outreach portfolio. As you read you will quickly see Greg is well-read in the annals of missiology and pays tribute to the legacy left us.
4. He is firmly grounded in BIBLICAL THINKING. Throughout the book Greg returns us to Scripture. Assumptions plus logic equals conclusions. His assumption is that all the church does should be founded on the Word of God.

I suggest you begin reading with the final chapter, <u>Direction</u>. In this chapter Pastor Greg lays out specifically what he encourages your church to consider and why. The remainder of the book explores our mission history and optional strategies and why they are lesser in practicality, effectiveness and for health within your local church.

If your church goes GLOCAL you'll never go back.

Dr. Gene Wood
President/Founder
Word4Asia Consulting International

Preface

In my hometown we have a fantastic old deli called Groucho's. I've been going there for at least 45 years. On the menu is a sandwich known as the STP. No one really knows what STP stands for, but everyone knows what's on it. A fat sub roll, with micro-sliced roast beef and turkey stacked high, topped with melted swiss cheese and sprinkled with real bacon bits. They bring it to you hot, with their signature— but secret— Formula 45 sauce on the side to dip your sandwich. No one knows why they call it the 45 sauce, but everyone knows what it tastes like. It's akin to a thousand island dressing, but 1000 times better. The STP...if you've been to Groucho's you've had it. If you haven't, I feel sorry for you.

In the mission world, STM stands for short-term missionary/mission. It is the acronym juxtaposing LTM, or long-term mission/missionary. I'll talk at length about the STM, but I propose a new term, STP...the short-term project. Many well-meaning, evangelistic missionary minded Christians are familiar with STM/STP but have fallen short of really grasping it. The word "mission" and its different forms has become somewhat ambiguous in describing people doing God's work out there somewhere. I would like to define, in a narrower scope, why and how we go and what, specifically, we do. The continued nebulous approaches to God's mission are undermining Truth. Vision for the accomplishment of the mission is sparse. Generally, no one takes chances anymore, and no one really sees it as holy. Mission work has been transfigured (not in a good way) into doing good deeds.

Churches need to do more projects in obedience to the Great Commission and for the sake of the Gospel, rather than going just to go. Good works and feel-good endeavors are a dime a dozen in twenty-first century church work. Doing good stuff is not a bad thing. I enjoy doing good for others, but Christ's dangerous-on-all-accounts command to go and make disciples has been replaced by an altruistic "go and make yourself feel good that you are doing good." I seek to take on this giant task by simply calling your attention to how it's happening, then demonstrate using experiences and accounts, how you, your church, or your small group can get involved in God's project of glorifying His Son Jesus.

Just recently, my wife and I returned from our Christian joy and work in a land located on the opposite side of the planet from the Southern United States. It's nine thousand miles away. Clandestine in nature and aimed to protect our brothers and sisters, we will not disclose exact locations. But in running a mission organization disclosure is almost necessary at times— to update our donors, those who pray, our church, and the participants. So, in a place you know well (you'll figure it out by the end of the first chapter), in cities and towns you've never heard of, usually characterized by being in the middle of nowhere, a normal question from those Christians of another world arises: How can we be like American Christians?

Painfully, not trying to discredit, discourage, or even make a judgmental theological statement on someone's salvation, I attempt to answer their questions. Because when I compare their commitment to Christ to ours, I have to seriously ponder what makes us real Christ-followers. Comparatively, we live in the lap of luxury. I'm talking about the American church. Our church buildings are carpeted, cooled, and commonly large enough to handle masses. The church buildings in the middle of Asia may have concrete floors, but if not, the dirt floor is okay to them. If you travel there in the summer and you are used to 72 degrees while worshipping, then take a portable fan with you because the ones they have mounted in the ceiling usually only blow the breeze around a little. And if you don't do crowds, then don't even bother getting on the plane because personal space is a commodity not for sale in the East.

Looking around, rapidly trying to process the sights and sounds, knowing they are sincere, I try to intelligently diagnose their inquiry. Upon learning their plight, trials, and woes, I have a serious dilemma, "Why does God trust them to suffer and hurt for Him more than He does me?" Believe me, it's not a position I envy or necessarily want to be in, but the facts are there, their persecution is more like the early believers than anywhere else on the earth. More of them know and depend on the presence and power of God than most of us. And if you want to argue that point, then I've proven mine.

If you are a Christian, then understand you are a missionary. Here's another question for you: Are you wholly committed to the risk to go courageously to share Jesus? You have a mission to carry out the Gospel to wherever and whomever. For most of us, our commitment to share Jesus and to make disciples can be a thousand times better than it is now. If you have never gone on a STP and experienced the power of God working mightily through you and your team, I feel sorry for you as my brother or sister. Please take time at least once in your life to enjoy the STP.

GD Dowey
Columbia, SC

INTRODUCTION

Great Commission work among western churches for the last three hundred years, known as "missions," has changed and is still changing today. Churches of past generations, those which started before the 1980's, settled into a systematic plan of going to other regions, nations, and lands. They joined in cooperation with other like churches to go to places where the Gospel had never been preached. Those called out, the men and women tapped to go, were labeled long-term missionaries, or LTM for short. Mission organizations providing financial support for the missionaries sprouted up out of the increasing demands to cross the oceans with the message of Jesus. Churches by and large participated by including a line item on their budgets, and cooperated with congregations similar in doctrine, to send more and more ambassadors for Jesus. Our Lord told us to go, and we responded boldly.

Over the decades and centuries, a few of these LTM became famous, usually posthumously, once their work was published by their family members. But for the most part, the men and women crossing denominational boundaries are unknown to the modern-day church. Going, giving up the American dream, and dedicating yourself totally to God's work is only admirable at best among most Christians. Their work orders were outlined in the book of Acts. Paul's missionary journeys set the stage for missions and modern missions. To "Go [therefore] and make disciples of all nations, baptizing them in the name of the Father and of the Son and of the Holy Spirit, teaching them to observe all that I have commanded you" (Matt. 28:19,20), involves preaching the Word (evangelism & discipleship), starting churches, and giving people the Word of God (Bibles). It must be continued today regardless of the methods relating to how.

Those early LTM struggled and suffered in foreign lands because of language barriers. They fought rejection, risking physical and emotional torture. They starved, yet they fed on being obedient to the words of our Lord and Savior Jesus by starting schools, hospitals, and orphanages, in addition to planting churches. They are largely responsible for translating the Bible into the language of the people of remote and desolate lands. Countless have been martyred, and maybe, just maybe, it made the last page on the local newspaper in their hometown. Long-term missionaries have been held in high esteem, and rightly so. Forsaking the American Dream of wealth, relaxation, and coziness, men and women of God ditched the hope of luxurious living for something better— God's plan. 'Out of sight, out of mind' was the silent motto among many people in regard to LTM. Their heroism was unsung and, in many respects, still is today.

In an age where preachers, pastors, and church workers become renowned and get rich via the Gospel, there have been tens of thousands that have been murdered for it. The reward of these LTM was exactly what Hebrews 11:35-40 promised,

> *Some were tortured, refusing to accept release, so that they might rise again to a better life. Others suffered mocking and flogging, and even chains and imprisonment. They were stoned, they were sawn in two, they were killed with the sword. They went about in skins of sheep and goats, destitute, afflicted, mistreated—of whom the world was not worthy—wandering about in deserts and mountains, and in dens and caves of the earth. And all these, though commended through their faith, did not receive what was promised, since God had provided something better for us, that apart from us they should not be made perfect.*

Advancements in modern day travel and communication have made things easier in some respects. Long-term doesn't have to be long term anymore. Short-term missionaries are a relatively new thing. Yes, they are called STM. What used to take months in just travel, now takes less than a day. Cultural barriers have been broken down by capitalism and free market trade. Churches that were once iffy about giving to missionary work outside of their congregations, now participate by organizing their own trips and projects annually. Larger churches have hired their own missionary pastor that plans and executes STM for the entire body. All of this is great news, but with it comes a caveat.

Notice that this introduction began with the words, "Great Commission." Every evangelical Christian committed to carrying it out knows that it involves going forward with Jesus' command to make disciples. When that charge becomes purely social ministry or we substitute some good deeds for preaching the Gospel, I'm not so sure that we can call it missions anymore. Let's continue to expand the Kingdom. Let's press onward to preach to the unknown people groups of the world; let's make sure we prioritize the making of disciples as the main thing we do. However, we cannot confuse the body by reducing the message of salvation in Christ alone with some cool 21st century travel to another country to repair a roof and pass it off as the mission of the church! Good deeds, operations of relief and love, and construction projects in the name of Jesus are wonderful, but they are not surrogate work for the real work of the missionary being obedient to the Great Commission.

Let me say it another way: Things are changing, but it's paramount that we don't replace kind deeds and works for the preaching of the Gospel and planting new works. The progress of the Great Commission is when we keep pressing to go where people have not been reached with the Gospel and to continue to reach people groups that have never heard about the love of Jesus. We go boldly. We go obediently. We go purposefully. We go in love, but let's just remember to go.

Chapter One
A RISKY BUSINESS

"God has entrusted the ministry of the Word to us, not its results."
-R.C. Sproul

"...Barnabas and Paul, men who have risked their lives for the name of our Lord Jesus Christ. -Acts 15:25-26

PHAN LI SQUEEZED THE VAN'S steering wheel a little tighter after she pressed the screen button on her smart phone ending the conversation with her brother. Tears promptly flooded her eyes, but she hurriedly wiped them away, struggling to mask her pain so she could concentrate on seeing the road ahead. Autumn, my astute Chinese friend and interpreter, yelled to me at the back of the extended vehicle in succinct, paused, Asian, pronunciation, "Pas-tor Greg... can you pray... for... Sister Phan?" I did not hear her because my head was bowed, and my eyes were closed... in iTunes reverence listening to "Revival" by the Allman Brothers.

It was late on Sunday afternoon, and my team had just finished a Bible distribution somewhere in the rural, Far East near the border of DPRK, otherwise known as Kim Jong-un's North Korea. Tired, my feet were aching from the seemingly endless treks throughout the hillsides giving out the Word of God to jubilant, poverty-stricken recipients. I was desperate for "me" time as I processed the last 72 hours of experience after experience of the emotional, frenzied scenes of seas of people receiving a Bible for the first time. The expressions of gratitude on their faces and the constant Mandarin response of, "Xie, Xie", had overloaded my sensory perception. My mind was congested with the fact that we had just fed the poor in spirit...for life. All I wanted was some peace and, sensing love everywhere, I was feeling it as Gregg Allman preached the repetitive, yet fanatical tune in my ear.

The mission was over, we were on our way to meet other nationals and Chinese Christian Church (CCC) leaders for a meal, to let loose, hang out, and relax with a new network for another incredible Asian feast. There's something about the garlic aroma escaping open-aired Asian kitchens that makes me crave the authentic cuisine. The smell is heavenly, yet indescribable because I don't know how to explain the incomparable flavors of silkworms, scorpions, or cicadas that were dished on my plate. Needless to say, if you've ever had it, you can never get enough of Peking Duck.

Back in the van my head was slowly bobbing up and down while my foot tried to keep time tapping the floor, oblivious to the looming commotion with my Chinese friends. Autumn persisted until someone sitting near me shook my arm for me to look up. Slowly raising my head up, I fished the earbuds out of my ears and said with a curt, "Yeah...", and I heard her assertive tone for the first time, "Pas-tor Greg, can you pray...for our dri-ver, Sister Phan...and her mother? She just received...phone call...her mother very sick...in hospital." My two-pronged response was not as godly as it sounded. I asked, "How far are we from the restaurant? We should just wait until we get there to hold hands and pray outside of the van." That sounded spiritual didn't it? Isn't that proper Christian demonstrative form – to hold hands in a circle while praying? C'mon, I was trying to be pastoral, wasn't I?

Truth was, I was perturbed by being interrupted. My translator expressed this confused look on her face, but she had been instructed to listen to her leader, and I was the leader. She answered me sounding dissatisfied, "Oh, okay...sure...Pastor Greg. We will be there...approximately 36 minutes." The Chinese are sometimes too precise for my style. I went back to my sounds hoping to recover the selfish quiet time. But before I could get the earbuds back in, I heard a loud mobile phone ring with that tacky Xiqu music. Xiqu is traditional Chinese opera, and if you have never heard it, well, it's hard to explain...YouTube it. It was the ringtone on Sister Phan's phone. Before the dramatic, sorrowful scene unfolded in the van, I knew immediately the impending dialog that was about to take place on that mobile device. Deep inside my mind and heart it felt as if the Holy Spirit had dialed my number instead and the wireless connection was crystal clear: "You messed up Greg."

Mandarin is a musical language, but there was nothing melodious about the sounds I was soon to hear. I knew it...I knew it...Sister Phan's mother had died. It all took place in less than 120 seconds after I postponed the prayer request. Two Church of Christ guys from the Midwest, sitting in front of me, turned around to look as if to say, "You blew it!" Sister Phan pulled the van over and, turning the ignition completely off...she wept and wailed for what seemed like an hour. We all just sat there letting her grieve and convulse while some of the ladies sitting near her patted her on the back, and then, *then*...I decided to pray.

BLOWN

It's the bottom of the ninth, two outs, with two men on base, and you are up 2-0. The closer comes in. He's the guy, the relief pitcher, the fireman, the stopper. The closer, they call him. He's the guy that you count on to sew up the victory and take you to the clubhouse. He takes his warm-ups, spits, and nods his head no a few times before affirming the catcher's sign. He winds up...the stretch...here's the pitch...foul ball. The catcher gives him another sign, and he kicks toward home plate...strike! Now the count is 0-2. If there are any risk-takers out there, put your money on this guy now because his winning record speaks for itself. The sign, the pitch...wait, oh no, he leaves a hanging curve ball out over the plate...crack...back, back, back.... It's a walk-off home run. They all round the bases and there is a mob scene at home plate. In baseball, they call that a blown save.

How many blown saves are there in the church today? Doing and going on the mission and committing to the Great Commission is a sure thing. Jesus has done the work for us on the Cross (Jesus Saves!), and all we have to do is walk in obedience or start throwing strikes, so to speak, yet we leave the mission hanging and when that happens – crack – we are way, way back, with backs against the wall, and we are losing. We let the enemy walk off another homer on us. We leave the mission hanging by undercutting the Gospel, or worse, by just not going.

THE FUNDAMENTAL TASK OF THE CHRIST-FOLLOWER IS TO INTRODUCE PEOPLE TO JESUS AND TO HELP THEM GROW UP TO CHRISTIAN MATURITY.

Your Christian life will never be complete until you zealously grab on to the risky Great Commission. The fundamental task of the Christ-follower is to introduce people to Jesus and to help them grow up to Christian maturity. Listen, Christian, the church will not complete its mission of winning souls and making disciples in your community until the Great Commission is fully exercised through you and your church. It's risky because not only will God take you beyond your comfort zone but it will cost you your self-worth, exposing you to become God's worth. Living out God's mission is dangerous, but it's the life He expects for His followers. Taking on God's mission without being under His directives and commands is like being absent without leave from the military. You are still a soldier on paper, but you have jeopardized the mission and weakened the ranks.

STP INTRODUCTION

I have found the best way for me and my church to accomplish Missio Dei, God's mission, in the twenty-first century: to be a proponent and participant of short-term projects (a.k.a. STP). It is a project that is planned with the heart of those early mission trips of Paul in the book of Acts. They should be planned accordingly, becoming an undertaking for the entire congregation. Short-term projects are events in the name of Jesus, but are simple. Simple because they go to the very heart of the Gospel to evangelize and make disciples. Simple because there is a difference in today's short-term mission trip and the STP. Short-term mission trips led by local churches have become popular, yet they are generic to the Great Commission. Just going somewhere in the name of Jesus while providing staples to the poor doesn't necessarily mean a church is accomplishing

God's mission. A lot of the services performed by short-term mission groups are just the foundation of what Christians should do. Many churches already do kindly gestures for those in need and erroneously call them missions. It's called ministry. In contrast, the STP should be laser-focused on carrying out the Great Commission. By continually calling attention to the reason, the Gospel, we are outlining the purpose of making disciples. And while leading this way, it may just get us ready for revival.

Gospel projects and STP's are simplistic in nature, but churches constantly struggle to do them. Why? Understand, we didn't sign up for God's mission, He chose us. He ordered us to go into all the world and preach and teach Jesus. In other words, it's not the plan we would have chosen for ourselves. Our response, however, should be one of obedience and one of blessing because He has commanded us to join Him. What motivates us to go? I promise you it will not be your profession of faith. What matters is that He possesses all of you and me! It is my possession of faith, and faith alone. Does He possess all of you? The inner baptism of your soul needs to be just as real as your outward one. Baptism doesn't save us. Only faith in what Christ has done for us on the Cross can save us. Faith alone.

A. S. K.

It is up to you and me to discover the intricacies and complexities of living out a missional life. God is not going to write them in the sky, send via text, or speak to you in emoji; nor is He going to ship it to you overnight Fed Ex after you pray ten minutes for it. This isn't Wile E. Coyote ordering those absurd contraptions from ACME to catch the Road Runner, receiving them immediately. Those details are only found out by living a devoted, committed, and praying life in Christ. In Luke 11 Jesus outlines how to discover this life:

ASK, SEEK, KNOCK.

Jesus tells this micro story with mammoth implications about a man knocking on his neighbor's door late at night wanting to borrow three loaves of bread to feed a guest. The house was quiet, the kids were asleep, and the owner of the house was no doubt drifting into R.E.M. sleep when there was a relentless banging on the door. It was not a discreet knock and thank God modern doorbells and cameras were not available. By now the other neighbors were perturbed about the situation. Can you imagine, "Please, please, if you just give me three loaves of bread, I will leave you alone. C'mon! Please! Pretty please!" The word used in the Greek for the incessant knocking means "shameless persistence." The Lord Jesus is giving us the command and luxury to shamelessly seek Him by constantly coming to Him in prayer and asking. But as our cowardice interferes, we shrink back from rightly being ushered into the throne room to encounter His majesty. How many have shirked their duties as missionary voices and become shamefully inconsistent?

AWOL, Aimless, ABSENT & Awry

My brother-in-law, Charles, was relocated from the South with his business corporation to Utah back in the mid-1980's. In a phone conversation with my sister, Cheryl, soon after their move I asked her what she had learned about the religious front by being in Salt Lake City. She told me about the Jack Mormons. Yeah, seems that the Mormons have difficulty with people who signed up to be a part of their religion but have lost interest. Some Mormons don't go to church anymore! We didn't see that one coming. A Jack Mormon is a Mormon gone AWOL. They are absent without leave from the Mormon religion and do not observe the religious rituals. Come to think of it...I know a lot of Jack Christians. They have gotten it all backwards. Which led me to flip it around and create my own acronym for their lack of commitment:

LOW-A

It means "Looking Occupied...Wandering Aimlessly."

A majority of Christians are absent in the mission work of the church. We are not devoted to discovering the joy of adventure in serving the Almighty. Maybe, we are in church several times a year looking like everything is all right between us and Jesus. Only it just looks like we are busy while wandering nomadically in a religious circle with no purpose in sight.

As an online slang dictionary defines *jack* as meaning "nothing," I wonder if it is too early in this book to state that most Christ-followers are doing jack when it comes to mission work? No, it's not. Why? Look at the faces at your church. Do you see people looking occupied, while in reality they are wandering aimlessly in this world? The twenty-first century American Christian is gifted (more than our Christian forerunners) in creating an eminence front that looks like we are busy carrying out Christ's command to make disciples of all nations but, sadly, a majority of professing believers are clueless when it comes to doing mission work.

I suppose we can assume mission work has gone awry in America. Well-meaning Christians have been hijacked by false claims to the Gospel by fake leaders. Instead of intense, rousing news stories about the difficulties of sharing the Good News of Jesus Christ in resistant nations, we hear outlandish true stories of crazy self-professed and selfish Christian leaders. Television evangelists are asking for $54 million to buy a new jet. The reason? Allow me to quote: "I really believe that if Jesus was physically on the earth today, he wouldn't be riding a donkey...He'd be in an airplane preaching the gospel all over the world." No joking, Paul may have taken this guy out with just one punch...well, Paul would have at least punched him with a combination of spiritual blows to the heart.

The nation that once led the world in sending missionaries is now seeing our missionary forces dwindling in number. What do we blame? Our lack of faith? Inaccurate interpretation of the Scriptures? Poor organization? Inept theology? Inability to adapt to the times? Yes, and one thing is obvious over the past several generations: it is easy to get off track in being a true servant of the Lord. Even the way we raise money for mission work has turned into a circus philosophy straight from P.T. Barnum.

Once, long-term missionaries (LTM) from the past were asked to sacrifice and suffer for the Gospel. Leaving one's home for years, along with the comforts of American life, and forsaking the thrills of entertainment, were built into their spiritual long-term contracts. Giving up the American dream for the purposes of the Gospel was stringent criteria for "going." It was risky business. Now that we've created short-term missionaries (STM) that are asked to participate by flying to the other side of the globe, it's billed as a "sight-seeing, fact gathering, prayer walking" adventure called missions. They come back and complain about jetlag or how bad the food tasted. When asked about the trip, they respond, "Oh yeah, it was great." Sadly, the results are minuscule. Why? There is no vision, only accolade seekers.

BIGGER RISKS

Your presence in another country does not necessarily indicate mission work, nor does staying home mean you are dodging your responsibilities. One of the best missionaries was one who never really stayed on the mission field for a long time. Luther Rice, the famed missionary of two hundred years ago, set sail to Calcutta, India, with Adonirum Judson, but soon returned to the United States and spent the rest of his life raising money for mission work. Prayers, encouragement, wisdom, leadership, money and ability to gather resources, and the sharing about the work that friends and family were doing, inspired and provided in massive ways for those chosen to go. You see, when we participate in mission work, we all go whether we leave home or not. So, how do I get in on this risky business? By taking the biggest risks of all! Try these on for size...

The biggest risk of your Christian life may be just keeping Moses' Commandments 1-4. Principally, they focus our attention on God and His holiness and away from our selfishness. They are about worship and obedience while warning against the evils of idolatry. By becoming a member of a church that worships with a great passion for God, and devotion to the Great Commission, you will sell out your so-called friends, your supposed days off, and your alleged false dreams for something that is real.

The biggest risk to your bank account will be to get involved in God's mission for your life. Going on short-term projects, supporting mission causes, and praying to be a part of a Great Commission church may cause you to live a middle-class life. Hurts doesn't it? Christians should face up to it and get on with God's business.

The biggest risk to your family life will be a commitment to God's mission. You will lead them and steer them towards God important experiences instead of taking them to endless weekend baseball, basketball, and dance tournaments. The risk isn't involving your children in extracurricular activities, it's taking them to God. They may just commit to Him, and He may just call them to something really great.

The biggest risk to your ego will be choosing to clothe others, feed street people and beggars, spend your money on those that don't and can't work, forgo that new car in favor of a used one, and to visit dirty people in prison. It's not Great Commission work, but it's not just social work either. It's Christian ministry. Loving others by leading a lifestyle of giving should be part of the norm for every Christ-follower. Christian obedience and mission work are not glamorous, and shame on those who try to make it so.

The biggest risk to achieving the American dream comes by committing to the mission of reaching lost people with the Gospel. You can't do both? Why? Time...it's running out and there is only so much of it left for you. Jesus says you can't serve both God and money. What are you waiting for? It's time to go!

The biggest risk of all is for you to do SOMETHING. Doing nothing is a massive holy risk that I am not willing to take. Neither should you. Ask God today where your holy risk is located. A holy risk puts you in a great position to live out the Great Commission.

ON TO GOD'S POSSIBLE MISSION

Tom Cruise's stance on Scientology is idiotic, but the dude can still fetch a mean action scene in the dramatic motion picture series, *Mission: Impossible*. Deadly operations, near misses, and the sound of explosions have you on the edge of your seat, senses engaged, simultaneous tensing of the muscles and nerves, absorbing you into this superficial, impossible super-secret spy thriller. But it's those opening lines, especially in the television episodes of the 1960s-70s, that really draw you in: "Your mission Jim [remember Peter Graves?], should you choose to accept it...," delivered via reel-to-reel tape, if you know what that is. After the mission was explained, the tape would "self-destruct in ten seconds." Also included was the treacherous warning: "should you or any member of your I.M. [Impossible Mission] Force be captured or killed the secretary will disavow any knowledge of your existence." Often, the impossible mission was to cause the overthrow of some despot or vile dictator. And just like a good story, there is character change, a plot twist, and the apparent ridiculously impractical resolution. The writer, producer, and director's goal: You, shaking your head at the end saying, "That...was...impossible!"

God's mission for you and me is to boldly preach and courageously live out the Gospel of Jesus Christ in such a way that others shake their heads in wonderment. Of course it is difficult. Of course there are spiritual near misses and relational explosions going on and off all around us, but it is never impossible. The Christian knows everything is possible with God. Have you noticed that just about every theme, story, and character development in the Bible seems impossible? Creation begins with what scientists for years have called an impossibility. The Latin phrase for God's creation by that divine fiat (let it be done) is *ex nihlio* meaning "out of nothing." We cannot comprehend that event. We just take it in by faith. The Cross of Christ causes us to wince in stupefaction, questioning the why and how.

IT IS DIFFICULT… BUT IT IS NEVER IMPOSSIBLE.

The flood and the ark, the plagues and the exodus, and Jonah and the big fish all seem like tall tales to a majority of the world. Yet, it is the impossibility of them all that points us to our great God. He thrives in it. The impossible realm is something nebulous, and what we call supernatural, while God calls it home.

Abraham's call upon his life, and the promise that his lineage would be as great as the number of stars, started out as speculative. When Moses was standing before God at the burning bush and was told he would be the emancipator of God's people from Pharaoh, the thought of "ridiculous" must have crossed his mind before submission. On paper, Peter, James, and John's resumes would send a typical twenty-first century corporate headhunter in another direction, but the Holy Spirit develops their unbelievable character, changing them to become believable carriers of the Gospel. From alpha to omega, God's message of the mission is entirely humanly unimaginable, and if it could be read in one sitting like a short story, many would receive it as preposterous.

The fact is the Great Commission goes much deeper. It is risky. It's more bananas than we can imagine. It's not an "aha" moment of finally seeing that Jesus has issued an imperative for us. No, it is understanding that when we bow the knee to Christ as Lord and Savior, we bow to allegiance to His call on our lives. So, here is the question early on: have you gone? Not just on a mission trip, but have you committed to go with Him wherever He leads? Plainly, has your heart already gone with Jesus and wherever He takes you? If not, now is the time to pledge your love for Him and go.

ON THE BORDER OF RISK

I was in a church meeting near the border of Vietnam, giving out Bibles to locals, and I was asked to preach. That's unheard of in that area of the world. I reminded the pastor that it was against the law for me to preach the Gospel in a meeting, and he quickly let me know he would take the blame for any problems. It turned out to be a major blessing for me. While there, the pastor related to our team the history of the church in his region, mentioning a cemetery nearby where several American missionaries were buried. I excitedly begged, "Please take me!" We traveled a backroad and then climbed up a hillside through brush. Chinese cemeteries are often not as well manicured or perpetually cared for as they are in our country. The grass was knee high, the climb perilous, and after finally reaching the peak I discovered an old graveyard long forgotten, and one you will likely never see. The writing on the tombstones was almost indecipherable because of the neglect. The carvings were weathered, and the stones were crumbling. I got out my mobile phone and took a picture. I could barely make out the words:

> **TIL HE COME**
> **Loving Memory of**
> **Rev. Henry Zehr Missionary and Christian**
> **April 11th 1876 to April 10th 1904**

He didn't make it to his twenty-eighth birthday. I got back home and Googled Reverend Henry Zehr and buried in the corner of a back page in a small town's newspaper was a passing article on him. He was sent by the Christian Missionary Alliance group. Born in the Midwest, he came to Christ as a teenager, answered God's call for a mission in the Far East, began to study Mandarin. He contracted smallpox in southern China and died on the mission field. That's it. From what you know about mission work overseas a hundred years ago, you can probably fill in the blanks.

As I stared at his fading tombstone, I thought about how many other Christ-followers had obeyed God, left the comforts of their homes in America, and maybe met an untimely death while sharing the Gospel. How many of them were there? Hundreds? Thousands? How many of them suffered, maybe writhed in pain at the hands of those who rejected the Gospel? How many were ignored, spat upon, or sucker-punched by locals? Nearby Zehr's burial place, was a grave marker for the three-year-old child of one the missionaries from a hundred years ago. I can't imagine the torture of knowing the risks to the health of your family but going anyway, let alone the pain of burying one of your own children on the mission field. Beside the child's grave was the headstone of a pastor's wife from the early 1900's, and as I made my way precariously around the overgrown, brushy mountaintop, I saw many, many more.

Years ago, the calling to follow Christ in a foreign country wasn't met with "God, protect me from harm and give me traveling mercies." No, it was, "I have decided to follow Jesus...no turning back, no turning back." These days, the very first prayer request churches have for their traveling missionary group is for "safe travel."

> **"It is a sad sin when we take God's mercies and use them in rebellion against Him."**
> **-CH SPURGEON**

It's a great prayer request, and David often prays for safety and security in the Old Testament, but it was not likely first on the long-term missionary's prayer list two hundred years ago. And it was probably not on the Wednesday night prayer list at all two thousand years ago as Paul made the decision to go to distant lands.

What does "Til He come" mean? The prophet Hosea mainly spoke to the Northern Kingdom of Israel, sometimes called Ephraim and represented by the city Samaria. The great British preacher, C.H. Spurgeon, talked about God's people in Israel in Hosea: "It is a sad sin when we take God's mercies and use them in rebellion against Him." Mutiny & insurrection describe Israel here, as Hosea writes, because the people had become hard towards God. He calls them back and in the KJV, in Hosea 10:12, he begs them to seek the Lord once again: "Sow to yourselves in righteousness, reap in mercy; break up your fallow ground: for it is time to seek the Lord, till he come and rain righteousness upon you." Ironic, it seemed to me, standing over Reverend Zehr's fallow grave, gazing at the tombstone, knowing his heart was soft for the Chinese people and that he had sought the Lord fully despite the dangers...even giving his own life. Zehr knew fully the phrase in Hosea, "...til he come...." Do you know it? If you do, then there is no turning back...no turning back.

STILL SELFISH

I can't remember where I was, but it surged through me like a lightning bolt. Someone was praying for those soon to leave for the mission field and the prayer went like this, "Father, please give them traveling mercies...." The rest of the prayer trailed off for me as I wondered if the Apostle Paul and Barnabas prayed for safety on that first mission trip. Maybe it's me, but asking God for safety on a mission trip is like saying, "Okay God, I'll go, but you have to promise me that you are going to keep me from harm, make things go smoothly, make sure I stay emotionally stable, have plenty to eat, get plenty of rest, have extra money to spend on souvenirs, and bring me back to my comfortable life...and if you don't I may not go next time."

Jesus dispels this kind of innocuous thinking as the time drew near to the Cross. "As they were going along the road, someone said to him, "I will follow you wherever you go." And Jesus said to him, "Foxes have holes, and birds of the air have nests, but the Son of Man has nowhere to lay his head" (Luke 9:57-58). Many times it's uncomfortable following, going, or even staying home for Jesus. He calls us to take the risk of faith. If you believed He has called you, then you will believe He will protect you, or maybe not. Read this book and you will not discover reckless souls on the mission field asking to suffer or be martyred...of course they were afraid. No, you will see men and women who were like Daniel in the lion's den, or the Hebrew boys in the fire. They understood that the risk was not in obeying God and going to a far-off land, but the risky business would have been if they had decided *not* to go! Saying "no" to God is far riskier than going to a terrorist-minded country or to a godless region. Just ask Jonah.

To risk, you must begin somewhere. I cannot imagine getting to heaven and seeing Jesus face to face and not have risked anything to obey Him. What does risk look like? It looks a lot like the church when they gathered around Paul and Barnabas, "So they commissioned them. In that circle of intensity and obedience, of fasting and praying, they laid hands on their heads and sent them off" (Acts 13:3 MSG). Your first step of risking with God is risking with a church that has a vision to reach their community AND the world. Churches that go outside their little community are churches that have a risking faith. Quit identifying with the mega, "Me" churches, and looking to get your fill. Stop looking to be entertained and look to be empowered. Start by looking to be a part of a church that goes to change the world when the odds are against them. That's a 'live by faith in Jesus' church. They are not gamblers, no, they trust God is going to do what He wants to do through them. You need to be a part of one of these churches.

Maybe, just maybe the greatest distance He will ever take you is 50 yards, across the street to be a fantastic missionary to that neighbor who is far, far away from God. It is possible, you know. No, it's more than that, it's probable. I think that the first word that pops into most people's heads when they hear the word missionary is *distance*. Think of it this way: God probably has you living where you live in order to be missional to that person who is far away from God and in desperate need of the Savior. My friend, Gene Wood, says, "God put two-thirds of the population of the planet in Asia, don't you think He meant something by that?" He has you where you are for a specific reason.

On a daily basis you see your neighbor getting out of their car, checking their mail, and walking their dog down the street. You most likely see them at the grocery store once a week. Have you ever asked yourself why you keep running into this person? It may sound crazy, but Jesus has ordered it for His purpose. I believe God always puts His will for your life and mine right in front of our faces. He is a Sovereign God, so don't you think He knows what He is doing by ordering your day and your steps? The greatest little labyrinth you need to solve is the short few inches between your head and heart.

A BETTER WAY

Mr. George Muller, the incredible faith filled minister of the Gospel in 19th century London, established his own mission organization on biblical principles because he and his friend in the ministry, Brother Craik, agreed that many of the other mission groups were heretical in their approach to evangelism and raising money for support. Muller writes in his autobiography that the goal of other English mission societies was that the "whole world" would be converted. Muller and Craik believed this to be unscriptural. Those mission societies cited verses from the Bible, but Muller says they basically had a poor understanding of God's Word. He laid out in his *principles of the institution* by saying, "The world will not be converted before the coming of our Lord Jesus, but while He tarries, all scriptural means should be employed for the ingathering of the elect of God." Maybe Muller's theology is different from yours, but one thing is for sure, everything he did was ordered directly from God's Holy Word.

Muller believed it to be unethical, and refused, to raise money from non-Christians. He said he would not ask them for money but would only ask believers. He believed God would use their new ministry to help the "children of God in those societies to realize their unscriptural practices." Being criticized for starting a new mission movement instead of joining an existing one, Mr. Muller further states, "We consider every believer to be called to help the cause of Christ, and we have scriptural reasons to expect the Lord's blessing on our work of faith and labor and love."

Surrendering your life to the Great Commission will do something to you. The more you go, the more you are exposed to the realities of life on this planet.

After repeatedly going on mission causes and many times being dismayed by the purpose, progress, and outcome, my wife and I decided to start our own mission/ministry organization. Our goal is simple: Give out the Word of God, the Bible. Giving away Bibles is a good thing, isn't it? I believe in sharing the Gospel, and I believe in starting churches, but putting a Bible in someone's hand who has never owned one is a particularly moving thing. If you make it your mission in life to give out the Word of God, I promise you the Holy Spirit will open all kinds of doors, and you will never be confused about God's will. Everyone admires the people who go on medical missions, disaster relief missions, and construction missions. They are called, it is needed, and God is glorified in their work. Are you on one of those teams? If not, then consider giving Bibles away…you can't go wrong. I believe He has called so many of us to call attention to the Bible because it is the Word of God. It is God talking to us and we need to listen.

The very least commitment you can make is that when you receive a graduation, birthday, or wedding invitation you resolve to always buy a Bible as a gift. I do it all of the time. It will say as much about you as it will say to them. They may receive it asking, "What is this?" or, "Where is my $100 Amazon gift card?" But years down the road, after the designer purse has been donated to charity or sold in a garage sale, the engraved Cross pen/pencil set is tucked away in a box in the attic, or that other painstakingly purchased gift sat unwanted on a closet shelf for years before being tossed...there will likely be that Bible. It might be dusty and faded, but maybe, it just may be, God's better way. His patient plan will unfold in that loved one's life.

IMPLAUSIBLE MISSION

Back to my Far East adventure with Sister Phan Li...after all the great work we had accomplished in training pastors and giving out the Word of God, I sort of blew it with a sorry attitude. What was I really risking? What kind of selfishness was I experiencing at that moment when called upon to intercede for a woman on the doorsteps of death? I don't remember. Was that live rendition of the Allman Brothers so important that I couldn't push the pause button for a five-minute prayer? Who says, "No...let's not pray now...let's pray later for a dying woman and the comfort of her daughter?" I had failed in my mission, I had failed in missional living. Maybe my prayer would not have rescued the ailing woman from death, but at the very least, and perhaps the most, I should have prayed on the spot for Sister Phan Li. Sadly, I've come to realize that it's a common thing to avoid God seeking prayer. Failing to respond to God's call has consequences, but the benefits, if you allow God to open your eyes, will lead to massive spiritual booms in your life. Or, as Christians put it, "you can grow in your faith."

I'm sure you have failed God. Very sure. You may have promised Him uninterrupted attention and perfect church attendance this morning in your quiet time if He would only.... I know, I've done it. Please hear this: nothing positions your spiritual life for peak maturity like acknowledging that you are a failure (sinner). It's called repentance. The great Reformer, Martin Luther, advocated a confessional lifestyle. John Calvin said, "Repentance is not merely the start of the Christian life, it is the Christian life." Repentance should occur daily and involve more than words. You need a physical turning around— from idolatry to following Jesus. Idolatry is the adoration of anybody or anything more than you adore God. The body of Christ is constantly met with convicted individuals who feel a need to step up with mission-minded activity. Sure, it's a fantastic thing to see people respond to the Word of God and worship while having an insatiable desire to please the Father. So let's set the stage right up front here with a statement that you desperately need before you step into the missional world: *Confession comes before mission.*

We've been tasked with an impossible mission, not an implausible one. What's the difference? It's not what the difference is, but who is the difference maker. In the theophany described by Doctor Luke in his Gospel, Gabriel visits the Virgin Mary, tells her she is favored by God, and announces the Savior. Mary's response is not just a simple question of improbability or doubt, but one out of biological absurdity. She asks, "How will this be, since I am a virgin?" Spinning through Mary's mind like an engine turning over 5000rpm was, "If God is going to favor me, then why give me an impossible mission?" I know that, because Gabriel responds with the statement we all clutch when we are faced with incredible odds. When we are backed against the proverbial wall of despair we pull out of our God-fearing little hearts, hoping it's true, "For nothing will be impossible with God" (Luke 1:37).

Yes, He has called the Christ-follower to be involved, but you and I have to confess and possess that He is King and Lord of all before we start the mission. By now, maybe you have done enough Bible study to earn doctoral credits, speak a foreign language fluently, and have more of a mission heart than Mother Teresa. Others have gone on mission trips, and participated in the mission of their respective churches, and still more have given tens of thousands of dollars, perhaps more, to the cause of Christ.

What is missing in missions? What's missing is confession of our inability to do it and our continual confession of our sin before a righteous God. Confession means we are on the right track to knowing Him and carrying out His Commission. Without confession, there is no foundation in what we do. We lack truth, and when this occurs, our mission is implausible.

Scripture speaks to seeking God: "...no one seeks for God" (Rom. 3:11). This strange line in Romans is talking about sinful, unregenerate man, seeking God. When you become a Christ-follower, you are to seek God galore! Jesus says, "Seek and you will find" for you to continually seek out God in every aspect of your life. Seeking begins every day with confession.

Every Christian should have a mission that is connected and interconnected to the Gospel of Jesus Christ. Your spiritual gift mix is given to you by the Holy Spirit for the building up of the Kingdom, namely the church. Another purpose of this book is to help you utilize God's resources— a call, a church, prayer, provisions, and experiences – by networking your God-given gifts to carry out God's mission. In Latin, it's called *Missio Dei*, and it is synonymous with the call upon Abraham's life, seen in the Great Commission in Matthew 28:18-20, Luke 9 & 10, Acts 1:8, and Acts 16, among others, and continuing to the culmination of the Gospel when Jesus returns.

A Simple Lesson

Sister Phan dried her tears, wiped her face, started the van, and thirty-six minutes later we arrived at the restaurant (I told you so). When I finally made it out from the back of the van, she fell into my pastoral arms and I held on to her as she cried more. We prayed. For a split second, I felt vindicated about my failure in delayed prayer, like I had somehow redeemed myself, but only for a second. Just as I finished praying, Reverend Cho, Phan Li's pastor whom we were meeting for dinner, walked up. Phan Li grabbed his shoulders, sobbing. He comforted her and hugged her for a moment. I was anticipating the normal chatter and rhetorical loving speech to come from the pastor. Pastors just know how to be the soothing superman in these difficult moments don't they? But this pastor wasn't just another pastor. It was there I discovered something new about the simplicity of mission work. Going, and being God's ambassador, is more than kissing babies, delivering a pallet of water, and patting brothers and sisters in Christ on the back while offhandedly promising them prayer. When you risk with God you get to encounter things that money can't buy, and handshakes can't deliver. I watched and listened, and I grew more as a pastor and believer in the next ten minutes of listening, through a translator, than I had grown in years.

The Great Go Mission

Pastor Cho pulled away from Sister Phan after letting her cry for a minute, and he put his hands on her shoulders, squaring her up, looking into her eyes assuredly with a smile, and said (as Autumn translated for me), "Sister Phan, your mother is with Jesus now. She was a Christ-follower, and is with Him. You must have trust and faith in this truth. For years you have been learning about the love of God and how He never lets us down. You've risked your life for Him, and He has never left you nor forsaken you. Sister, now is the time that you need to live it! He will give you peace. Rejoice in that fact!"

If you could have seen my face, I am sure it reflected an *aha* moment. For about ten minutes, he spoke honestly and reassuringly to her about the truth of what the Word of God says for those who are in Christ. He gave her assuring words that her mother was with the Lord. And then, as he backed up, the dear sisters of the church gathered around Phan Li, loving her, and weeping with her to give comfort. Crying silently in the background I thanked God He had allowed me to experience this sacred event. I will never forget it. It was the whole Gospel in action.

I decided right then and there…if this is what mission work is all about, then I'm going to spend the rest of my life doing this as often as I can. I'll jeopardize everything to be involved in God's work of giving out the Word of God. If I can experience real moments of life in adventures on the other side of the planet, then I am going to give my money, use my time off, and sacrifice everything I can for this calling. It's perilous but oh, so worth it. I may never experience retirement. I doubt I will ever get to the point of comfort and security and get to ride off into the sunset or sit on the beach, going through the money I put aside years ago. The rides will be bumpy. My usual upset stomach will just have to endure the potential embarrassing times that "I have to go now."

My visa and passport may confer approval from governments that I can go, but it's a simple call in my life that gives me permission to go on God's mission. It's a co-mission. It's the GO mission. God calls me to go, He plans my route, He executes the agenda, and I only have to say, "Yes, sir" as He leads me. If He calls you, then He will give you the power. A revival of truth broke out in the Far East that afternoon, and indeed, love was everywhere, real love…can you hear it, can you feel it, do you know it? Risk more for Him and you will.

Chapter Two
UPSIDE-DOWN WORLD

"If you believe what the Bible says about Jesus, the world will hate you. But if you start preaching a Jesus that is not the Jesus of the Bible, the world will love you." -Paul Washer

"...they dragged Jason and some of the brothers before the city authorities, shouting, "These men who have turned the world upside down have come here also...." -Acts 17:6

LEGEND HAS IT THAT THE Apostle Peter was crucified upside-down, but who really knows? Early church father, Eusebius, refuted the apocryphal text from the second century that records Peter saying, "I request you therefore, executioners, to crucify me head-downwards in this way and no other." The contested words, although laced with credibility, lie in the absurdity of the whole transcript. It's one that contains the ridiculous story of Peter raising a tuna from the dead to impress on people to believe:

> And all the people saw the fish swimming, and it did not so at that hour only, lest it should be said that it was a delusion (phantasm), but he made it to swim for a long time, so that they brought much people from all quarters and showed them the herring that was made a living fish, so that certain of the people even cast bread to it; and they saw that it was whole. And seeing this, many followed Peter and believed in the Lord.

Being inquisitive, there are two questions I must ask; did ancient assassins take requests like the deejays on our local radio stations? Would making the daily catch come back to life be the best sermon illustration a preacher could find considering it would be after Jesus arose?

The real point of this supposed head-down crucifixion (and I tend to believe it), is to point out Peter's humility in following the Lord Jesus to a cross. One would suggest that he simply didn't believe it was suitable to be martyred in the identical way as the Lord. Knowing it was going to be crucifixion on a Roman cross, we assume he scrambled to beg for a point of difference in deference to his Master.

An upside-down approach to missions is exactly what we need in the twenty-first century. Far too many have been trying to do God's work right side up. In other words, they have been trying to go by worldly methods, bowing to worldly means. You can't do that and be true to the Gospel. Genuine meekness is elevating Jesus to His rightful place in our lives, high and lifted up.

All we really need to know about Peter's response to the Lord Jesus is found in the Holy Canon of Scripture. The Bible painstakingly paints the radical change that takes place in Peter's life and it specifically involves him abandoning his pride. There is authenticity and integrity in the indisputable transformation that occurs in the once, twice, three times a denier. True, the tuna story brings up interesting observations from this crazy fanatical counterfeit incident in Peter's life. However, translated to our culture, the real question is, what have you done that singles you out as a true follower of Christ? We don't need more sensationalism. What we need is plain, self-denying, God-seeking, repentant and confessing Believers who are going. Going where? Going wherever the Great Commission takes you. Obedience is always center stage for Christ-followers.

The proverbial light bulb coming on in someone's head to signal an awakening is seen in Matthew 16, and it's ugly. Jesus is unveiling the dangerous plan to go to Jerusalem. It is upside-down thinking for us. He was going to the Roman gibbet, to give His life for the ransom for His chosen, those that belong to Him. Jesus' precise and short description of that dreadful day came as a shock to Peter's ears (Peter was used to doing things right side up) and he begins to censure the Lord.

The Great Go Mission

> And Peter took him aside and began to rebuke him, saying, "Far be it from you, Lord! This shall never happen to you." But he turned and said to Peter, "Get behind me, Satan! You are a hindrance to me. For you are not setting your mind on the things of God, but on the things of man (Matt. 16:22-23).

We learn up front there is no reprimanding our King. Did you notice how Matthew put it? "And Peter took him aside...." Think about that. What kind of pride and gall do you have to possess to pull the Lord Jesus aside to give Him a piece of your mind? A turning point in Peter's life occurs here. This is a remarkable makeover spurt in Peter's spiritual growth. Jesus didn't softly and tenderly admonish the poor disciple. No, the Lord moved him out of the way. It was up to Peter to get back in line. Peter's little conception of the world was turned upside-down and that was exactly where it needed to be.

When God calls you, the change doesn't occur instantly. The real transformation, as in Peter's life of conceptualizing and comprehending reality, is about to commence. God calls all true followers to a different style of life and it requires humility (and a lot of it) to do mission work and ministry. Before you make your reservations and pack your bags to go, learn this: Unless your mission and ministry world exists right where you stand today, then don't go looking for it in Inner Mongolia, down south of Mexico, or even in the next state over. Being a missionary means going deeper with God on the call that has been graced on your life right where you are, right now. Let Him take care of the rest of the travel for you.

We are all unique in this world, and I surely don't mean to dampen your call to ministry or the mission of God. However, the old preacher's charge to youthful wannabe ministers is true: If there is anything you can do besides go into ministry – do it! If there is any doubt whatsoever in going, and going on mission with God then don't go. Realize your understanding of the Gospel will increase, and you will discover that the world you thought you had figured out is really upside-down when you grow in godliness.

> **"DOING WORK IN THE NAME OF THE LORD JESUS IS NOT TRENDY AND SOCIALLY HIP"**

Peter's fresh angle of meekness in seeing the world, is maybe the view you have been seeking. An upside-down world is reality. It's where we live as we walk through the twenty-first century. Why? How? Our social calendars keep us too busy to consistently consider God's work for us on the weekends, much less on the other side of the world. Giving our vacation time and hard-earned income is equivalent to breaking a sacred vow unto our sanctimonious selfishness. Doing work in the name of the Lord Jesus is not trendy and socially hip. Accumulation of *more* is the name of the game. Taking selfies with a drink in your hand and posting them on Instagram is the new social status of "making it." To the Christ-follower, worldly ways are upside-down, and if we court the friendship of the world, we are compromising our relationship with the Lord Jesus.

My quiet time approach to God is one where I often read the Bible, sensing and *imaging* (not imagining) certain phrases as dynamic scene-building crescendos that are over the top cornerstones shaping my faith. One in particular is that scene from Acts 17 when Paul goes into the synagogues in Thessalonica and preaches Jesus suffering, crucified, and being raised from the dead. Many came to Christ in faith, yet in their jealousy the temple leaders formed a mob to attack Paul and his cohorts in the Gospel.

When they didn't find Paul at one of the believer's homes, they dragged the owner, Jason, out into the street to blame and abuse him. And there is that line that shakes me every time I read it, "These men who have turned the world upside-down have come here also..." (Acts 17:6b).

In reality, the world was already upside-down. One of Jesus' most faithful disciples desired crucifixion upside-down to display his unpretentiousness. It's one where everything was created by our Maker, Creator, and Almighty with perfection, and in one egotistical movement, everything was turned upside-down.

The emergent, contemporary church has followed suit in erroneously turning the congregants of Christ and the mission upside-down. We've made it about us. That is twisted and warped. Our job, in following the Great Commission, is to right the world in our mission work, using an everyday ministry of loving people to align with the Scriptures. We are righting the world when we obey the Gospel.

The Great Go Mission

ALWAYS GO TO THE PSALMS

In Psalm 81, Asaph the Psalter opens with a boisterous shout to God. He calls for singing aloud and raising voices to the "God of Jacob!" But the tone of singing joyful songs to God quickly detours into something else, and things turn miserable. The Hebrew hymns spoken by God's people are suddenly distorted. They are grumbling and critical of their Rescuer. God acknowledges the cry of the people, and He says, "I relieved your pain, I delivered you from it, I answered your call, and even when you complained about the water, I provided." God admonished them for not listening and reminds them of who He is, "I am the Lord your God..." (Psalm 81:10).

This dire test occurred back in Numbers 20. It was a wilderness location called Meribah. In Hebrew, *Meribah* means a "place of strife." Discord occurs when you are a million-plus people out in the desert, having run from your captors, possibly seeing mirages, while your tongue sticks to the roof of your mouth, and your throat is parched. You need water! We don't know if they were running out, or had completely depleted their jugs, but we do know that there is constant complaining to God. It's something we are very familiar with despite the circumstances. *Meribah* may describe some facet of your life, but don't let it derail your mission. Our discontent fights against our desire to follow God into and onto His mission. Be prepared.

God told Moses to speak to the rock for water to come forth. Moses, peeved at the people and worn out from the heat and perpetual wandering, strikes the rock twice with his staff. Water gushed out. What's the problem? Whether he talked to it or struck it as in Exodus 17:6, the result was the same. There is a huge dilemma here: Disobedience to God. Moses should have known— perhaps he did— that God was present at the rock. Speaking to the rock would mean he was actually speaking to God. By striking the rock twice, Moses demonstrated his anger against God and the emotional uneasiness he felt as more and more time passed in the desert. It shouldn't be a surprise that God's penalty to Moses was severe. It was at this point, the place of strife, that Moses learned he wasn't to complete the mission to enter into the Promised Land.

How many individuals and churches do you know that began with the proper vision yet failed to complete it. Did they depart further and further from the truth of the Gospel? No, you don't see it pasted on website walls or in the halls of social media. However, you do see many people just fade away from church attendance. I've witnessed many would-be missionaries throw in the towel. Church closings are almost too staggering to report these days. Missionary attrition is at an all-time high. All of this facilitates a rapid, downward spiritual spiral. Individuals stop giving, they stop serving, and they stop growing. Churches stop giving, they stop serving, and they stop growing.

Meribah is a real place in the modern church. Strife and confusion will undoubtedly define your mission work should you decide to continually cry foul to where God leads you and what He leads you to do. I've heard many people say, "God has told me to go here or there, and I'm wrestling with it." Truth: you and I don't get to *wrestle* with God over His will for our lives. Much of mission work and the mission calling is truly going to places never explored, and doing things never attempted, while seeing the power of God manifested regularly. Why does anyone want to go and do what someone else has already done? I believe at the very core of a missionary should be someone who is wild at heart, yielding in unconditional surrender, and ready to risk being led by the Holy Spirit.

The Psalter continues this powerful word in number eighty-one...

> Hear, O my people, while I admonish you!
> O Israel, if you would but listen to me!
> There shall be no strange god among you;
> you shall not bow down to a foreign god.
> I am the Lord your God,
> who brought you up out of the land of Egypt.
> Open your mouth wide, and I will fill it.
>
> (Ps. 81:8-10)

God warns, cautions, and gives caveats pointing us to their destructive and painful conclusions. If Israel would have just listened. If we would just listen to Him and look to Him for our fill and fulfillment. The point is this: if you are reading this book then you want to do God's work. You believe, based on your background and continual growth in godliness, that participating and achieving the Great Commission is for you. However, your struggle is attempting to do it your way. Your conversation with God goes something like this, "God, I will go anywhere! But God don't send me over there." Maybe your talks with Him are filled with, "Father, I want to be involved in bringing many, many to faith in Christ... but God, can we do it via some social media posts, because that is where and how I feel the most comfortable." Or, "Dear God, I'm ready to go wherever and whenever you send me and to discover your direction... but God, I'm tired of waiting."

The Israelites waited 430 years for Moses to show up! Waiting is part of the basic call upon your life to be on mission with God. Waiting on the Lord is referred to over a hundred times in the Bible, and we are told to specifically "wait on the Lord" over twenty times in the Psalms. Waiting, then bowing in obedience.

> But my people did not listen to my voice;
>   Israel would not submit to me.
> So I gave them over to their stubborn hearts,
>   to follow their own counsels.
> Oh, that my people would listen to me...
> (Ps. 81:11-13a)

The first part of verse 13 of Psalm 81 burdens the missionary heart. It's that last line that gets me. It's that one line that should keep Christians on their knees just a little longer, especially the missionaries, and principally those called to ministry and to preach the Word of God. You see, all believers have felt the heart strings pulled by the suffering of brothers and sisters in Christ in third-world situations. We have read about God's mission to rescue the lost, but when it comes to following the blueprint (the Great Commission) we, instead, seek our own counsel. We settle for modern approaches. We make excuses while assigning culpability to someone else when failure arrives on the steps of the church.

Read the entire Psalm slowly. When you get to verse thirteen, you will realize something about God. The Psalter has done a fantastic job of conveying the steps the Almighty has taken to rescue and comfort His chosen. However, there is disappointment from God the Father that after all of the "things" He has provided, they still act flippantly in response to their king.

This is a book about missions... so why the hard-hitting sermon to the obedience to God at this point in the game? First of all, you always need a sermon about submission to God. Second, you need a case study or testimony. It's more than a sermon. It's a call back to the basics in winning souls, starting churches, and doing genuine mission work. There's so much "religious" fluff and stuff done in the name of Jesus that doesn't have anything to do with the Great Commission or winning souls. We are fraught with desperation for more and more examples of correct missiology.

UNDERGROUND

After finishing one of my legal clandestine (yes, I know it is an oxymoron) Bible distributions, let's just say in Asia, Reverend Lieshi, my host, extended an invitation to a Bible study and prayer meeting at his home late one Sunday night. My team was exhausted from traveling thousands of miles over the course of a week, yet I sensed this was a special invite and we needed to attend. Arriving, we walked down a dark hall, up three flights of stairs, and down another hallway before it opened up into a bright, good sized classroom-looking living area. The smell of Chinese tea was wafting through the air and we were invited to enjoy Oolong and cookies. In no time, more and more people began filing in and they soon crowded the room. Although everything we were doing was considered legitimate, this had all the markings of an illegal, underground church meeting.

The Right Reverend opened the group with some words as my interpreter, Autumn whispered the translation to us. By the expressions on each face you could tell that they were all engaged and had no other place they would rather be, unlike most meetings back home. I was a little surprised when Pastor Lieshi asked me to come and share, to speak, and preach. I wasn't prepared, and the Apostle Paul's words to Timothy were ringing in my ear... "I charge you in the presence of God and of Christ Jesus, who is to judge the living and the dead, and by his appearing and his kingdom: preach the word; be ready in season and out of season; reprove, rebuke, and exhort, with complete patience and teaching" (1 Tim. 4:1-2).

I fumbled through some thoughts, Bible verses, and words, and then asked if they had any questions. The first hand went up and the Chinese gentleman said, "Tell us about the American church...we want to be like you! What is your church, and all-American churches, like?" I hate that question. I am often embarrassed with the American church and our self-absorption and promotion. Let me be transparent also, I am ashamed about our lack of risk-taking for the Gospel. After all, I don't know anyone who jeopardizes themselves by getting imprisoned, beaten, or killed for the Gospel at home like these brothers and sisters in Asia do regularly. We've

The Great Go Mission

neatly packaged Christianity, insulating ourselves from the cold deaf ears of rejection, and consistently have bargain basement sales on church membership. Our contemporary pitch to the masses is that all you have to do is "make a decision," "pray the sinner's prayer," and "be baptized." It leads people to believe that they have been rescued or justified in Christ, when more times than not we have only signed up a bunch of hipsters to hang out with us each Sunday morning to listen to the band. As I surveyed that crowded room, I saw face after face of people who were indeed sold out to God and would go wherever He would lead them.

    I fielded questions for an hour and thought we were done for the evening. Reverend Lieshi then asked if I would pray for everyone in the room. Many had come that night with specific burdens for their children and family members. Others had struggles with their job and money problems just like us. And (as in America) I thought I would gather up everyone and ask that we hold hands and I would lead everyone in a spirited prayer so we could be dismissed and go find an ice cream cone for Sunday night dessert. Just when I extended my hands to grab the nearest one to me to start the human chain, Reverend Lieshi firmly, yet kindly said, "Pastor, I want you to pray for each person and family individually." He instructed me to sit in a chair at the end of the makeshift platform. He was very kind about it, but he was being the pastor to his people. He then called for his people to come one at a time and to sit at my feet and tell me their prayer need. He asked me to take my time and pray for each one. "What? Who does this in America? How long will this take?"

    We started. I was trying to settle in and to comprehend the great honor that had been given to me. It was a humbling experience to see people come and kneel and wait expectantly on my prayer for them. After about a half hour, I was worn out getting up and down and putting my hand on their heads and praying. As another family got up to go back to their spot in the room and the next sat down greeting Autumn, my interpreter, I motioned to my friend Dr. Don Kenney to join me. He had already consumed two gallons of tea with our team while waiting and praying on the side. I whispered in his ear, "Don, I'm worn out...you come and lay hands on them and pray silently (in a whisper) while I concentrate on their prayer request and I will continue to lead in praying for them out loud." Three hours later, the last person came and sat down and she began speaking in Mandarin to Autumn. I asked in an expedited way so I could get some rest for the night, "What is her prayer need?" Autumn said, "She doesn't have a request, she wants you to know that she has been sitting in the back of the room praying for you all night as you have been praying for them." Read between the lines here, the people had come risking their lives for prayer, and Don and I, and our team were blessed by God more than all the people in the room that night because they were praying for us. As I reflect, I see it was a holy time, it only happened because of a holy risk, and Reverend Lieshi showed us how to take God-ordained risks. Once again, I was the learner, or the one being discipled on my STP.

A Holy Risk

Let me encourage you to get on with your life of, with, and through Christ by taking holy risks. Warning: If you are a Christian, remember, the greatest of all risks is taking no risk at all. And it is exactly where the majority of Christians live... on No-Risk Boulevard, Peril-Free Avenue, No Threat Circle, Safety Street, or Security Road. The opposite of risk is certainty. Does this mean we have a risky hope (second oxymoron)? This question could present a problem for us as Christ-followers. If we need to risk with Jesus, and risk means taking a chance, haven't we learned that our hope in Christ is a sure thing? That's why I call it a holy risk. Taking a holy risk may just turn your life upside-down in order to turn someone else's life right side up. What is a holy risk?

A holy risk completely occupies the space in which you live or where you have been called...with Jesus. Inhabit this world with Jesus because the Holy Spirit has inhabited you. This type of a risk disregards your personal desires and wants in favor of obeying our great God. Taking holy risks involves coming out of our religious comfort zone and relying completely on the Holy Spirit to guide and direct us, come what may. It is a thorough understanding of hope, real hope in Christ. As the writer says in Hebrews 6:19, He is our anchor!

Our Occupancy

Jesus tells a fascinating holy risk story in Luke 19. It is the *Story of the Ten Minas*. The disciples had allowed their imaginative anticipation to get the better of them. They were looking for the Kingdom of God to appear

The Great Go Mission

any second. So, the Lord tells them this parable about a nobleman, royalty, who had to go on an extended trip to be crowned a king (Can you see Jesus' prophetic analogy yet?). He called in ten of his workers and gave them minas, or talents, a unit of money, and he told them to do business with it until he returned. There is no time limit mentioned by Jesus as to when the well-to-do owner would come back. Instructions were clear... work!

Often, the King James Version translates certain words that just seem the perfect words to meditate upon and to study. That Old English rolls of the tongue for the preacher-type. We find such a gem here in Luke 19:

> And as they heard these things, he added and spake a parable, because he was nigh to Jerusalem, and because they thought that the kingdom of God should immediately appear. He said therefore, A certain nobleman went into a far country to receive for himself a kingdom, and to return. And he called his ten servants, and delivered them ten pounds, and said unto them, Occupy till I come (Luke 19:11-13 KJV).

What is Jesus' purpose in telling this story? Look carefully and you see that Luke doesn't waste any words. He lays out the foundation for the parable. There had been talk among the Jews about God's kingdom appearing any minute and Jesus is correcting their thought. Adding fuel to this message, it was the season of the Passover. This is the major Jewish festival, so the people are looking for something grand and significant. What's the hitch in talking about the soon-coming of the Kingdom? Nothing if you are just talking about it. However, it's a massive problem if you become enamored to the point where you quit living life, thinking it's coming at any second. When you stop seeking and stop serving and start selfishly indulging to pad your intellectual spiritual superiority, you begin swerving from the truth.

Here's the dilemma for so many: they harbor a belief that they are rescued and safe with God with nothing to do. Sitting back, watching others engaged in the Gospel, they believe their ticket has been punched, allowing them to relax and make excuses about their lack of Christian involvement. So they play this mind game with themselves, convincing themselves that everything is satisfactory. They attend church... a little, give a little, serve a little, and seek a little, thus justifying their sin life. They skip worship, they skimp on giving, they take baby steps away from God. Before you know it, in their feeble attempt to explain the world away, they say "well, Jesus is coming back soon and I don't need to do anything because I'm saved, and everything is all right with Him and me." Then they discover they have successfully proven to themselves that He is meaningless. Such a person is far, far from God. They've explained away their need to be busy serving the King.

> **WHILE SEARCHING FOR SOMETHING ELSE IN THE CHRIST-HONORING LIFE, WE OFTEN MISS THE SIMPLE CALLING OF OBEDIENCE THAT GOD REQUIRES OF US.**

I've encountered many people who claim to be amateur scholars on the book of Revelation. They have their so-called eschatology, theology down pat. They know what they believe, and that's good. But they are also fantastic in living a neglected godly life. They say, "Pastor, I know what I believe. I'm a Pre-millennialist, Post-tribulationist, Rapture-believing Christian, partial Preterist, partial Rapturist," and all the other -ists. At the exact same time, many of these people are terrible husbands/wives and parents. They are horrible friends too. They exhibit immaturity in basic love and forgiveness of others, and their mouths are sewers spewing lewd and licentious remarks. While searching for something else in the Christ-honoring life, we often miss the simple calling of obedience that God requires of us. And that's the thing Jesus is stating up front here, even before He gets to the heart of the story.

Let me show you the problem with this thinking: What if Jesus is not coming back in the next five years? Ten years? Twenty? Where does that leave you? Think about that...all of us who grew up in the 60's, 70's, and 80's when it was stylishly popular for preachers to pound on the pulpit

The Great Go Mission

preaching, "Jesus is coming back soon so you better turn or burn!" They expounded on the fact that Jesus' return was imminent (maybe it is; I'm praying it is), so you had to get things in order with God. Scolding the heathen, that you better get your heart right before Jesus returns, is an excellent sermon. But when the hearers stop at "I'm saved" and that's it, we have problems among the brothers and sisters. The goal for the Christian life is more than just several experiences with God. It's all about knowing Him...so we keep seeking. Am I promoting good works theology? Heavens no! I'm as reformed from a deformed theology as you can get. Nineteenth century pastor and theologian A.W. Pink said,

> The nature of Christ's salvation is woefully misrepresented by the present-day evangelist. He announces a Saviour from Hell rather than a Saviour from sin. And that is why so many are fatally deceived, for there are multitudes who wish to escape the Lake of fire who have no desire to be delivered from their carnality and worldliness.

No wonder we don't want to do anything! You and I, in Christ, have been rescued by Christ. We are righteousness. We have been freed from sin and its dirtiness. That cleansing leads to right living which should lead to taking holy risks. You have been saved by grace to *do* good works, not *by* good works. No, good works don't impress God to the point at which He excuses your sin and lets you into heaven. We are rescued by Him and now—now, we live for Him and to Him. One more time:

> And he called his ten servants, and delivered them ten pounds, and said unto them, Occupy till I come.

I particularly like the King James Version of Luke 19 because of this word: *Occupy*. Occupying space would be a good place to start. God gives the servants the space, He defines the space, He outlines the space, He determines the dimensions of the space, He funds the space, and He says, "Occupy the space until I come back." It's precisely what He says to you and me today. Occupy! Don't just sit back and let it happen. The word in Greek, pay attention because it's a fantastic word, is: πραγματεύσασθε (pragmateusasthe). What does it sound like? Pragmatism. We need to be pragmatic...is what Jesus says. We need to be practical! The servants came

33

in, the Master gave them the money, and he gave them the command – πραγματεύσασθε. It means that those who hear and believe the Gospel must live and share the Gospel and that, my friends, is a holy risk. That is faithfulness. We have to proclaim it. Could it be that godly pragmatism is what is missing in your spiritual journey? What are the practical applications of following Christ, or how can you occupy your world for Christ?

FAITH TAKES PRECEDENT OVER SAFETY

The nobleman returns, but now he returns with a crown on his head. He is the king. I suppose royal title holders are treated with a high regard and respect, but obviously, the king is esteemed to the maximum. He calls the workers into account, to give their reports of their "occupancy."

The first one, with the ten minas, is thrilled to inform the new king how he risked it all and the payoff was huge! He doubled what he had by avoiding the pitfall of safety. His measured steps of real faith with a real hope catapulted him to a place of giant faith. Think about it. There is story after story in the Scriptures where faith is chosen over security. The early church patriarchs, all the way through the Reformers of the church, risked life and limb just to stand on the Word and propagate the Gospel.

The second, the one with five minas, had the same result as the first. He had also taken a holy risk and he doubled what he was given by the king. This teaches us that it's not about you and how many minas you are entitled to, but what degree of responsibility you have been granted. We fail miserably when we try to figure out why and how the servants were awarded differing numbers of talents. We succeed greatly when we concentrate and commit to using the talents to bring honor and glory to God. Each of these servants risked it all like it was Las Vegas when no one was looking! And God rewarded them.

PUTTING YOURSELF FIRST CONDEMNS YOU IN THE END

There's a twist on life that Jesus is overtly hinting at here. Think about others first and you will be gratified in living this life that you live. But if you continually elevate yourself to gratify and hold on to "everything" in your life, then you will lose it. Jesus warns us, "Whoever finds his life will lose it, and whoever loses his life for my sake will find it" (Matt. 10:39). Cut to the chase, quit living a selfish life, Jesus says. Obey the Master and occupy the space and occupy this life by doing something with what He has given you. *Occupy* is a great translation here. The modern translations of the Bible use terms like "do business" or "operate" with the money. I like "occupy" because it defines the whole of Christian life.

If you are at the ballgame, then occupy the space as a Christ-follower. Be mindful of your mouth, your actions, and thoughts. If you are driving and someone cuts you off and then flips you off, then by not getting up into their space and reciprocating their actions. You see, HE lives in your space if you are believer. The term *occupy* applies to all of your life, and that is the way Jesus intended for the message to be received. Wherever you are, let your words reflect Christ. Wherever you are, let your actions reflect the righteousness of Christ. Occupy the space He has given you rather than looking down the road thinking someone else will show up to help you out. You have all you need to live this life with Christ. Has God entrusted you with gifts? He has. Use them. Don't live out this life without discovering why He put you in a church community.

GOD'S GENEROSITY IS HIS TO DISTRIBUTE AS HE SEES FIT

So, the third servant was called before the king and came stammering and stuttering, looking for a legitimate excuse. There was none to be found. The servant's excuse was not even flimsy! It just flopped. He said, "'Lord, here is your mina, which I kept laid away in a handkerchief; for I was afraid of you, because you are a severe man. You take what you did not deposit, and reap what you did not sow'" (Luke 19:20, 21). The king then says, "Your own words condemn you." In other words, if you wanted to be lazy and not do any work, then why didn't you put it in the bank and let the money do the work for you?

God's generosity is His to give away as He pleases, and our response should be to occupy that space with everything we have. That is why Jesus emphasizes this word occupy, and why it's so good in the KJV. We are to occupy this life, our body, this world, our mind, with Christ. Paul says, "For who has understood the mind of the Lord so as to instruct him?" But we have the mind of Christ" (1 Cor. 2:16). When Jesus is concluding the parable of the ten minas, He gives an important piece of information about the return of the master. The master was pleased when the servants actually occupied their space and worked for an increase. The master was disappointed to find the one servant preoccupied with himself. What's the lesson? A continued path of preoccupation will always lead to regret and remorse. A life using God's gifts and talents will bring about a life of honor to our God and bring meaning in a remorseful world.

Here's the truth that Christians need more than ever in this world today: God gives... but God will take away when we play, shirk responsibility, and then just lie to Him. Don't believe me? Then just take a look at the entire Old Testament and the repeated failures of the Israelites, God's own people, to be true to God.

Taking holy risks with God's resources, His power, and His authority and directions is the only way to progress in a world that loathes our Savior. This is the exact lesson that Peter learned. He went from talking a good game to living a risky life. Peter's transformation in Christ caused him to capitulate his safety for taking big risks that would turn the world right side up. These risks for you and me are going to have to be supported by continual prayer, measured dependence on His indwelling Holy Spirit and, at times, fasting to seek Him intimately.

Making our way toward the middle of the twenty-first century, be assured that the enemy has reloaded and made his own commitment to his heinous, devious plot to destroy God's plan of redemption in your life. Don't be fooled, Satan has moved the gates of hell to the front door of the church in these last days. So, make sure every step you take is a deliberate one, and obedient to the call upon your life to follow Him wherever He takes you. It's only in that risk with Jesus you will see Him prevail in your life.

REVEREND LIESHE...A NEW BEGINNING

He knew the risks. After all, as a Christ-follower in a communist country you are warned, lectured, and warned again of the consequences of selling out to Jesus before the party— the communist party that is. But Reverend Lieshe pushed ahead anyway sacrificing comforts, livelihood, and safety. He knew what a holy risk was all about firsthand. Being responsible for over a quarter of a million people in his district requires a decision that is without guile, ego, or greediness. Tirelessly, he led the sheep to lie down in green pastures beside quiet waters.

The Great Go Mission

My friend and contact in the Far East called me a few weeks ago and said, "Lieshe is dead." I waited in silence to hear the whole story. Sadly, we were only privy to parts of it. I was shown the document compiled of Lieshe's personal notes outlining his frustration at being denied basic rights for his church to operate. There were some bogus rules enforced about entrance and egress for the church building and the continued pressure from the local government to close the doors. It was a phony charge and a cover-up from the real assault on the church. In those notes he recorded his anxiety and vexation concerning the leadership of his people. My friend Lieshe was a seasoned veteran in ministry. He was strong in the Lord, but the relentless battering from the enemy, and hounding him to the point of mental torture was getting to him. By his own hand he stated he wanted to give up, but he wouldn't. He said that he would be willing to be the first "martyr" in his region for the Gospel. The police report said he had jumped off of a seven-story building to his death. Do you believe that? I don't.

Recently, disgraced American financier and multimillionaire Jeffrey Epstein, who was accused of sex trafficking minors, died from an apparent suicide inside in his Manhattan jail cell... they say. Epstein was closely associated to political figures that wanted to remain anonymous when it became apparent that some of them were named in his escapades. So, immediately after Epstein's death, social media was abuzz with reports that his suicide was highly questionable, and that maybe he was murdered to keep him silent. There were Tweets galore that defended the probable murder because he was on a 24-hour suicide watch. The rumors and conspiracy theories ran rampant. Maybe there was a fiendish plot? Who knows?

And who knows what really happened to my friend and fellow minister of the Gospel. There was no video of Reverend Lieshe jumping off of a building. For a country where 5G technology is about to rule the world, with ubiquitous cameras and censors touting that they can locate anyone anywhere in their country in less than five seconds, why would you not have video footage? No one in his church was allowed to attend the funeral. The funeral was quick and government controlled. Everything Lieshe had been fighting with the authorities to accomplish was immediately granted to the church hours after he died. The funeral occurred, then the benefits given to the church were revoked.

Last week I saw a report on the news warning people about the dangers of summer swimming in the lake. The reporter said, "Be careful because often when someone is drowning it doesn't look like what you think drowning looks like." The reporter was trying to say that usually a person doesn't flail their arms six feet out of the water and scream to a decibel level where everyone can hear them crying, "I'm drowning, help me!" It's rather quiet. Being murdered for the Gospel of Jesus Christ in the twenty-first century doesn't look like it did five hundred years ago. Back then they burned you at the stake or severed your head in the public square. They gathered your acquaintances around so that they could see what it meant to disparage the kings and governments, as adversaries spit and threw vegetables at you. It was loud. Not today. It's quiet today. People just disappear and are never heard from again. Don't you find it strange that in our high-tech world we rarely see videos of Christian missionaries, pastors, or teachers, suffering and dying at the hands of their captors? Let me give you a quick warning: It may be happening only on foreign soil momentarily, but it is coming to an American town sooner than you think. And it will be quiet.

Pastor Lieshe knew the holy risk he was taking. Maybe the challenge and call to follow God in a dangerous climate got the best of him and he just had to find a way out? Maybe he quit? Maybe he was telling the truth and he just couldn't take it anymore? Or, maybe those weren't his notes at all? I know this: he was a man of God. He loved Jesus. He loved his church and would have died for her. And he did. Maybe, just maybe he had counted the cost. Maybe he knew what it meant to occupy fully the space that God has given to each one of us. I believe he did. Here's a thought: Live a righteous life, take holy risks, and if it costs you your life... well, then you're home.

GLOBAL + LOCAL = HOLY RISK

I am on a perpetual mission trip because I am a Christ-follower. Short-term mission trips, Short-term projects, and "Holy Risks" never stop coming for the Christ-follower. Retirement is not an option. We've got one chance to turn my community from upside-down, up to the right side. It's essential that we continue to bow down to Him, and every morning continue to get on our knees and thank Him, confess our sin, and ask Him to lead us to participate in His Kingdom's work again— all while being amazed that He allows us into His presence. I am on mission with God for the sake of the Gospel of Jesus Christ, obeying His command found in Matthew 28 - The Great Commission. Are you?

You've probably heard it before. *All* Christians are missionaries. Serving God locally and globally is not up for negotiation. Allow me to introduce to you a new way of thinking when it comes to mission work: *Glocal*. About thirty years ago, someone coined this straightforward phrase out of two words, "global" and "local." Glocal thinking makes the short-term projects approach to missions logical and practical.

Glocal thinking enhances our obedience to go wherever and whenever. The Apostle Paul highlights this same type of obedience in one of his prayers for the church in 2 Thessalonians 1:11-12, "To this end we always pray for you, that our God may make you worthy of his calling and may fulfill every resolve for good and every work of faith by his power, so that the name of our Lord Jesus may be glorified in you, and you in him, according to the grace of our God and the Lord Jesus Christ." The *call* here is important to our salvation. It is a step of obedience and discipleship. It propels us into the mission. The call is a constant theme of Paul throughout his letters in the New Testament.

Our duty is to grow up in Christ to maturity, and to live up to that calling while relying on Him for the power. It's risky. Maturity in Christ is not like downloading the latest upgrade on your electronic device. No, Paul urges us in Philippians 2,

> Therefore, my beloved, as you have always obeyed, so now, not only as in my presence but much more in my absence, work out your own salvation with fear and trembling, for it is God who works in you, both to will and to work for his good pleasure" (Phil. 2:12-13).

Pray for God to help you to expand your ministry and mission for the Gospel cause. Trying harder by gritting your teeth to be a better Christian is not going to cut it, and it leads to failure. Crying out to God to work in our lives is the answer. Let's start getting down to the risky business:

- When was the last time you honestly prayed asking God to send you to someone to help and share Christ?
- It's risker than you know, but have you ever studied the Gospel in another culture?
- How are you doing in loving the people God has put in your path?
- What mission cause are you praying for in real time?
- Have you ever candidly asked yourself if you would suffer for the sake of the Gospel?
- Are you asking God to work in you to bring about His global kingdom initiatives?
- Have you been obedient to God in one missional act over your entire lifetime? Think...what was it?
- When was the last time you gave your hard-earned money to a real mission cause? Did it hurt to give? It should.
- Why don't you ask God right now...not holding back...giving yourself completely to Him...to do what He wants to do in your life?
- Why not consider planning a short-term project in your church? Or join one where someone is already going?

If someone says, "The Bible is boring" then they've never taken time to explore its holy pages. Hollywood can't and never will capture the adrenaline-charged moments, the breathtaking realness, and spine-tingling significant words of the book of Acts. We will just have to do our best to picture in our minds, so we can understand the constant dangers those early Christians and church leaders were engaged in hourly. The first missionaries were launched into the deep hazardous waters of a dark domain armed with the Light of the World. As Luke, writing in Acts, said, "...our beloved Barnabas and Paul, men who have risked their lives for the name of our Lord Jesus Christ" were holy and wholly sold out for the Gospel.

Chapter Three
FANATICS & ZEAL

"Young man, sit down. When God pleases to convert the heathen, he will do it without your aid or mine!"

-Reverend John Ryland Sr. to William Carey
at a Baptist Associational Meeting, September 30, 1785

"Do not be slothful in zeal, be fervent in spirit, serve the Lord."

-Romans 12:11

BRITISH ROYAL NAVY CAPTAIN JAMES Cook was slaughtered by natives on the Kona shores of Hawaii on February 4th, 1779 after attempting to retrieve his stolen dingy. Cook was an explorer, navigator, and cartographer in the middle to latter part of the eighteenth century. He had mapped new territory called Tahiti and other unknown islands. The rest of the known world used Cook's maritime parchment maps and expertise to marvel at this vast planet. However, in a small town north of London there was a far more significant use for those diagrams. Something holy and absolutely spectacular was about to materialize for the glory of God. Just as Cook had launched his adventure to new worlds, Christianity was about to be launched in a whole new way. Not since Pentecost after Jesus' Resurrection, when His disciples gathered in the Upper Room in Acts 2, has there been recorded such an unimaginable spiritual movement as the one about to break out in that little municipality in England.

Modern Day

Modern day descriptions of Christian movements usually start with mega-conferences in massive auditoriums, manufacturing pulsating music louder than an AC/DC concert. They are swarming with church-leading earth-shakers popular for being modern spiritual gurus. Many of them are paid exorbitant sums of cash to address the feverish jamborees. I like loud music, I love the conferences, and I get into listening to God's preacher expound the Bible, but I have a problem with the anticipated outcome of some of these meetings.

The American metric for measuring greatness and God-like development begins with crowds mashed into massive auditoriums on sensory overload. The busy-ness and seemingly spiritual chaos of the moment creates a frenzied havoc where young would-be ministers gather to devour ideas like it's feeding time on a catfish farm. Lavishly decorated booths in the hall are equipped to look, you might think, like contemporary money changers in the temple. Expectations are lofty for you and me to sprint from the auditorium on adrenaline pumped highs to go into all the world. Yes, Scripture does tell us that when the Holy Spirit showed up in Acts 2 the room was indeed crowded and it was noisy, but the subsequent movement of God's men and women afterwards was palpable, meaningful, and productive in a different way than what we typically see today.

The power and presence of King Jesus has been traded for hype and hysteria. A fervent, oft anguished, decision to go, led by the Holy Spirit as one ponders and nurtures what Scripture declares, is replaced by you being convinced that all your wants will be met if you take the step and come to the front. Listen to me, every Christ-follower is called! I'll say it again: *every* Christian is a missionary. Every child of God is to be fulfilling the Great Commission. You are called by God-of-the-Angel-Armies to go, to serve, to give, to die spiritually, and to die physically if necessary. We are to engage the world we live in with the life-changing Gospel. Why aren't you doing this? What is your excuse? Where has the modern-day church missed the boat when it comes to charting new waters? Could it be that we've lost the heart of the mission? It's no wonder Christians brood over whether or not they really want to be missionaries.

Thirty-five years ago I began to experience the Holy Spirit's work in my life for carrying out God's mission. My problem was that the course I had charted in my life was leading to the usual doldrums of ministry... towards burnout. Real transformation had to occur in order for me to live the real life God had for me. The Great Commission started evolving in my life to the point of my truly understanding Jesus' life and death, and Resurrection... that's the Gospel. I prayed earnestly for God to send me to another country to minister. At that time, I had recently returned from Hong Kong, Singapore, Malaysia, and Indonesia and found I have an affinity for the Asian culture... and cuisine. New friends from my graduating class were being sent left and right to the other side of the planet, most to parts unknown. I wanted to go, too. God didn't send me then. I was disillusioned. Looking back, I had more equipping to do.

Our God is a great God and His ultimate timetable is marked by perfect precision. He had a completely different schedule of events for shaping my life. It would be another ten years of praying and maturing before He would quicken my dispatch. As I continue on this journey, I want to help you discover God's real mission, and God's mission for your life. It is a good thing to realize that what God wants to do a year, five years, or ten years down the road for you is better than your jumping into something that doesn't matter. First things first...absorb some history of the mission of God...

BIRTH OF A MOVEMENT

Unknown to Captain Cook, God used his bravery and globe mapping abilities to start a heroic, Christ-centered revolution of vast proportions in evangelism and discipleship, to become known as missions. A man we would probably nickname Bill today, and his little brotherhood of fourteen men, were sitting in Martha Wallis's cramped parlor in Kettering, England, and came up with a temporary name for their newly minted mission project: *The Particular Baptist Society for Propagating the Gospel Amongst the Heathen*. Up to this moment in the 1790's, organized missions as we know it did not exist. During this same period, the great hymn writer William Cowper (pronounced "Cooper") lived twenty miles down the road, and was penning "There is a Fountain, Filled with Blood." Bill, née William Carey, who is today called the father of modern missions, was being moved by the Holy Spirit to start something for the glory of God. Carey referenced and marveled over Cook's geographical accomplishments— a new map— as the

GPS catalyst to start a mission work to reach hitherto unreached people groups. Reading the legend, or map symbols, of Cook's voyages initially drew Carey to begin contemplating missions. For maybe the first time on record, one of God's servants looked at a modern map as a diagram for how to actually be able to go to the ends of the earth. They passed a hat and took up a little more than thirteen pounds...just over $400 in today's U.S. currency value. And they were off!

True Mission?

Missions, the most white-knuckling, adrenaline charged job in days gone by, is today... a detractor's yawn. Today's combat soldier doesn't see as much action as one of God's called missionaries did two hundred years ago. However, over time, the missionary has become regarded in many circles as a religious nut... a fanatic. Years ago, zealous men and women, those who were God's Great Commission warriors, risked their lives by going anywhere to share the Gospel. If you grew up in church, did you ever imagine there would come a time when people would be hating on missionaries? You've arrived! We hear these things today:

"Why can't we just leave those people alone?"

"Who travels to an island full of primitive people without some kind of protection?"

"There is no way he knew what he was doing."

"He could be taking a disease to them that their immune system can't handle!"

"Even though I share his faith, (he) had no business going to those people."

"That guy was an idiot...he got what he deserved."

Thousands weighed in on social media in November of 2018 after missionary, John Chau, illegally gained access to the North Sentinel Island in the Bay of Bengal. He was immediately killed by bow and arrow by the island's indigenous people. The Sentinelese have violently resisted contact from the outside world for centuries, meeting the unwelcome with deadly force. Why did Chau go? Surely, he knew the risks? Did he just want to die? Rod Dreher, a Christian writer, wrote a blog in The American Conservative and said, "Chau could not have preached to these people," Dreher wrote. "Nobody speaks their language. How on earth could he have witnessed to them?" New York Times World tweeted about Chau, "He was caught up in a dangerous set of ideologies that helped drive him to do something so unwise." There were scores, maybe hundreds more hateful Tweets chastising Chau and the Evangelical Christian community with insensitivity to the Sentinelese and questioning our missionary training and preparation. Yet, someone appropriately declared something like this on social media, "This planet is not good enough for the likes of John Chau."

Chau is not the first valiant, maverick-like, missionary and he won't be the last. God has raised up men and women that *get it* and intrepidly go where few dare to venture. They *get* not only an indoctrination of the Great Commission, but resolute allegiance and action to the Great Commandment even if it means death. Very few people have possessed a combined commitment of boldness and obedience to Jesus' mandates. Maybe it's Carey, the trailblazer of world missions, that we have to thank for opening the door. His youthful stand for radical evangelism "to the end of the earth" in the midst of seasoned pastors' resistance was the line in the sand he crossed to open the door for us.

Very few people have possessed a combined commitment of boldness and obedience to Jesus' mandates.

At an associational pastors meeting on September 30, 1875, a young William Carey made an extreme comment that would be echoed in the actions we find in John Chau: to go and evangelize the lost even if it is to the ends of the planet. In other words, Carey wanted to be totally faithful to the Gospel. Surely, Paul's words to Timothy must have been somewhere on his mind, "Let no one despise you for your youth, but set the believers an example in speech, in conduct, in love, in faith, in purity" (1 Tim. 4:12). Met with immediate opposition by Reverend John Ryland Sr., Carey was called "a most miserable enthusiast" and Ryland further rejected Carey's zealous call to action by dismissing him with, "Young man, sit down. When

God pleasures to convert the heathen, he will do it without your aid or mine!"

ZEALOUSNESS

As a Christ-follower, my blood starts pumping and my mind fixates on bold, life-threatening, missionary stories. These folks are the real heroes to be celebrated, not the skinny jeaned, supercool pastoral dude that's monetized his online minister's store to afford himself a new BMW. No, the stories I have read about my intense, sometimes fanatical, brothers and sisters in Christ cause me to reflect on my own inadequacies and failures to participate in the most die-hard, revolutionary movement of all time: the calling to forsake any trust in this world and turn to our Lord Jesus. My dilemma arises as I discover their bravery and courage from the comforts of my warm and cozy office, listening to Pandora while sipping on my hot double espresso. What am I to do with this information? Am I living an authentic Christian life? Where did they get this enthusiastic allegiance? How can I get that excited? Simply, what can I do?

Open the Word of God and discover what Jesus was looking for when starting His army of kingdom shakers. What were the attributes necessary that Jesus had in mind as He chose those twelve men? It's rather confusing and contradictory when you consider what most churches today look for in a pastor or staff when hiring for a ministerial position. The large, affluent churches demand graduates of higher education as well as experience. Medium size churches with medium size budgets settle for a little experience, and some education. The tiny churches settle for no experience and sometimes no education just because they are desperate for someone and something. And all of it is handled on a professional website with resumes being exchanged with electronic handshakes, while sizing up congregational size to determine what kind of salary one might earn. That's some good fodder for the polemic question: "Is the modern-day church a business?"

Jesus' freshman team was made up of several fishermen— Peter, James, John, and Andrew— you know, the guys that are up at 4am working, scruffy (and didn't care), and dressed in layers to help control their temperature throughout the day. Their wives probably spent a small fortune on laundry detergent to no avail. There was Matthew the tax collector (we

The Great Go Mission

all have our own personally motivated detestation and loathing of the IRS type). Then Judas. Let's just skip him. And there were a few others, but there was one in particular that stands out to me: Simon the Zealot. Absolutely nothing is known about him, but everything can be assumed from the name, zealot. He is mentioned in passing four times: in Matthew, Mark, Luke, and Acts.

Simon the Zealot was probably given the name because he had a certain zeal about his feelings regarding the Roman occupation of Israel. Think about it from his perspective: A Zionist, having a world power trespassing on his homeland, encroaching more and more upon his rights to be a free Hebrew citizen of Israel. Ironically, it is still happening today. Surely Jesus had some differences of opinion with Simon the Zealot and his politics. Maybe others would have balked at Jesus' choice calling Simon an uncontrollable fanatic. However, there was something in his rowdy behavior, as in the others, that would and could be developed into an influencer and leader of many other disciples.

In contrast, if you read about the Reformers, you will discover that the word "zeal" is not a good word to describe a modern-day Christ-follower. Too much of an assumption about feelings is associated with the word. According to many theologians, a zeal for Christ may just put you at risk of abandoning truth in favor of emotion. You know, when you feel the goosebumps about something spiritual, you immediately neglect or forget what the Bible says because you feel it! It is never a good thing to let feelings take precedence over truth.

The other disciples may not have had a contributing modifier to their name like Simon the Zealot, but you can be sure they had passion. Read about them in the Gospels. Acts is where they made the most noise. Observe Peter's misdirected and uneducated fervor. Jesus was keen on making that rag-tag group of boys His men. They were being fully equipped, getting fully ready and charged to do Kingdom work. Jesus had a precise plan when He assembled them. R.C. Sproul points out in his commentary on Mark's gospel, that "the Twelve represented the church in miniature." These diverse backgrounds are a microcosm of that which the church must be. How fanatical are you when it comes to bucking the humanistic beat we seem to march to every day? Are you prepared to resist the status quo? Is your zeal for Jesus real?

That first century passion was contagious. In addition to the band of the original twelve there were also many other men, and women such as Mary Magdalene, Susanna, and Joanna. Christ's church is not one-dimensional, and not just one race, sex, or socioeconomic class; rather, it includes men and women from every nation – multi-dimensional. Jesus takes your unpolished skills and shapes you into His shining light in darkness. In our search for biblical unity in this lost culture, we need to be reminded that only Jesus can bring harmony to sundry backgrounds. We have to be careful not to dilute the Gospel or to try and add anything to it.

If you feel inadequate in serving God, can you identify what you are lacking? What is that void? What skill sets do you need? What will enable you to become a fully devoted follower of Christ? The answer is zeal and being real. Men and women of Scripture have these two common features between them. Zeal is an outward expression of an emotion and truth. Being real and exhibiting zeal are what permitted Peter and John to stand boldly in front of the Jewish leadership as recorded in Acts 4.

Stop right here. Reflect, and be careful to understand the combination in this definition: Truth is paramount. Unchecked emotions lead to fanaticism. B.B. Warfield, in his work, *Perfectionism*, identifies this modern-day, created emphasis of having a certain emotional feeling from following Christ. He traces it back to the "Western Revivals" in Ohio in the mid-nineteenth century. Charles Finney, a popular evangelist, thought normal church was boring, so looked to spice things up. He taught that emotion is what moved people to 'make a decision.' Fervent and exciting preaching was deemed the real thing that stimulated the crowds to make decisions to follow Christ— and decisions he got. Finney is credited with creating the modern-day altar call. He called it the "Anxious Bench." It was there he hoped to get an emotional response to his invitation to make a decision for Christ. Questions loom...were people truly regenerated or just exhilarated by fanaticism? Was the zeal real?

If you are contemplating doing something great for God, and you are hesitating, then maybe it's zeal you are lacking. *Real* is necessary for genuine zeal. Real zeal for God is indispensable to your quest to serve Him. Make certain that Truth is the source of your zealousness. Acts 5 gave clarity to genuine zeal. Peter and the apostles are hauled in again to the high priest, they were scolded once more and commanded not to preach Jesus. Peter's

The Great Go Mission

response is priceless, "We must obey God rather than people" (Acts 5:29). What is the source for this real zest for Jesus? Is there a prerequisite for those wanting to fulfill the Great Commission? In order to be zealous for God, you have to be jealous for God. Not jealous *of* God... *for* God.

PLANS FOR REAL ZEAL

In one of my graduate classes our instructor, Richard Blackaby, was reflecting on his dad, Henry's, legacy. Henry Blackaby, author of *Experiencing God*, had just turned eighty, and Dr. Richard Blackaby was telling us about his father's spiritual habits. One specific quality stood out over the usual things we hear about someone having the typical spiritual disciplines in their lives. The advice Henry Blackaby gave his son was to always operate out of the overflow. What's the overflow? Due to our frenetic, crazy schedules, we squeeze in time with God the best we can. Admit it. You grab five minutes of Bible reading while choking down some pop-tarts and, more times than we would like to admit, prayer becomes our Melatonin for insomnia. Inversely, Dr. Blackaby advocates spending so much time with God, that to live for Him is just an overflow. The best way to live the Christian life is to live it "out of the overflow."

If you want to succeed in mission work, let it be an overflow from your time with God. Instead of trying to pack God into your overcrowded calendar, plan dedicated time with Him so that the Holy Spirit overflows in your life. It's the only way to develop genuine zeal for Him.

The majority of both long-term and short-term missionaries, servants of God, pastors and church staff try to live on an empty tank. I see it all the time. Running out of fuel sidelines you. If the spiritual life of Christians were measured like we measure the gasoline tanks in our cars, then the red light would perpetually shine, indicating we are about to run out of gas. You cannot be on mission for God with an empty tank; don't be fooled. Do not attempt to serve God on your own strength. If you try to use your own power, you will fail. You can't fan a little flame for God and expect to become a fanatic. The outcome will not be good for people running on empty and, surely, you won't be running very long.

IF YOU WANT TO SUCCEED IN MISSION WORK, LET IT BE AN OVERFLOW FROM YOUR TIME WITH GOD.

We learn how and why Jesus called those twelve men. They were learners. That's what disciple means in Greek – learner. Serving Jesus in this post-modern world means you and I have to live out of the overflow of God in our lives. You are still learning. Elijah was flooded with God's power on Carmel, but then he let his tank get dry. Simon the Zealot was a moldable disciple in Jesus' eye. He wasn't where he should have been, but Jesus was going to make Him into His man, rich with Godly zeal, by filling his tank. You are probably not who you could be. Are you living out of the overflow of God in your life? It's the only way to truly live the Christian life. Overflow happens when you:

- Spend time in prayer with God every day and don't look at the clock.
- Read the Bible every day and study how to apply it to your life.
- Belong to a local church and believe in the godly vision.
- Discover your spiritual gift(s) and feed them for growth.
- Serve in your church and do it with joy.
- Tithe and give cheerfully to the vision/mission of your church.
- Avail yourself to God to go wherever He sends you.

Step up real zeal:

- Read a Psalm every day! The Psalms will transform your life because you will begin to see the Holy God you worship and serve like you've never seen before.
- Get on your knees before God...bow to Him.
- Ask Him to do the impossible in your life and to challenge you to come out of your comfort zone.

→ At least once in your life, give away a significant sum of money to God's work.
→ Lead someone to Christ and disciple them.
→ Go somewhere— to a different city, to an international spot— and observe.
→ Risk something or go to someplace risky.
→ Beg God to send you!

ZEALOUS MAN

God's man Elijah had seen Him move in very powerful ways. The most recent was how God reigned down blazing fire on Mount Carmel. Wicked King Ahab of the Northern Kingdom was out for Elijah's head because Elijah had delivered the news of a long-lasting drought. God demonstrated His power. Our God acted in the manner of an ancient fight promoter to prove His power even over the elements. It all came to a head when Ahab ordered 450 prophets of the Baal god to the mountain for the showdown with God's lone prophet. Elijah called to the people, "How long will you go limping between two different opinions? If the Lord is God, follow him; but if Baal, then follow him" (1 Kings 18:21). There was no answer. Elijah continued,

> I, even I only, am left a prophet of the Lord, but Baal's prophets are 450 men. Let two bulls be given to us, and let them choose one bull for themselves and cut it in pieces and lay it on the wood, but put no fire to it. And I will prepare the other bull and lay it on the wood and put no fire to it. And you call upon the name of your god, and I will call upon the name of the Lord, and the God who answers by fire, he is God (1 Kings 18:22b, 23, 24a).

God's challenge and terms were agreed to by the false prophets. And the action began.

Elijah, being the gentleman, ordered them to go first. He told them to select a bull, cut it up and put it on the altar, then call on Baal to consume the sacrifice. From a God-fearing perspective, it must have been a hilarious sight. Can you imagine watching this from heaven? Those fake prophets prayed and called upon Baal for hours. At one point they leaped up on the dead bull and called louder. Elijah, having fun with this, mocked them and said, "Yell more. Your god is preoccupied, perhaps he's in the toilet, or maybe taking a nap and needs to be awakened!" They continued to scream out, and the false prophets became desperate. They began cutting themselves as if to say, "Look Baal, we are bleeding for you down here... do something!" Nothing. Elijah didn't interrupt, but he just let them go on making bigger fools of themselves, Baal, and Ahab.

Next round: There was no need for a bell to signal for action because Elijah stepped in and called God's servants to come close to watch and help. Elijah took twelve stones in homage to the twelve tribes of Israel and built back the altar. He gathered wood and stacked it under the altar. He cut up the sacrifice and laid it on top, then dug a deep trench around it. He gave orders for the people to fill four water jars and to saturate the dry altar. He said, "Do it a second time." He said, "Do it a third time." And the water filled the makeshift channel surrounding the sacrifice.

If you know the story, you know this is where it gets electrifying. Elijah prayed this powerful prayer to the only God, his God, and our God. He prayed,

> O Lord, God of Abraham, Isaac, and Israel, let it be known this day that you are God in Israel, and that I am your servant, and that I have done all these things at your word. Answer me, O Lord, answer me, that this people may know that you, O Lord, are God, and that you have turned their hearts back (1 Kings 18:36-37).

And the fire fell. The rest of the story is a power-packed one, as the people of God rose up and killed all of the prophets of Baal and Elijah told Ahab to go... watch it rain now.

But it took an ugly turn when Jezebel, Ahab's wife, makes a threatening do-or-die statement: "The gods will get you for this and I'll get even with you! By this time tomorrow you'll be as dead as any one of those prophets" (1 Kings 19:2 MSG). Elijah tucked his tail between his legs and took off. It's one of those verses in Scripture that makes us turn our heads like a dog does when it hears a loud siren. What, Elijah? Why? You just led God's people to victory in the Middle East Super Bowl. Cheerleaders, motivational speakers, and lobbyists from all over the West would have been beating down Elijah's door for coaching on how to be a winner in a world that hates you. Yet he runs from one single threat. I don't want to exhaust possible answers as to why, but we must explore Elijah's answer to God's ultimate question, "So Elijah, what are you doing here?" (1 Kings 19:9 MSG)

"Woe is me" was Elijah's tune sitting in the desert under a shade tree. His complaints about life had reached to heaven and God's question is a real one for those engaged in God's mission. Elijah answered, "I have been very jealous for the Lord, the God of hosts" (1 Kings 19:10). Jealous? It seems like a strange word to be used. Eugene Peterson translates the statement as, "I've been working my heart out for God, the God-of-the-Angel-Armies..." (1 Kings 19:10 MSG). Jealous and zealous are the same here. Remember Simon the Zealot? Jesus saw the potential in Simon, as a disciple, to take his misplaced zeal and to put it in its proper place. Elijah, on the other hand, had things in the right perspective but lost focus. A zeal or a jealousy for God is a life-long journey to seek God and His truth. Our zeal for the Gospel, no matter how dynamic and devout, is no good without being grounded in God's truth.

REAL CHRISTIAN ZEALOTS

In a strikingly similar story to John Chau's, on November 20, 1839, missionaries John Williams and James Harris set sail to the coast of the small island called Erromango in the New Hebrides, which is modern-day Vanuatu, located a thousand miles off the coast of Australia. Warned not to go, and to keep away from the vicious natives and cannibalizing people of this island, Williams and Harris braved it anyway. Word was they had seen God move on other islands and believed He would continue His great work among these people. Even though they knew the dangers, they were unaware that the Erromango community had recently been provoked by an attack of outsiders. Several weeks prior to their arrival, an Australian sandalwood trader had brutally killed two boys that happened to be the sons of the local chief. That vicious attack resulted in the resolve of the community to violently oppose any white-skinned outsiders.

Williams and Harris were attacked within minutes of setting foot on the island, and after being clubbed to death they were eaten by the islanders as part of a sacred ritual. You read that correctly... they were eaten.

Somehow, even without the Internet, word of their fate quickly spread. They were accused of being foolish and crazy and imposing foreign standards upon unwilling communities living in "primitive bliss." But the story doesn't end there. Twenty years later, another missionary, John Paton took his family to the island, ministering and leading many of the Vanautu island people to trust Christ. It doesn't stop there either. For two thousand years many, many have given their lives for the cause of the Gospel.

Living out the Great Commission isn't difficult when you understand Jesus' words, "Foxes have holes, and birds of the air have nests, but the Son of Man has nowhere to lay his head" (Matt. 8:20). It could have been Jesus' way of saying, "Home is where the heart is, but you better make sure you know where your heart is!" However, He is saying a mature believer devoted to the Great Commission doesn't begin their journey by measuring out their home or planning for retirement... they realize they are already dead and are not afraid. True discipleship involves a struggle and spiritual warfare. The critics were complaining that John Chau must not have been planning on coming home. I disagree. He knew he was punching his ticket to go home... either to be with the Sentinelese for the rest of his life or to go home to the Father, it didn't matter to him. Total obedience to Christ is as foreign as is a Martian to this selfish world.

If I said to you that I was a Las Vegas Raider fan, and a member of the Raider nation, then you would know I was a fanatic. Those are the fans that paint their faces black and white and dress up like modern day warriors similar to Mad Max. We are suspicious and wary of fanatics. They make us uncomfortable. But if I tell you I am a fan of college football and the South Carolina Gamecocks then you will smirk a little and say "bless your heart" while boasting about your Crimson Tide, Fighting Irish, Seminoles, or Nittany Lions. *Fan* is the shortened form of fanatic. Is that what we've done as Christ-followers? To take the fanatical feeling out of it, we have not only created a new word but given it a new definition. Many would say today, "I'm not fanatical about Jesus, but I'm a fan." What does that say? A lot. It's time we become fanatics about Jesus again.

The Seven Promises for becoming a fanatic for Christ

If you design and discipline your life to meet with God every day, longing for the overflow, then I promise you it will grow into an incredible and fanatical love affair.

If you absorb the statement, "your spiritual life will never grow above your prayer life", and begin to pray every day for mission, then I promise you will fall in love with God like a fanatic and you will crave the opportunity to talk to Him, and to listen as He speaks to you through His Holy Word.

If you read the Bible every day, and read through it each year, then I promise you God's Word becomes indispensable for your fanatical living and lifestyle, and you will want to give away the Gospel to others.

If you make worship a priority each week, then I promise the Holy Spirit will make you a priority in dispatching you for fanatical ministry work.

If you serve in some capacity in the church on a regular basis with all humility, trusting your leader, then I promise you that you will never feel insignificant and your fanatical service will become contagious.

If you tithe, give, and then give some more, I promise you will never feel like a failure in ministry, you will never feel as if you have wasted your life, and people will call you fanatical for God.

If you lead one person to Christ, just one person, I promise you that you will lead more and more, and you will die feeling that you could have done more. And you will be correct.

Reality

Now that I have your attention, let's begin to shift to reality. Your reality. I just hung up the phone from talking to my good friend Adam about getting involved and becoming all God means for him. In short, the Holy Spirit is changing Adam's life. He is undergoing spiritual transformation right before my eyes. His questions were the same questions I hear all too often: "Where do I start? What do I do? How do I find out exactly where God wants me? What is God's will for my life?" I realize you want to make a significant contribution to God's cause, but one thing that stands out to me about every Great Commission hero of mine is that self-promotion was absent from their ministry. My list of spiritual giants of the past were not famous by today's standards. They were obedient. They were zealous. They were fanatics in their own right. They had this unsurpassed passion for going as far as the oceans would carry them. They didn't search for notoriety to sell their books and ideas. They continued their search to know God by going in God's name. They were playing the game of life and the only audience member that mattered was God alone.

Reality starts when you and I get over our self-seeking ways in order to get under Jesus authority. *Compromise* has no place in God's work, and it may just be the most despised word by God Himself. Compromise leads to you and me settling for less than God's grand design for us. In my zealous younger days, I purchased a poster, and had it framed (it still hangs on my office wall), of a guy standing while everyone else is bowed down to the king and his entourage walking in parade. It reads at the top, "No empty words, no white lies, no token prayers, no compromise." Compromise comes when we entertain sin. Letting sin hang around only invites trouble later. If you don't believe that, then ask David who had to deal with Saul's inept and failed engagement with the Amalekites in 1 Samuel 30. Puritan preacher John Owen said, "Do you mortify; do you make it your daily work; be always at it whilst you live; cease not a day from this work; be killing sin or it will be killing you." If you want to be an ambassador for Jesus, you have to quit any games with God. Indulge me. I have one more incredible mission story before I get down to the basics concerning your mission and mine.

BRUCHKO

You probably haven't heard of Bruce Olson, a.k.a. "Bruchko," but he too, is a risk taker. His remarkable story is told in his autobiography, *For This Cross I'll Kill You* (later renamed *Bruchko*). It was one of the first missionary books I read cover-to-cover, thoroughly engrossed in his almost unbelievable adventure. Here, a nineteen-year-old Midwestern boy of the early 1960's wanted to be a missionary. No, it wasn't something he selected to fit his fancy during the high school job fair. Olson was called by God to go at an early age. He recounts in his book about going to an interdenominational missionary conference when he was just sixteen and encountering a Mr. Rayburn, a missionary to New Guinea. He recalls

The Great Go Mission

Rayburn speaking of the extreme poverty he encountered there. Then Mr. Rayburn made his appeal and plea to the audience, describing the rat-infested scene in Melanesia, the southwest Pacific. He painted the evangelistic canvas that only missionaries can do of the damned — the lost without Christ and dying in their sins while the rest of the modern world sits idly by in the comfort of their home. His depiction of the apathy of the American church in the 1960's grabbed young Olson's attention. Rayburn went on to condemn the mere talk about missions, laying the responsibility and the blood of the heathens at the feet of today's church.

Bruce Olson was hooked. His problem was that there wasn't a mission organization in sight that would touch him. Hudson Taylor, the great English missionary to China experienced the same rejection due to lack of training or education. And so did countless others. Bruce didn't want to continue his college studies and he had no time to get into long-term training; he was ready to go... or so he thought.

He secretly took a bus to Chicago to obtain a passport because he knew his parents wouldn't approve. He bought a one-way ticket to Venezuela. Through a friend, he found a missionary there who agreed to pick him up from the airport and show him around. Bruce had $70 in his pocket and didn't know a soul in South America, but felt God calling him there. He didn't know one sentence in Spanish. It wasn't long after he arrived that he found a room and started wandering the streets of Caracas. He met someone, was asked to enroll in the University and there he was, a tall blond-haired American standing out among all those Venezuelans. And true to form for seemingly every missionary I've ever read about, Olson got sick. His fever hit 103° before a simple medication prescribed by a doctor, and paid for by a fellow student, rescued him. Through several more introductions, he met a man in the Department of Health, and was offered a job teaching English to potential students going abroad to study at Harvard. It was this meeting, however, that "Bruchko," the name given to him by the Motilones, learned about this unreached Indian tribe.

Braving the jungle and almost massacred by the Motilones, Bruchko, led by the Holy Spirit, made the seemingly impossible mission connection. The tribal chief embraced and worshiped Jesus, Bruchko labored and translated the Scriptures into their language, and more and more impossible stories followed and still continue today as Olson has passionately given his life to ministering and reaching this South American Indian people group.

THE LESSON

What is our takeaway from the stories we have read so far? Is this zeal for the Kingdom hereditary? I crave these life and death stories for the Gospel, and my fascination never fades. What is it about these called-out saints that make us proud to call them our brothers and sisters in Christ, but also makes us ponder our own lack of effort? Heroes of the faith, which all missionaries are, need to be regularly recognized and celebrated for their bravery! But the truth is, these servants don't want the recognition, accolades, or awards. They know they've already received it when they simply bow down to the Lord Jesus.

What advances for the kingdom of God would we have ever made without missionaries? Our Christian dilemma is apathy. No, the modern-day church doesn't have disdain for missionaries, and we haven't really forgotten them. Rather, the twenty-first century American church views them as an insignificant other, a dying breed, or maybe as orphans that the church literally left on the doorsteps of others a long time ago. At this point you may be fostering your argument against my position but follow the trail.

Thom Rainer's work, *Breakout Churches*, speculates that eighty percent of the 400,000+ churches in America are declining, have plateaued, and/or have lost their purpose. Churches, for the most part, have grown stale. The statistics are often camouflaged by the great church growth stories of a few megachurches. While we are lamenting the fact that our culture is going to hell in a handbasket from the moral decline of America, we tend to forget the ripple effects. The church is cutting the evangelism and discipleship budget to the bone because the worn out 1950's buildings geared to accommodate the Sunday School programs of yesteryear are unusable or in disrepair. Staff downsizing is necessary to keep up with providing senior leadership salaries. And in our lost effort to preserve and sustain the ship, missionary support is a line item done away with altogether by small and medium sized churches. They've been fooled into thinking they have to keep up with the Joneses with their budgets. Slowly, but surely, the American church is turning inward rather than going outward.

The Great Go Mission

Rainer says missions giving among the core groups— the Baptists, Methodists, Presbyterians, and Assembly of God churches is down almost 50% from the 1960's. The decline in missions giving precedes the decline in church attendance. Did you understand the previous sentence? It means our church attendance is sadly spiraling downward as it follows the budget cuts. Further statistics say three-fourths of American life has lost the Christian influence that the church once supplied. Even sadder, a majority of the emerging and contemporary churches lack any effort to simply *go* and share the Gospel. What's happening?

Because of our one-sided focus on the declining church, our inept definition of God movements and a lack of "jealousy" for true discipleship in the American church is causing our focus on Jesus to persistently diminish. If the American church were compared to athletics, it would be analogous to the giant spectator sport, the NFL. If we continue with just a few players and coaches who are involved on the sidelines and on that artificial green football field, then I will quote the colorful coach, and now retired, Jerry Glanville. He once remarked, "This is the NFL and that stands for "not for long" [if you keep doing it that way]." The majority do not comprehend the decline in funding. The resulting tragedy is a reductionist philosophy of cutting out mission giving to prop up and propagate the local church. Does that mean the heart of mission work is gone? Not so fast. There's a remnant.

OUR INEPT DEFINITION OF GOD MOVEMENTS AND A LACK OF "JEALOUSY" FOR TRUE DISCIPLESHIP IN THE AMERICAN CHURCH IS CAUSING OUR FOCUS ON JESUS TO PERSISTENTLY DIMINISH.

New Frontiers, New Opportunities

I walked into the Cigar Box in Jasper, Alabama, the day after Christmas. I was in Jasper visiting my in-laws for the holiday. It's a small town on the far peripheral northwest side of Birmingham that functions as a lunch or gas stop on your way to Tupelo. Nothing to do, I strolled into the newly opened cigar place. Yeah, I smoke a stogie every now and then just like one of my heroes, the Reverend Charles H. Spurgeon, and the founder of my seminary, Dr. B.H. Carroll. It's true.

The owner, Shawn, welcomed me better than any church I had ever attended. His hospitality and handshake were as genuine as I have ever received. Honestly, my saying that I was a pastor and STM may have had something to do with the free cigar he offered me, but that's not important. I chose my favorite cigar from the humidor, sat down with his three buddies, and we began to discuss mission work. That's right, mission work. And that in itself is another book.

I was puffing on my cigar with three brothers in Christ, talking about how they all were involved in their own mission projects in Europe, Latin America, and Cuba. Each man went into detail describing his passion for going and sharing the Gospel, teaching children about Jesus' love, and giving away their hard-earned money and time. Passionate about serving God while "going," they talked about how they once worked on the staffs of various churches but left their positions because the Great Commission wasn't being accomplished in their respective churches. One man was driving a school bus during the year and using his extra money to fund his mission work in Spain, the Ukraine, and Scotland during the summer months. Another was new to mission work and was about to start seminary. My new friend, Shawn, had opened a t-shirt printing company, but needed to do more to fund his mission work in the Caribbean, thus the Cigar Box.

Before I left that Cigar shop, I was invited to church, invited to come back, and invited to go on a mission trip to Latin America with them... and they were serious. I have discovered something and will talk about it in the rest of this book: They are out there. People on mission for Christ are out there doing it... sharing and preaching Jesus. What about you? Where is your zeal directed?

In the last book of the Bible, Revelation, addressed to the last ancient church mentioned, Laodicea, and among the last words John the

Revelator writes to them he says, "Those whom I love, I reprove and discipline, so be zealous and repent" (Rev. 3:19). In these last days, let's not forsake a basic thirst and zeal for the Lord Jesus. Distressingly, there is a continuous quest to institutionalize the Great Commission, thinking that it legitimizes our efforts. In other words, we've become cultured and tolerant of being asked to keep our Christianity to ourselves. Government and civic groups are pushing Christians into the corner more and more. If we don't develop a zeal for Christ, then we will be unable to come out with holy fighting. God can do it without any help from you and me, but friends, that is the point I am making – He *desires* for us to do it. You had better start getting jealous for God or you will not make it. Get jealous and zealous.

Chapter Four
A CASUAL THEOLOGY = A CASUAL PLAN

"My main ambition in life is to be on Satan's most wanted list."
-Leonard Ravenhill

"To this end we always pray for you, that our God may make you worthy of his calling and may fulfill every resolve for good and every work of faith by his power..." -2 Thessalonians 1:11

"DETROIT MICHIGAN, THE HOME OF rock 'n' roll!" yelled Rock & Roll Hall of Famer, Bob Seger, during the taping of his album, *Live Bullet*, in September of 1975. Detroit is also home to Motown, Ford, and GM, as well as the Pistons, Tigers, Red Wings, and Lions. However, with the influx of Muslim immigrants from the Middle East, it has become one of the foreign mission hotspots in the good ol' U.S.A. The Greater Detroit area is home to one of the largest, oldest and most diverse Arab American communities in the United States. The city has shrunk by hundreds of thousands in the past two decades, but it has begun a renaissance of sorts.

The demand for the Gospel to be preached there again is colossal, and churches need to be started by the hundreds. Perspective from the outside is that many Christian leaders have given up because it looks impossible.

The Holy Spirit led me there several years ago. It started out as one of those useless fact-finding missions I found myself involved in again. Apparently too often, I find myself in the back of the van on my mission endeavors. The mission, as explained to me, was to get the church I lead and shepherd to be involved in helping new church plants near downtown Detroit, spilling over into Ontario, Canada. Trying to make sense of this seemingly nonsensical journey, I inquired of the goal to get other churches onboard. My question was met with bewilderment. "Goal?" Therein lies the problem. Goal-less equals clueless when doing God's work. Before I learned how to correctly do mission work, I was involved in several failed mission endeavors that failed for being goal-less. Just going someplace in the name of Jesus doesn't mean you are being obedient to the Great Commission. Nike made millions with "Just do it," but our attitude of "just go" has resulted in a shrinking budget, lifeless involvement, and a dwindling movement.

WHAT DO YOU BELIEVE?

Tom Fillinger is president of IgniteUS, a consulting ministry for leadership, discipleship, and reform of the church. He says we all have a *Directional Theology*: What you believe is taking you somewhere. Your theology, what you believe about God has a destination— is transporting you somewhere. It matters what you believe. Whatever your theology, understand, you are in that philosophical vehicle being lifted or lowered to another level. It may be a level of understanding or misunderstanding. The experience may be good or bad; up or down. Here's the lesson: Don't worry about *comprehension* more than you concern yourself with God's *apprehension* of you. Don't merely grasp a strategy, but instead allow the Holy Spirit to grab you and immerse you in His Word.

Here's the obvious answer to knowing God's will for your life:

> Thus says the Lord: "Let not the wise man boast in his wisdom, let not the mighty man boast in his might, let not the rich man boast in his riches, but let him who boasts boast in this, that he understands and knows me, that I am the Lord who practices steadfast love, justice, and righteousness in the earth. For in these things I delight," declares the Lord (Jer. 9:23-24).

What is a good first step in knowing God's specific mission for me? Know Him. Strive to be an eager student of the Word of God and seek to digest its principles and truths in which to live. Repeatedly in the Old

The Great Go Mission

Testament the nation of Israel is admonished to follow the Lord while being reminded of God's statutes. This must be the message to the modern-day church also. First and foremost, the Bible must apprehend you— and hold you to the point of having a passion for God's dynamic mission. If you are going to begin praying about your involvement in mission work today, your appetite for God has to come from His Holy Word.

First and foremost, the Bible must grab you...

LTM stands for long-term missionaries and missions, STM for short-term missionaries and missions. LTM is how we have done it forever, at least for the last 250 years. Mission organizations were created in order to "send" would-be missionaries off to another land. To *send* meant being able to pay for the mission endeavor, to organize a missionary plan, to prayerfully support the missionaries, and to pay the missionaries' salaries. In addition, it means to act as home base for the sent missionary— and for the financial support— to prove their validity to foreign and domestic governments. Like all American commerce, some mission organizations were legitimate and succeeded, while some were poorly managed, therefore failing pathetically.

Hudson Taylor felt the call in 1854, at age nineteen, to leave England and to go to China for the long haul. Here was the conundrum: he had no money, no training, and couldn't find a sending mission group. He waited a year or more while training as a doctor when, finally, a group took a chance on him. Disappointingly, young Hudson found out too late that it was actually he who had taken a chance on them. Anxious about the assignment, and the potential of this "startup" organization (uh-oh, getting that feeling yet?), he jumped in full force only to become disillusioned when he arrived in Shanghai. This first journey alone took five and half months by boat, and you can be assured it was economy class. Where was the bathroom on those old boats? Could you upgrade to economy plus? Upon arrival, he encountered other missionaries who had suffered burnout within short periods of time. He, himself, was stricken with sickness after a few years and had to return to England to recuperate before returning to China. Taylor believed in the God of the Bible resulting in a legitimate, solid faith in Him and His mission.

A lot of current missionary movements are still operating as if the conditions of the world are the same as they were two hundred years ago. On his voyage Taylor braved seasickness, a contemptable crew, and a near shipwreck while sailing to China. When he arrived and looked up the three men who were to help him get started, he discovered one had just died, another had just left for England, the third was missing, and the stipend for housing he was promised had vanished. Hudson Taylor did not speak Mandarin upon his arrival and, to add to his present hopeless situation, he was already worn out from the lengthy cruise. But it did not stop him.

The zeal for going and doing mission work can be contagious and energizing. Just reading and hearing the stories of risk from the giants of the past is empowering to you and me, and to those who will be called in the future. But for all the courageous pilgrims who have braved the opposition, pain, and tragedy, there have also been many who have quit. Recent statistics show that seven thousand leave the mission field every year. Carlton Vandagriff of the International Mission Board (IMB) wrote a blog post in 2017 listing *Five Things That Make Missionaries Leave the Field*:

1. Excitement without calling
2. Spiritual immaturity
3. Poor health
4. Children's needs
5. Sexual sin

Three out of the five have to do directly with theological issues. The pep talks and motivating stories are not enough to sustain the person involved in God's mission. Does it sound like I am trying to discourage you? If you are debating the mission field down the street, in the next state, or in another world, don't go if God has not dealt with you in a deeply personal way. Do not attempt to do LTM or STM/STP without a firm grasp on God's direction for your life.

Days Gone By

Lottie Moon was an incredible servant of the Lord in China 150 years ago. She followed her sister to China, but her sister couldn't handle the stress of a missionary's life of being away from home. For some sad reason Edmonia Moon developed a mental condition that greatly affected her

The Great Go Mission

health and returned to America, only to commit suicide years later. We don't know her spiritual state, but we desperately need a theological foundation if pursuing mission work. What is your theology of salvation? It's called soteriology. Delving even further: what does it mean to go? What is the Holy Spirit's involvement? Why should you go? How do you recover when things go south, or the enemy gets to you? If you stay home, then where is God working in your life to carry out His mission? Where do you turn when the feelings of failure invade your ministry? Even worse, what do you do when you just want to die?

I like great movie quotes (so do you— admit it). You know there are not many sequels that have lasting words, but Rocky III does. My wife says it must be a guy thing, but Sylvester Stallone as Rocky Balboa shaped many young men when it debuted in 1976. Rocky overcame the odds of being a smalltime boxer and won it big! Now, in the second sequel, part 3, Rocky is getting old. He is facing the realities of his inadequate physical stature and that Mickey, his trainer, had been carrying him for years by scheduling easy opponents. Rock has this conversation with the old man:

> **Rocky:** You really don't think I got nothin' left, do you?
> **Mickey:** Well, Rock, let's put it this way. Three years ago, you were supernatural. You was hard and nasty. You had this cast iron jaw. But then, the worst thing happened to you that could happen to any fighter. You got civilized. Don't worry, kid. You know, presidents retire, generals retire, horses retire, Man-o-War retired. They put him out to stud. That's what you should've done, retire.

Mickey's lingering words, "you were supernatural" and "you got civilized" have more than just a superficial meaning for us. They are metaphors for the turn in modern missions. Once upon a time we were supernatural, so to speak, in our approach and someone brazenly said, "We were ten feet tall and bullet-proof." We were galvanized by our agreement on God's Word. The Holy Spirit guided and directed our planning and execution of ministry as we prayed fervently. Fasting and prayer was the staple of long-term missionaries. Now, it's money and sightseeing (for the STM).

The Great Commission is God's charge to His people about His desire. The evangelistic purpose of going was front and center. Couple evangelism with a heart for discipleship and it was TNT. It was dynamite! Our motto could have been: "Every man dies, but not every man really lives," long before it became a motto in pop culture! We were not on side streets of worship wars, arguing for a new wave of the Spirit, pushing the prosperity gospel, nor battling for the next recipe to build a mega-church. No! Men and women left their homes braving the elements, poor transportation, and lack of food; raw to the elements, without adequate funding, forsaking all others... to exalt God! Now, just like a Triple Crown winner of the past, all we can do is talk about the glory days.

THE REAL GOAL

Recently, someone posted on social media: "GO" in huge letters! Then underneath, in small letters, "and make disciples." It should be the reverse. Let's take a moment and understand the Great Commission. It does not tell us to go. Let me repeat that: it does *not* tell us to go. If I were standing in front of you preaching this, I would likely say it another ten times to get your attention, and maybe shake you! Look at it:

> **Go therefore and make disciples of all nations, baptizing them in the name of the Father and of the Son and of the Holy Spirit, teaching them to observe all that I have commanded you. And behold, I am with you always, to the end of the age (Matt. 28:19-20).**

Wait! I thought you said... I did. Go back to the beginning of the paragraph to confirm it. Okay, now that you have done that... and at this point you think I have lost my mind, here's the problem: We are looking at a word instead of the function of the clause, to put it in grammatical terms. It's a clause... among several other clauses. "Go" looks like a command straight from the lips of Jesus, but that is not what it means here. A verbal command is not what Matthew wrote.

Your interpretation of "Go," as if you're being cheered on to get up from your place of laziness, is not the proper translation. The message of the Great Commission is lost in translation. Sure, it's a co-mission, but it's

The Great Go Mission

also a GO-mission. Here's what Jesus said, from the Greek: "As you are going...make disciples of all nations." Or an even better translation to clarify – would be for you and me, "Having already gone...." Jesus is not holding a pep rally here at the end of the Gospel of Matthew trying to hype up the disciples to obedience like they were at a Zig Ziglar conference. An imperative command does not exist at the beginning of the Great Commission found in Matthew 28.

Sometimes I believe we confuse Jesus' command in the Great Commission with Knute Rockne's half-time speech to the University of Notre Dame football team. Since they didn't have recording devices so readily available in the 1920's, Rockne recreated what he said for a newsreel,

> We're going inside of 'em, we're going outside of 'em – inside of 'em! outside of 'em! – and when we get them on the run once, we're going to keep 'em on the run. And we're not going to pass unless their secondary comes up too close. But don't forget, men – we're gonna get 'em on the run, we're gonna go, go, go, go! – and we aren't going to stop until we go over that goal line! And don't forget, men – today is the day we're gonna win. They can't lick us – and that's how it goes...The first platoon men – go in there and fight, fight, fight, fight, fight! What do you say, men!

Isn't this a great rallying cry? It makes my heart palpitate like I watched the movies: Rocky, Rudy and William Wallace of Braveheart all rolled into one! And if you are a sports enthusiast, especially football, you would love to hear these fighting and encouraging words from your coach. However, again, that is not what Jesus was doing. He was not pushing a hard sell of hysteria to the twelve. He simply stated the purpose of His mission in which He wants us involved. The power is in the Word, not in our acting, nor ability. The power is from the Holy Spirit, not from our good works. Theology, what the text says and our correct rendering of it, matters. Your theology will take you someplace, but make sure it's the right place.

Are you acting like Rocky? Think you have "nothing left?" Following God on His mission for your life is something supernatural. Please do not become civilized to the point where you sell your soul for idols and financial security. Resist the quick Internet sales of *How to Grow Your Faith in Ten*

Easy Steps. Receiving the truth from the Master is where you need to begin. Remember: what you believe about the Bible is leading you somewhere. When you feel or sense God's clear direction, ask yourself: is that perhaps where you *want* to go, or is it where God is taking you? There is a huge difference. God takes us where we need to go, not where we want to go.

The focus of the Great Commission centers around the mission for your life. It is a plan...God's plan. At the end of the Gospel of Matthew Jesus is about to ascend to the right hand of the Father and, as He is leaving, he imparts final instructions for us to understand. In our modern-day vernacular, it would sound differently than a pep talk. Don't misunderstand me, I'm not saying He was subdued and relaxed, speaking in hushed tones about it, but I'm sure He wasn't standing on a soapbox firing up the crowd like Coach Rockne. I'm sure He was not acting like He had just returned from a John Maxwell conference, inflecting his voice and bellowing, "Go, go, go!" Here it is. This is what I believe Jesus said: "As you have already decided to follow Me (as you are already going), then here is what I want you to do," and here is the focal point: "share with others about Me and the message, while making enthusiastic, joyful, following learners who walk and talk like Me!" Jesus' statement and command is a good plan for your life. It is the only plan for life.

CASUAL = CASUALTIES

The cavalier and flippant approach to the Great Commission amounts to massive attrition. Waiting for someone to yell your pseudo battle cry to "go" is wasting time. And hearing the supposed cry to march as "onward Christian soldiers" has reduced the cause to sightseeing while beefing up the tourism industry - it's called Christian tourism. It's surely the evidence of what was once a radical movement gone casual. Mission work is just the latest victim of wrong ecclesiology. In other words, wrong church.

It is wrong for the church and organizations to send volunteers and would-be missionaries into the field without a complete understanding of the mission. Current statistics point to good people doing good things in the name of Jesus. It may be good, but it's not the goal. The very heart of the Great Commission is at stake when short-term missionaries are not spiritually educated and equipped. In addition to the planning of short-term projects, preparation must go beyond a quick overview of the culture,

The Great Go Mission

although historical awareness and a cognitive picture of the political climate greatly enhances the mission. Plan, plan, and then do more planning while getting a grasp of what is going on. Presently, while writing this, I am only a few weeks out from a glocal STP with my wife and we are getting daily reports of drastic governmental policy changes directed toward the church and to what they call the "western" influence. When I read their words of warning and policy, I say to myself, "They are talking about me!" It is incumbent upon me to be aware of the changes and how they affect my planning.

A casual response to the Great Commission may not produce a tumultuous display in your life, but it may well have cataclysmic consequences in the future. Be responsible by praying through a STP or the mission and understand the directional signs from the Holy Spirit. Here's a great way to tell if you are serious about the STP: Is your checklist for the actual goal(s) to be accomplished for the mission of the same importance as your packing, planning, and flight arrangements for the STP? If you haven't spent time praying over the goals and how you are going to achieve them, then you are not packed. I have found several manuals touting the importance of planning and, upon further inspection, 90% of them are about making travel arrangements!

SPIRITUAL PACKING LIST FOR STP:

- ☐ Publicly, plainly stated & written goal(s) for the STP. Don't complicate it.
- ☐ Attain individual & corporate prayer support before, during, and after the STP.
- ☐ Make sure you have your spiritual passport with you at all times. In other words, make time for personal devotional time during the STP. You will need the spiritual energy while you are there.
- ☐ Purchase a journal and record the events that shape the journey. In real time, record your happenings and stories to reflect upon when you get home. It will also serve as a reminder to pray for those you met and ministered to because I promise you when you arrive home, you will want to resume

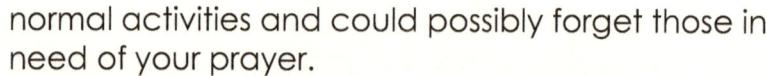

normal activities and could possibly forget those in need of your prayer.
- ☐ Purposely and Pointedly, look into the eyes of those you are ministering to and see beyond your selfishness and realize God has put you face to face with someone who needs Jesus.
- ☐ Plan another trip by setting a tentative date when you return home. Keep it fresh on your mind.
- ☐ Be positive and encouraging by forgetting about tracking personal baggage. Forget social media while you are away...concentrate on what God wants to do through you.

The Christian life is about a relationship with Jesus that transcends all others. Mission work ought to be the same focus... relationships. Our desire should be to reach people where they are, which demands we connect with someone. Your desire to preach the Gospel has to be grounded first in your relationship with God. Pack spiritually...accordingly. Do you thirst after Him, looking forward to gathering with like believers to worship and spur each other on? After all, we are asking them to enter into the relationship of all relationships with the King of Kings.

Planting a Church Plant

Sitting in the back of the van (I know), I asked the mission leader this question, "How many churches are committed to helping start new churches in Detroit?" Out of the whole state of two thousand churches, there were only a handful, one handful. I shouldn't have been upset with the lack of participation, but I was. Understand that Detroit was only one of many mission fields for which we were asked to help with church planters. Other metropolitan areas of America were being shopped, too. However, this creates another STM dilemma.

Down South we say it like this: "There is hunting with a shotgun and there is hunting with a rifle." With a shotgun the pellets (shot) spread out, to hit multiple targets. You use a shotgun to shoot birds. On the other hand, a rifle is used to hit the bullseye. STM cannot be done with a shotgun. You will miss the target 100% of the time. Sadly, shotgun style is also the way the modern church does evangelism, but that is for another time. STM

The Great Go Mission

lends itself to specialization or to a narrower target. LTM's are lifers. LTM's are different breeds. They are in it for the long haul. They learn the language, the culture, the traditions, and the customs. They can afford to spread out, take timely steps, and learn in order to reach many different people in one nation. STMs or "Short-term Projects" (STP) cannot do this. You usually get one shot. STPs have to concentrate on one locale and only a few days, at the most, to be effective. They need to penetrate that locality by a real sending capacity. In spiritual fighting words: Give it all you got!

In Detroit, my church committed to helping three church planters. Since I am a shy-type relationship person and have to feed off of like feelings, I gravitated toward a young quiet guy I met. I heard and liked his testimony, and the risk factor, of moving his family to this crime ridden city that was making a comeback. He intrigued me with his vision. The Holy Spirit was pushing me to engage with him.

Another leader was someone I had absolutely nothing in common with. He was just over the border in Windsor, Ontario. I don't know anything about Canada, and not to be mean, but who goes there? He loved hockey. I hate hockey because I'm from the South and I never knew it existed or saw a game until the 1980 *Miracle on Ice*, when the U.S. Olympic team defeated the Soviet team. Still, to this day, it's the only entire professional hockey game I've ever watched. I don't even know the name of the positions outside of the goalie! Again, the Holy Spirit drew me to this young guy whose testimony of being far from God, and now being an unashamed evangelist and pastor, grabbed me.

The last young man's vision was as far from my comfort zone as you can get. He was married with two children living in an old neighborhood, the ones that we might label "the 'hood." He has a long beard akin to Billy Gibbons of ZZ Top. His plan called for winning street kids to Christ, having them move in and live with his family, discipling them, and one day starting a church. So, we decided to help each of them launch their respective churches.

It was not a laidback effort, and we are not a megachurch with gobs of money. Our zeal is to be laser focused on gospel-centered mission work. Paul's words to the church at Corinth:

> I planted, Apollos watered, but God gave the
> growth. So neither he who plants nor he who waters is

anything, but only God who gives the growth. He who plants and he who waters are one, and each will receive his wages according to his labor. For we are God's fellow workers. You are God's field, God's building (1 Cor. 3:6-9).

Our church prayed for the start-up churches in several of our meetings and worship services. We took up offerings and gave the money. We had an expensive sound system given to us for future use, and instead we gave it to the church in Canada. Our entire worship team traveled almost a thousand miles by air and highway, hauling our sound equipment to Detroit. We continue to send support and plan future days to go and give. We haven't made huge dents in the work yet, but we led in worship, we've prayed diligently for the church in Detroit, I've preached a sermon or two, and we celebrated God's goodness and blessings. Why? Our approach to ministry is far from casual, but we are deliberate.

Those pastors planted the seed along with several others. We came along and did a little yard work and watered the new garden. Now, as they continue to seek and serve this great God of ours, preaching salvation through faith alone in Christ alone, God alone is growing them. If God's Word has arrested and apprehended you, your church urgently needs to get involved in some type of short-term mission project.

AMATEURIZATION AND PROFESSIONALIZATION IN MISSIONS

When mission organizations were delineating a strategy for long-term missionaries nearly three centuries ago, the six-month boat ride was built into the itinerary. When faster boats were developed and then plane travel introduced, they then made adjustments to time. But they did not take into consideration the sociological changes that gradually accompanied the mission work. Short-term journeys and trips, as recently as only forty years ago, started making significant inroads into the way we look at missions.

Yet debate ensued near the end of the twentieth century over the advantages and disadvantages of STM as the number of short-term missionaries increased. Some of the LTM balked at these so-called interlopers and cried foul. Ralph Winter, founder of the U.S. Center for World Missions, is regarded as the first to use the term "amateurization" to

The Great Go Mission

describe young people, or the inexperienced, going on short-term trips. The long-termers (LTM) detested what they considered their flippant approach to the STM, and developed apparent apathetic attitudes toward them. And rightly so, because STM made serious mistakes that led to many unnecessary deaths and demoralization of missionaries and pastors. David Hesselgrave, co-founder of the Evangelical Missiological Society, points out that their "amateurism set missions back instead of propelling the work forward." The result: long-term missionaries looked down on the short-term newcomers. This advent of STM served to show more and eager Christ-followers who were able to "go," but does it matter? Does it continue to be detrimental?

Twenty years ago, I was invited on another one of those "fact-finding" missions, this time to Taiwan. My state denomination was anxious to get more of our churches involved in doing attractive missions on the island once known as Formosa ("beautiful island"). During the Communist Revolution in China in the late 1940's, the Generalissimo Chang Kai-Shek and the Kuomintang escaped incarceration by fleeing to this scenic island, taking the Republic of China (ROC) with him. Literally. Overnight they had dismantled thousands and thousands of idol shrines and reconstructed them on the island. Miss Bertha Smith, Southern Baptist missionary to China, was forced to Taiwan along with the ROC. Word has it (something I heard but can't corroborate) that the brilliant Miss Bertha purchased lots in what is now downtown Taipei for ministry, and years later the land was sold for unheard of dollars. I cut my teeth on international missions in Taiwan. Three times I visited Taiwan, walked the streets of Taipei, saw literally hundreds of Buddhist and Taoist temples while witnessing the pagan practices of burning money to please the false gods.

We primarily participated in prayer walks and arranged for several backyard Bible club meetings with children. Nothing else. Okay, there was a perfunctory prayer every now and then, but they were blessing-type prayers we had before we went out— like a preliminary exercise. Understand, I have nothing but great respect for the men and women (LTM) I have met who have uprooted their families, relocating them to the other side of the globe for the cause of Christ. But our team was made to feel like we interrupted the festivities. It wasn't intentional. They didn't mean to, and they were not malicious. They just didn't have time for "inexperienced" missionary wannabes from the southern United States. Parading around town and eating Asian fare was fantastic. However, I'm afraid we have developed a worthless Christian pastime that I call *Christian Tourism*. It's a cheap substitute for mission work. The long-term missionaries are thrust into the reluctant position of tour guide. And who can blame them for being reluctant? Short-Term Projects coupled with Long-term missionaries becomes like a sporting activity pitting one team against the other.

While I am on the subject: prayer is foundation, groundwork, and prelude to mission work, and I will talk about its necessity in the next chapter, but prayer-walking as the primary task of STM confuses me. Maybe there are those who can't walk and chew gum at the same time, and I believe in this walking and praying discipline...however, can someone explain to me how and why it has become the primary work for our short-term mission opportunities? I have a friend who says, "Greg, we can pray at home."

Categorizing missions at "home" and missions in a "foreign" country was never the New Testament's intention. Going is going.

Instead of orchestrating an elaborate mission trip to the other side of the world to prayer walk, our pre-planning prayer should lead to walking in the Spirit to share the Gospel in myriad creative ways when we get there. And one more thing... if we have prayer-walking, do we have prayer-driving and riding around? Do we have prayer-hiking? What about prayer-swimming or running? Prayer-skydiving? You get my point.

STP is the way of the future for missions, but it does not mean LTM is to be discarded. No, it's God's wake-up call for the church to see where updated travel and communication has changed the playing field as we share the Great Commission. It's a call for new planning. Categorizing missions at "home" and missions in a "foreign" country was never the New Testament's intention. Going is going. Following is following. Your commitment to Him is your commitment to go and follow wherever He leads you. The church has to climb up to the new venture of doing God's mission as one, both here and there. It confuses a congregation to present missions as alienated and segregated, yet we have done it for years. A huge theme of the Pauline epistle to the church in Ephesus is unity, so why is the church confused about the Great Commission and carrying out the mission of God?

DISCIPLESHIP IS NASTY

Mission work is ugly and dirty, and we have made the church and ministry "activities" too clean. Those first missionaries in Acts risked their lives, and they were labeled the first rockers – turning the world upside-down. Go to Detroit and observe what my new friends are doing by planting churches in the vilest places on earth and look at their faces with smiles and feel the joy in their hearts as they serve our Lord; then tell me you don't want to give your prayer, time, and money to that work or a work like it, and I'll tell you that you are neither serious about God, nor about the Gospel.

Drew Ansley, a church planter & disciple maker, was promoted by the Holy Spirit to go directly to the front lines of ministry. The front line in ministry, like the frontline in war, is no place for doubters, the mild-mannered, or cowards in Jesus (if there is such a thing). It is a warzone. Drew and his lovely and Jesus-devoted wife, Alisha, have bought a dilapidated house in one of those poor sections of Detroit like you see on the evening news. They invite new converts to Christ (often homeless students) into their home to live. I've toured Drew's home several times and he has shared with me that often he and his wife have to teach these teenagers general hygiene before they can move on to teaching them to become a disciple of Jesus.

Where most families would be concerned about the safety of living in those Detroit neighborhoods, and they should, Drew and his wife are safely in God's will. It is a freeing thing to know God's place for your life even if it's a place the world deems unsafe. Real mission work is a far cry from the painted pictures of modern church growth. Incredibly I just saw a poster advertising a church conference with the profile picture of one of the speakers with the caption, "How to market your church for growth!" Being a minister/missionary and doing discipleship is difficult and can be ugly, but this type of promotion is dirty and does not represent the Gospel of

Jesus Christ. The church growth movement needs more guys like Drew and Alisha that have clean hearts in the midst of a polluted society.

Mission Logistics

The logistics of God's mission (Missio Dei) are being debated while its purpose is suffering. The problem is in the incisive understanding of God's mission, and missions in general. For as far back as we can look and speculate, we have made a distinct difference in the two. Missions is something the church has catalogued and relegated to a type of ministry, whereas God's mission is the redemption of His people. But instead of further dividing the understanding of the two, the truth of the mission should be highlighted and celebrated often by extricating local and global missions.

Go to just about any church website and look for "Missions" on their home page, click on the word/icon, and you will find that it appears separated from what the church does locally. Missions appears almost to be a bastard child. It's a foreigner. It's like, "We love him and everything, but he has a place over there." Or, "If you have done everything else we have to offer, then you may want to give Missions a try...it's for a special kind of person!" What is missions? As perplexity pervades the mission scene, more and more are led astray in misunderstanding the purpose and gravity of Jesus' words in Matthew 28:19,20. What is the true objective of missions and where are we going wrong? Further, where are we *going*? God's mission is redemption and that leads to restoration. The paradigm shift has only just begun. The short-term mission trip and the STP will be studied for years to come to determine the impact on all fronts. But understand, missions first and foremost is biblical, then it is intentional.

From one perspective, the term *missional* originates with the Gospel and Our Culture Network (GOCN), a group of North American missiologists, who gathered to implement Leslie Newbigin's approach to doing missions. Newbigin, a missionary to India and missionary thinker, realized how pagan and given to humanism North America had become. He said the West must be treated as a mission field and the church has to adopt the posture of a missionary, or to be missional, in any hope of reaching the culture with the Gospel.

Christian Tourism is popular these days and masquerades as mission work. I propose that we stop sending just to send. Sending capacity, not seating capacity, is the future and measuring stick of an obedient, Great Commission congregation. God isn't trying to find a mission for your church. Stop measuring mission success by the number of people you involve in STP or LTM. He called your church and mine to His mission. Read the opening sentence to Paul's letter to the Romans and you will find Paul emphasizing that it is God's Gospel, not ours. Sending capacity means getting *missional* in our spiritual formation ways. Every believer becomes a missionary because it is the duty of every believer to share the Gospel of Jesus Christ. The believer thus takes the posture of a missionary, and as a result the church becomes missional.

Consequently, all STPs need to be inspected for desired impact as to the overall good and achievement of God's mission. Second, if we should all be going, participating, giving, loving, leading, evangelizing, and discipling, then why are we not taking advantage of the new Glocal concept of quick travel and instant communication? Third, STP will serve as a mode of transportation to develop a firmer grasp of God's Mission. It is necessary to read the Bible as a missiological text or else a spiritual schizophrenia will result, splitting theology and mission, which in turn results in tragic consequences for the body of Christ. God seeks us, not the other way around. His evangelistic heart and love are demonstrated even before He issued the call to Abram. In the garden, after the fall, the Bible says in Genesis 3:9, "But the Lord God called to the man and said to him, "Where are you?"

EVERY BELIEVER BECOMES A MISSIONARY BECAUSE IT IS THE DUTY OF EVERY BELIEVER TO SHARE THE GOSPEL OF JESUS CHRIST.

It is easy to see in Genesis that God's heart is missions from the very beginning. The Bible is indeed the story of God's mission, engaging His people for His glory. The rationale for STP is not to introduce just another enterprising missionary experience, or methodology, or to be involved in Christian Tourism. Rather, it is to realize that much of today's Christian mission is itself an anomaly to the reality and truth of the Bible. The Old and New Testaments do not contain a mission, but the whole Bible is itself a *missional* phenomenon. The Bible does not merely contain the Word of God, it *is* the Word of God.

WHY SHOULD YOU BE ALREADY GOING?

The call...the answer to the call...and, subsequently, the journey to wherever it takes you...all takes place from the beginning of Scripture and continues throughout. It seems God wants to know where we are at all times. Adam sinned, and hid from God. God came looking for Adam, and if you are running from the call of God upon your life, you can bank on it: God has sent out the search party. Answering for being AWOL will come into play one day.

FOUR TRUTHS IN THE BIBLE

There are four supportive truths from God's Word that show STP as a compelling foundation in which you should do short-term missional projects glocally:

From all signals in the Gospels...Jesus was Short-term project minded. His entire earthly ministry was only thirty-three years and the time He spent training, equipping, and making disciples was a mere three years. Yet He accomplished everything as ordered by the Father. Directly referred to by some as a Short Term Missionary, and called the "ultimate missionary" by others, Jesus introduced STM by preparing His disciples and sending them out (Matt. 10). Jesus modeled for the disciples everything they would need to do as they went (Mark 1:39, Luke 8:1-3). Bryan Slater demonstrates the STM Jesus approach by saying that Jesus introduced the disciples to STM, gave them specific STM training, prepared the way for their mission, and provided thorough debriefing following the mission. The biblical basis for Jesus' approach to missions epitomizes the missional heart of God. Missions and evangelism expert George Robinson calls the disciples "God-initiated, God-empowered, God-equipped, God-dependent, God-directed, and God-debriefed." In Luke 10:1 Jesus equips, then sends out, the seventy-two. He tells them what to do and where to go and explains the rationale for going. He then proceeds to give them a warning, tells them how to pack, and instructs them on how to handle rejection. Jesus, the mission trailblazer, sets the pace and practice of missional work of the disciple.

The book of Acts is Short-Term Project dominated. The acts of the apostles directly reflect the called life of short-term missionaries. While the New Testament book does not give us a specific plan, it does provide guidance. The local church "after fasting and praying...laid their hands on them and sent them off" (Acts 13:3). This is glocal: the local church undertaking global work for the Gospel. Barnabas and Saul (Paul) were deployed to move from town to town. The thirteenth chapter of Acts shows their movement to each city. Chapters fifteen, sixteen, and seventeen record the beginnings of a second short-term mission trip once the teams have been multiplied. I am finding that more and more missionaries are advocating for this biblical model of being sent by the local church, or by a small cluster of geographically close churches. It cannot be ascertained exactly how many mission journeys Paul took; however, Acts records at least three predominant trips (Acts 19) and possibly a fourth (Acts 20), while some claim as many as seven.

Paul had a Short-Term Project approach. The most common arguments against STP/STM are the financial cost and the validity. The question often arises over what can be accomplished by amateurs in a professional arena. Long Term Missionaries are the professionals, and they are called by God to go. It is argued that a person with little to no training may complete little on foreign soil in a few weeks. Yet Paul accomplished a great deal in an abbreviated amount of time. The veteran approach to missions was to plant oneself in a particular area, country, or continent, and minister there until death or retirement. But Paul never stayed in one place and never planned to do so. Robinson explains, "Paul, it seems, was a long-term missionary that worked through a short-term strategy." One caveat to be pointed out early in this project is that it is not designed to argue for replacing LTM with STP, nor to suggest that LTM is no longer needed.

Rather it is meant to highlight how STP is poised to become a glocal movement bringing revival to the local church, by making disciples that go deeper in their spiritual walk. The very word walk is a spiritual word (Eph. 4) defined as our truest form of personal transportation. Modern technology and travel have simply allowed local Christ-followers to more easily walk on the other side of the planet, in turn teaching and helping others to walk with Jesus.

God is equally Short-Term Project and Long-Term Mission oriented. He has always been moving, from the beginning, and He is not waiting around for us to move. From Genesis 3:15 and the proto-evangelium, the first gospel, to the time of Abraham when God stated His mission, to Jonah's STP, we find that even the Old Testament supports the fact of God moving with the mission mind. By the same token, adoption of a glocal initiative moves the modern-day church to be missional.

My church has responded with a biblical mandate to have a glocal reach, striving to help and guide local churches to achieve seemingly impossible results. The Great Commission commands disciples to go make disciples, and there is no longer a reason not to go. Sadly, in many cases, STMs have been nothing more than spiritual field trips for the retired, or Christian activities for the youth. This has left the church weak and denominational leadership wondering if the STM contributed with any significance to the work. Simultaneously, it has led to the undermining of sound theology. With the dichotomy of *missions* and *God's mission*, confusion has ensued and, in many churches, God's mission of Kingdom redemption and restoration has been reduced to theological discussions left to the spiritually scholastic-minded Christ-followers.

For sure, the key questions ahead lie in whether STP can be strategic, and whether they are even valid in carrying out God's mission. It is essential they be successful and have a lasting effect on cross-cultural work. George G. Robinson, IV, in his dissertation on missiology says, "The paradigm shift in missions toward an increase in STM demands further investigation to see what the true impact is for all parties involved." The essence of the Gospel does not allow us to be territorial. Exploration, movement, and obedience need to be the action words of the church in the twenty-first century. Robinson further reports that all of the players in missions, the missionary, and the missiologists struggle with the new strategy of short-term missions while wondering how anything can be learned or accomplished.

Yes. An army is exactly what we need for revival. STP is a valid movement and there is much to be learned through them. Their validity is both practical and philosophical, and even more importantly, they are biblically and theologically sound. God calls us to make an impact, bringing fresh faith and enthusiasm to the mission field. What does the goal look like? With a city like Detroit being a leading center for immigration, then it should be called the Home for Our Rock in Christ Jesus Steamrolling Hell, rather than the Home of Rock 'n' Roll.

Chapter Five
YOUR CALL

"God said it all in calling Abraham so that all clans and nations might be blessed because of him. After that, it was mainly a matter of working out the details."
-David Filbeck

"But the Lord God called to the man and said to him, "Where are you?"
-Genesis 3:9

MY WIFE AND I RUN a small, simple mission ministry we started several years ago. Small because it's really just us two and a small board of directors. Simple, because we raise money to buy Bibles and give them out to anyone that doesn't own one, both in the U.S.A. and on the other side of the world. Because of the sensitivity of places we go, we don't overtly advertise it, nor do we beg for money. We trust God for the resources we need, and we go. Part of our purpose statement is, "Giving a Bible to someone is a good thing."

A few years ago I found myself in a covert gathering at a site along the Changbai mountain range near Mount Baekdu, on the border of North Korea (DPRK). We were celebrating God's Word in a rural region where locals minister to Koreans who will frequently cross the border, then will return to North Korea to share the Gospel and to give out Bibles. It is a very hazardous way to live.

Pastor Han Chung-Reol, ethnically Korean but Chinese citizen by birth, was one of the men God had placed on the front lines there. He was 49 years old and married with a son and a daughter. His story of risking his life was portrayed in a short video produced by the Voice of the Martyrs. A few weeks before we arrived his wife, who was his partner in ministry as well, was captured by the North Koreans and tortured by waterboarding. They released her with a warning to cease all Gospel activity. Instead, she and the Pastor sent their children to stay with relatives in South Korea and they continued speaking boldly in the name of Jesus.

Pastor Han was fully cooperative with the Communist Party and pastored a government-sanctioned Three-Self Church in the area. Three-Self means self-propagating, self-governing, and self-supporting, but it doesn't mean that you are exempt from the oversight of the Religious Affairs Bureau (an arm of the communist party) of China. Pastor Han was staking his life on total surrender to Christ. One night he was lured from his home to a secret meeting place where he thought he would be ministering to others in continuing discipleship. However, he had been tricked by North Korean soldiers. The soldiers are known to cross the border offering money in exchange for information on Christians trying to spread the Gospel along the border. He was ambushed and stabbed to death and, to prove a point, they embedded an ax in his skull. All of this took place just weeks prior to my arrival.

Surmising the hurt from their sudden loss, and sensing their suffering, I tried to comfort them by praying for their continued efforts. A missionary friend, who will remain nameless because of the sensitivity in this area of the world, was able to minister to Pastor Han's distraught wife by helping with some money for the family and funeral. But what can you truly do? Pastor Han knew the risks, had endangered his life for the cause of Jesus, and was called home...another martyr. I ponder and reflect in awe that I was a handshake away from this faithful follower of Christ.

Your follow-up question should be, "Do I really believe God?" not "Do I believe in God?"

God had blessed me with the opportunity to meet and pray with many true believers in Asia that week. I sat for the longest time and contemplated on what happened in this man's life. What moved him from spiritual drinks of milk to strong draughts of God's Word? How did he become so enamored with Jesus that he genuinely lived out, "To live is Christ, to die is gain?" (Phil. 1:21) Be warned: the enemy wants you to skim by on half-hearted commitment because the apathetic, cool types of the religious sect seldom experience true "game time," as it is called in the sports world.

Playing the comparison is largely considered an emotionally dangerous trap in a secular, psychology-driven society. In this case it may be a great place to start when evaluating your call and your spiritual walk with Jesus. Instead of getting bogged down with comparing yourself to all your "friends" on social media, why not compare yourself to Pastor Han? Why don't we do the majority of our personal comparisons with the men and women of the Bible? Look at all of the other martyrs that were on the front lines in the last two millennia, and it may substantiate your effectiveness for Christ and your ministry. The Apostle Paul writes to the church at Thessalonica advocating comparison,

> We showed you how to pull your weight when we were with you, so get on with it. We didn't sit around on our hands expecting others to take care of us. In fact, we worked our fingers to the bone, up half the night moonlighting so you wouldn't be burdened with taking care of us. And it wasn't because we didn't have a right to your support; we did. We simply wanted to provide an example of diligence, hoping it would prove contagious (2 Thessalonians 3:7-9 MSG).

Your follow-up question should be, "Do I really believe God?" not "Do I believe *in* God?" Social media exists for the sole purpose of comparing ourselves to our peers to see how we stack up. I wonder how many bad moods and attitudes are decided by a sixty-second check of your homepage? Please realize that the end goal of discipleship is to look like Jesus, to be like Jesus. One of my biggest critiques in modern missions is our quest for the perfect mission opportunity instead of trusting God to take you where He wants you to go. Like a photo-op, too many are seeking to pad their Christian autobiography by adding their mission-op picture to social media. As a lover of short-term mission projects, I constantly search for better ways to be involved and for opportunities for my church to do them right. However, for every great story about a successful short-term mission team, there is an upsetting story about how churches have made mission work a secondary ministry.

In the Western world, we can enjoy the freedom of speech without danger of bodily harm. Every now and then there may be the risk of being called a few names, or told to shut up, but we are free from physical persecution. Human rights violations in the DPRK are horrendous. Pastor Han and the people he reached could not and cannot simply say, "Jesus loves you" to anyone on the street corner, or even to close friends, without being in jeopardy of a one-way ticket to a life in prison, breaking rocks... or a hatchet to the head. They daringly share Jesus because they believe God.

Your Contract with God

As much as we despise contracts when it is to our disadvantage, we adore them when they are in our favor. The first eleven chapters of the Bible seem to track sin and the ramifications on creation, but then something happens. God calls a new man, and it's a new contract. All Christ-followers have a call upon their lives. It all started with Abraham. When he was known as just Abram, he had the call of all calls directed to him. In Genesis 12, God told Abram to go, to leave home. The Hebrew writer affirms, "By faith Abraham obeyed when he was called to go out to a place that he was to receive as an inheritance. And he went out, not knowing where he was going" (Heb. 11:8). It is rare these days to find anyone that has this kind of faith in God— to just fill up your tank with gas, kiss everyone goodbye, and when asked, "Hey, where are you heading?" your answer is, "I don't know!" We would label that dude a kook. However, it was that kind of call and contract, woven into the fabric of all the Old Testament and New Testament, that translates into your call and mine.

Twelve chapters in, a man named Abram is inserted into Holy Scripture. He is at this point a kind of chosen one. It is revealed that he is the son of Terah, who is called out of Ur of the Chaldeans to go to Canaan. Perhaps negligently, Terah and his family stop in Haran, noticeably dissatisfied with where God wanted them to settle. Terah dies there and God calls Abram, consequently reflecting an important facet of God's character: to call men to Himself for reason. The choosing of Abram comes with a promise and includes God replacing Abram's land with a new land. In return for giving up position, protection, and security in his present kinship group, God promises Abram and his family posterity and His blessing. Here is what you desperately need to know: Abram was not merely

The Great Go Mission

to become a mediator like Moses, later was, of the Law, but he instead becomes the source of blessing for all. God promises to make Abram into a great nation, to bless him and to make his name great. Thus, the start of God's named people.

God called. Abraham responded immediately, much like the twelve of Jesus responded to the Master when He called. Abraham was clueless as to where God was leading, yet he followed. I find this incongruous with today's modern movement. Of the volumes of books written, and conferences played out, where vision is touted as being the beat-all, end-all tool for success, it's hard to define a vision when you don't know where you are going. I'm all for vision but I am also amused to read biographies of the all the men and women who did it wrong when it comes to vision and planning but who are held in high esteem as the heroes of the contemporary faith— and justifiably so. Maybe, just maybe, defining the call on your life supersedes realizing your vision.

Adoniram Judson, Hudson Taylor, and Bruce Olsen, to name a few, did it all wrong according to today's standards of missional work, yet they went. They suffered, they starved, and they were broken many times, but they came to know their call. Adoniram Judson went years before he saw his first convert on the mission field. Today, he would be offered early retirement and given a celebratory dinner with a few trophies and an honorarium. If you analyzed Hudson Taylor's global trip to China, you would discover a discombobulated travel itinerary that cries launch failure. He couldn't speak Mandarin, he chose a start-up mission organization that was poorly managed, and raising money was a huge weight hanging over his head. Bruce Olson, that modern-day missionary we talked about in a previous chapter, said he left home at age 18, bought that one-way ticket to South America, and just walked into the jungle. How was he not killed? Why was he not killed although the missionary to Ecuador, Jim Eliot, was? Whether they knew it at first, or after enduring heartache for years then becoming aware of it, those old guys we admire and desire to emulate *knew* their call.

Through the introduction of the Abrahamic covenant, the true character of God is revealed. It's merely the groundwork for His ultimate plan. He is shown to be a missional God. He has a heart of grace and a sovereign, loving plan to redeem sinners the globe over. Yet man, made in

89

God's image, sinned and defected. The result was God's Kingdom being splintered. It is in this contract with Abraham that we can see more and more of the character of God disclosed.

Get to the New Testament and He is perfectly reflected in His Son, Jesus. Did you miss the class when you signed up to be in God's Kingdom? There is a contract. Don't be confused, like I have seen in many others, when it comes to Jesus as Lord and Savior. It is totally incorrect to think you can merely be saved from hell by Christ, having heaven as your secure eternal home, yet delay bowing your knee to Him in complete obedience. When He called you to come out of sin and to repent by following Him, He contracted your life to be a total servant. I love the Greek name for us: δουλος (doulos). It means bond servant, or slave. My wife bought me a t-shirt with that Greek word scrolled across the front. I love it because it is my title, and yours as Christ-followers. You and I are called to be slaves to Christ. One more time... this is how the Bible puts it: He called you out of darkness into His kingdom of light. Are you living in the light? Are you living up to the contract? Have you bowed to be a slave to Jesus?

UNDERSTANDING THE CALL

I was a first-year seminary student struggling with a course of action for my spiritual commitment in a vocation. I had made it to graduate school, but now what? For one of the first times in my life I was little scared about the future. Having kept my life on cruise control up to now, my thirties were, dauntingly, on their way. I was searching for answers as I began my theological studies. My Greek and New Testament professor, Virtus Gideon, was kind to me, as he was to all of his students, and because of a mutual acquaintance I thought it best to start with him. Twenty-something and thirsty for vocational direction, I made an appointment with Dr. Gideon to talk about the call on my life. Understand Virtus Gideon was a scholar, always reading straight from the Greek New Testament, and he deeply loved Jesus. He was a sharp dresser for an old man; he was articulate and to the point. I remember well walking in the small office of that giant of a theologian, books all over the place and reaching to the ceiling. In his warm, deep baritone voice, he welcomed me to sit down. I was sure he provided me the same treatment as all of the other theology students.

The Great Go Mission

Dr. Gideon smiled and asked, "What's on your mind Greg?" Armed with my notebook and pen in hand, poised and determined to take down every word that wise old sage of God spit out, I asked, "Dr. Gideon," I cleared my throat, "what is a call?" Without hesitation or pause, looking like he had heard this question a million times, he looked me square in the eyes and answered, "Greg, a call... is a call." I will never forget what happened next. Immediately he spun back towards his desk in that black faux-leather, caster-wheeled chair and resumed his work. The interview was over. I mean, it was *over*! I mean there were no more words exchanged.

All of the blank pages I had hoped to fill with ink were left blank, except for that one line, "A call is a call." I excused myself, thinking I had asked the wrong question, and hurried off contemplating those words. Did he assume I was talking about something else? Did I miss something? Did he mishear me? Was the old man off his rocker? Maybe he had a deadline, and he just answered my question with the best one liner he had. Maybe it was time for lunch. He was my Greek professor and sure enough his answer to my life was Greek to me.

"GREG, A CALL IS A CALL."

It was a few years later that I realized Dr. Gideon's words were pure gold. Trying to figure out my life, I was clinging to that verse I learned at a young age, Romans 8:28: "And we know that for those who love God all things work together for good, for those who are called according to his purpose." What is God's purpose for your life? The Greek word for "called" is κλητος and is an adjective in Romans 8:28. It describes who we are before we look to find out what we are supposed to do. In other words, my crisis was not in finding out my next step, it was discovering who I was. Particularly who I was in Christ.

It was like finding a Van Gogh hidden in the attic. I would compare it to Jed Clampett, "...shootin' at some food, and up through the ground come a bubblin' crude!" Here's what Dr. Gideon meant: A call is unique. It is unique because we all are unique to God. He only made one of you. He gifted you and me to live out the call upon our lives. Although no one seeks God for salvation, and God makes that clear, God seeks us because He loves us. Jesus makes that distinct in the Gospels. Jesus also says we must seek to find that treasure even if it means selling all we have. We must knock on doors to have them opened, and to ask in prayer, to ask in our search, and to keep on asking. Your call is *your* call, not anyone's else's call. It's your call to be the saint or Christian whom God called. You are called, just like I am called to be an ambassador for Christ wherever you find yourself.

Your Call

Earlier I asked the question concerning God's geographical placement in your life and that is where you need to start. To what degree does it weigh in on the mission He has for you? Now, I want to shift gears slightly and ask: What are the resources He has blessed you with? Maybe you've never thought about how God has shaped you from a young age and how He has been planning and choreographing the upcoming mission He has planned for you. Think about these things, to name a few, and how God has carefully allowed them to shape you:

- **Church**
- **Marriage**
- **Network of friends**
- **Communication**
- **Education**
- **Books**
- **Music**
- **Family**
- **Financial resources**
- **Skill set**
- **Job/Employment**
- **Health**
- **Neighbors**
- **Problems**
- **Sickness**
- **Travel**
- **Entertainment**
- **Sports**

The Great Go Mission

Your call is shaped and determined by these things and more. But make no mistake, when Scripture refers to a call it is primarily speaking of your salvation/justification in Christ. He calls us and we repent; we turn around from our current path of sin and destruction and follow Him towards righteousness and holiness. One of the saddest lines uttered in today's world is, "I've done all right directing my own life up to now, I guess I will just continue." Your call may actually involve a total upheaval. God may be directing you to quit, pack up, and leave. Or, He may be calling you to stay where you are; to go out among your friends and neighbors, reaching them for the Kingdom of God. For the sake of the Gospel, at least be a missionary to the friends God puts into your life.

Whatever He is calling you to do, I promise that it involves you seeking Him regularly. I assure you it involves prayer, digging into His Word, and humbling yourself before Him as the Holy Spirit directs you. Don't do God's mission too fast, don't do it too slow, and don't lag behind in making the decision to already be going. Be careful because propping yourself up after a meaningful church experience, where you break out in goose bumps and have those *that-song-just-spoke-to-me* kinds of feelings, doesn't last long.

If you don't know the great missionary hero, the bold and radical Hudson Taylor, let me introduce you to him. He suffered greatly for the Gospel. He lost children and he lost his wife, all on the mission field. Experiencing civil war-type conflicts in China, long before the 1900 Boxer Rebellion (the Chinese Civil War against Imperialism), was a daily experience for him. Here is one thing you have to credit Taylor for... he knew his call.

Your mission is fleeting, and so is your time.

Once while traveling in the Hunan province of China I was alerted to the fact that we were near the original China Inland Mission (CIM), founded by Taylor. Taylor made eleven daring voyages back and forth to China from England in the 1800's in order to raise money to fund his work. He sacrificed his own health while giving his life for the spread of the message of Jesus. I was excited to visit the spot— the actual place— where his work took place 150 years ago. I walked around in the location that was presently a large courtyard for a Chinese elementary school. The kids were playing outside during lunchtime. I looked around trying to find some sort of plaque or memento of this dynamic ministry that took place on the spot I was standing on... nothing. CIM was gone. The organization had later become Overseas Mission Fellowship International, but the place where it all started had vanished. The dilemma is encapsulated in two lines: Your mission is fleeting, and so is your time. All that matters are the Gospel and you, on mission, to share it.

Stephen Olford was a holdover from the old days of preaching. He was once summoned to Los Angeles by Billy Graham to pray for one of Graham's crusades for a week. Olford said all he did for the entire week was pray for Dr. Graham and the crusade, on his knees in a hotel room. I was blessed to study under Dr. Olford before he was taken to glory. One of the most meaningful stories I've ever heard came from him.

It seems when Olford was eighteen years old he was a hellion of sorts. His parents were missionaries in Africa but were British citizens. Olford decided to leave the mission field in Africa and go back to Great Britain to college. He told us he had lived a wild life of drinking and racing motorcycles. One day he wrecked his bike and was in critical condition. His dad was summoned and Olford said the old man came into the hospital room and said something that changed his life. His dad, echoing the words of British missionary C.T. Studd said, "Son, only one life and soon will be past, only what's done for Jesus will last." Olford recovered and went on to be a major influence on many of the preachers of the twentieth century.

He asked himself a question: what have I done for Jesus that will last? A recent television commercial for a credit card asks, "What's in your wallet?" Have you taken an inventory lately of what's in your spiritual life? Look around you and see who is being influenced by the life you live. Are people responding positively to the Gospel because you have obeyed the call on your life? You see, although Hudson Taylor's place of doing ministry was gone his impact is still being felt in China. The Gospel message is eternal, with eternal consequences. Your whole life is going to be turned around when you submit to the mission of God. I'm asking you to explore the call of God. Listen to Paul's words,

> Therefore, my beloved, as you have always obeyed, so now, not only as in my presence but much more in my

absence, work out your own salvation with fear and trembling (Phil. 2:12).

Paul is not saying you have to complete more steps so you will go to heaven. He is imploring you and me to continue to walk with God in order to live out to the fullest extent of that call. Just maybe God is trying to get your attention today by showing you that you have something to offer. What's in your spiritual wallet?

ONE RISK

The mission has grown comfortable for the twenty-first century believer. Once there was a time when a person considering a lifetime of mission work had to ponder the perils and hazards of leaving home and moving to another country to minister. Going to the Amazon, the Outback, or to an unstable African country was to confirm one's calling, trusting in God's grace no matter what. Not now. The first item on the prayer list of a team preparing to depart for their short-term project is "pray for the safety of the team." Okay, but understand safety is not found to be a prerequisite in the book of Acts. Rather, just the opposite. The risk of life for the Gospel of Jesus Christ is prevalent throughout the New Testament as well as mission history.

Paul's resumé in 2 Corinthians reports he was shipwrecked at least three times and even spent a night afloat in the open sea, not to mention being whipped on the back 195 times. The book of Acts records the many perils of this disciple's life. Then, you add to this the many complaints from the "missions committee" and it was too much for Paul to keep his cool. Sure, when you have a family to support you have to entertain safety while answering God's call upon your life. But make sure you have dealt with the meaning of the call in your life first. Have you prayed through it? Set aside praying for Aunt Sally's diverticulitis and asking God "to be with you" and "to keep you safe." Instead ask God to help you live out, to the fullest, the call He has invited you to. Forget about seeking out the best mission-op for social media because volunteering to serve in any capacity for the sake of Christ is not for wimps, the weak, or the worriers.

Back to young Hudson Taylor. As a boyish Englishman in the mid-1800's he had a visionary drive to reach China. He was a pacesetter. The irony is he looked nothing like a modern-day missionary. He avoided the

> **VOLUNTEERING TO SERVE IN ANY CAPACITY FOR THE SAKE OF CHRIST IS NOT FOR WIMPS, THE WEAK, OR THE WORRIERS.**

limelight, and always had financial difficulties both on and off the field of service. But you can't use the lack of resources as an excuse not to go. God raised up this man with unique determination and giftedness. Missiologist Stan Guthrie says "[b]y today's standards... [Hudson] was an extremist."

Taylor's autobiography is a soul-shaping, personal story of how God called him to China. It gives great insight into his call, his campaign, and his commitment. He tells of borrowing a book about China from a local Congregational minister. The minister gladly handed Taylor the copy and asked him, "Why do you want to read this?" Taylor responded that God had called him to spend his life as a missionary in the Orient. When the minister inquired how Taylor proposed to get to Shanghai, Taylor responded, "Like the Twelve or the Seventy." Taylor was specifically referencing Luke 9 & 10 where Jesus sent the disciples out on a short-term mission. The old minister warned Taylor that "[s]uch an idea would do very well in the days when Christ Himself was on earth, but not now." Never mind the old minister's intended meaning because it foreshadows the focus of current missions and its institutionalized state.

Interestingly, from the time of Taylor (ca. 1830) until the close of the twentieth century, Christians could travel just about anywhere they wanted in the world, with a few exceptions, without significant consequence. Numerous other paragons of modern missions are known for answering the call of the Holy Spirit upon their lives, for how God used them in a powerful way in their time, and for shaping the future. Each had a tremendous grasp upon the Great Commission, both culturally and theologically, without fear of death or personal loss.

The Great Go Mission

FASTER & CONVENIENT

Short-term missionary journeys and projects are becoming more commonplace within our tech-advanced society. We are now able to travel faster and more conveniently than ever, whereas a century ago we banded together and cooperated locally with other churches to send support to a particular region or to a particular missionary. Maybe that missionary came out of our church, or from a church in our community or town. Looking back, we juxtapose the position of long-term missionaries (LTM) with that of the modern short-term missionaries. It was a big deal to the spiritual community to commission and "send-off" a representative of the church to a foreign land. They would be gone for years, and a lot of training went into the endeavor. There was cultural training and language training, not to mention the theological preparation that took place, perhaps taking several years to complete.

POSSIBLE MISSION

When 007 is called into M's office at the beginning of a Bond feature, it's always for a mission. The *Rambo* series was all about a former Green Beret going on clandestine missions to rescue those held captive. The *Mission: Impossible* series brags about the intensity of each movie. Boring. Seasoned church-goers yawn knowing the term *mission* entered into our lexicon centuries ago but has been boring us to tears ever since. Go way back to the 1970's when I was in my early teens, sitting in church during the announcements, and the pastor said, "Next week we have a very special treat for you…Missionary [name] is going to be here on furlough (the old term for missionary vacation) all the way from [country] and they will be speaking [bored to tears]." You may as well have told me and my teenage friends, "I hope you enjoy skipping church next week because there's something better on TV" or, even better, "Stay home!" I've seen plenty of eating utensils and wooden bowls from the Amazon, too many chopsticks from Asia, and enough warrior masks from Kenya or Uganda to satisfy me for a while. Mission work for you is very possible, but no one wants to even talk about it because the church has depicted it as monotonous— an impossible way to find fulfillment and spiritual satisfaction, let alone something daring!

The problem is that we label and rank activity in the church. And, sadly, missions falls dead last in a long list of church "activities." Of course! It's not a church activity and never has been. Can it be that our purpose as a church and as Christ-followers has been hung up on incorrect definitions? It's a *mission*. That means life-threatening! Quit thinking of it as religious activity assured of safety and understand it for what it really is... it is risking your life. It's God's call to you. Realize and understand our God thrives on you and me wanting to be a part of an impossible mission that is only possible with, in, and through Him.

HIDING IN THE JUNGLE

My mousy approach to Sino-Korean ministry was evidenced by my visit, but because of Pastor Han's tragic death I was re-examining my call. My secret thoughts and reflections on that short-term mission project took me to a place of deep reality. As I gazed at the GPS on the dashboard of the Toyota I was riding in on that trip, I could not decipher the characters in another language, but I could see the red lines outlining the countries and saw I was now less than three miles from the North Korean border. Kim Jong-un had tested a ballistic missile only weeks before. Recent world news depicted the mental instability of Kim. My then sixteen-year-old son, Jack, was sitting in the front seat. "How real is this?" I asked myself.

There's no heroic story to share here. I didn't get captured by the North Koreans and tortured for the sake of the Gospel. We didn't dodge bullets on a dusty dirt road. We just hit a few potholes and bumps. No blood and no checkpoints. I didn't get to play basketball with Kim. No scenes from M.A.S.H. No prisons and no soldiers. Only peasant-looking people with dirty faces smiling and welcoming us to sit and stay a while and enjoy some sunflower seeds (that's all they had). Our short-term project was successful— we were able to hide among the demons. We went to give out Bibles to the poor, to pray with them, and to encourage them in the Lord, and that is what we did.

From the very moment Adam and Eve went into hiding, our great and holy God went looking for them. Jesus is the Good Shepherd who leaves the 99 in search of the one. Our God is on a mission. The entire Word of God describes this mission and, happily, He calls us to be in on it. Are you hiding in the jungle of life, the mountains of personal momentum,

The Great Go Mission

or on the sandy beaches of your own vacation and relaxation? God's first question to you then is, "Where are you?" He asks this question because He wants you to come out of hiding. And my friends, that is the Gospel of Jesus Christ – He calls us out and calls us into. He calls us out of sin, into a relationship with Him. He calls us out of our selfishness and into His shared mission to rescue the world. He calls us out of the world into a cosmic mission to go wherever He sends us for the sake of the Gospel.

There are ten truths that empower and energize me and that I have instilled in the congregation of Fresh Church, the church I started in Chapin, South Carolina, over the years. I refer to them often as we address this ever-changing methodology to mission work. This is what gets me going and keeps me zeroed in on the Great Commission and our mission work:

- → There's just something about the name of Jesus that calls us to go.
- → Obedience to the Great Commission is simply sharing and making.
- → Going and giving is a good thing, staying and stashing money is not.
- → Missional thinking keeps us grounded in theological/biblical orthodoxy.
- → The goal is biblical and achievable...and that motivates me more.
- → Every Christ-follower should be involved in some kind of missional activity.
- → Short-term glocal projects are very viable even when long-term projects are not.
- → Suffering for the cause of Christ and the Gospel is common and expected.
- → Joy is unspeakable, and obviously a by-product of going and giving.
- → Expecting others to celebrate your missional achievements is illusory.

Recently, I listened to a podcast of Sinclair Ferguson on what it means to be a Christian. I always tune in to these broadcasts with my pen in hand, my leather journal, and a good listening ear, tuning out the distractions and ready to take copious notes. Too many of us believe that it's too difficult to live the Christian life and keep God's commandments. It's not (Deuteronomy 30:11).

Ready to write as Sinclair began his study on the Christian life, I couldn't believe my ears. He quickly pointed to John 8:12, "Again Jesus spoke to them, saying, "I am the light of the world. Whoever follows me will not walk in darkness but will have the light of life." He then expounded on this verse for twenty-six minutes... and that was it. No frills, no fantastic voice inflections, and no drop-the-mic stories. He simply reminded the audience that the Christian walks in the light. Let me repeat it: A *Christfollower walks in the light*. There is much darkness in this world. Jesus doesn't lead you to light... He *is* the light, and when you follow Him you will find the "deposit entrusted to you." (1 Tim 6:20; 2Tim 1:14)

MISSION IMPLAUSIBLE TO MISSION POSSIBLE

You will have to search long and hard to find any information about John Fling, but he was a really big deal among the poor in downtown Columbia, South Carolina in the 1970s, 1980s, and 1990s. John was a member of the little church in the city where I pastored for a couple of years. The local newspaper dubbed him the "Everyday Santa Claus." John was very faithful to church each time the door opened. One of nineteen children with no multiple births, he was born to an assistant sharecropper in Georgia. He had a full-time job running car parts, but most of his time was spent just loving on the poor. I will list some of the things John did, but it's impossible to completely exhaust everything he did.

Digest this statement: John didn't own a house, a car, a television set, a computer, or a mobile phone. He met presidents, rode on Air-Force One, and talked with governors and mayors regularly. He gave away approximately a quarter of a million dollars a year, maybe more. He never inherited money and probably never made above $40,000 annually. Each year around Thanksgiving he would drive around town and find the children whose parents were unable to celebrate Christmas with gifts for their children, and John would give them homemade $50 tickets to use at the local K-mart. Many adults also received tickets so they could buy necessities. The manager at the local K-mart would then open early on a Sunday morning with just one register open, and only several folks were allowed into the store at once. The line of people would wrap around the

The Great Go Mission

building as the poor, the indigent— those who many would refer to as "lowlifes"— gathered to spend their $50 tickets. John would be at the cash register making sure no one used the gift money to purchase cigarettes or things that weren't essential.

Since I was the pastor, John assigned me to the duty of getting on that microphone that they used for the blue-light special and have an opening prayer. To walk through the store and see the children of those down-and-out families smile as they poured the toys into the shopping carts was priceless. Sometimes they got to the counter and went over by $10 or $20, and John would wave them through. At the end of the morning, on that one cash register, they would total it up and John would write the check for $100,000 or $125,000... whatever. John was almost as poor as he was at 70 as he was when he was growing up. Where did the money come from? Early on in life John started sharing food and clothes with the children of the neighborhood. Years later, corporations and companies would give John money as charitable giving. Why? Because John never took one dime of overhead. One hundred percent of the donated money went to people in need.

A regular day for John would be to load up his truck with clothes and go to one of the low-income neighborhoods and have a "free garage sale." The truck would be emptied in seconds. He would then go to the bank and get dollars and quarters, drive through poverty-stricken areas where the children were playing and throw the money to them out the window. He fed a man dinner every day for ten years— each day John would go to the local restaurant, Lizard's Thicket, and pick up a meat and three for an old, lonely man who was on a very fixed income.

John bought a bus for the church, so the elderly could go on trips together, or so they thought. The real reason he purchased it was to pick up a hundred children each week and bring them to church for Sunday School to hear about Jesus. A local author wrote a little book about John when he was alive, depicting his lifestyle, generosity, philanthropy, and love for the children of South Carolina. It's interesting how God used this unknown, uneducated, and non-political factor to minister to so many. I could write pages and pages about John Fling, just from stories that I personally witnessed. He was an original.

John died about twenty years ago. The ministry died with him. I remember having several meetings with concerned local officials who wanted to continue John's successful ministry. Their idea was to form a committee, to update John's financials and 501(c)3 status. They wanted to add an office, phones, and build the work into a giant goodwill and benevolence missionary society complete with a massive staff. It never happened. Why? The uniqueness of John's altruism was found in John's heart, not his brain. The passion was in the person, not the corporation.

He was also a very wise man, avoiding greed, avoiding popularity, and able to spot a fake in an instant. The true ministry was in John's call and his heart for those that were like him. For amusement, John would take you through his back yard to a literal falling-down shed that stunk from mildew, to show you all his trophies. There were hundreds of 8x10's hanging on the walls with notable world figures. In just about every picture, there was John, dressed in his "uniform" of blue work pants, white shirt with his name on it, and his blue hat that read, "I love to tell the story." As important and big as John's mission was, I'm sure all the accolades are boxed up and in storage somewhere, if not buried in a trash heap.

BIGGER TO SMALLER

A few decades ago, the church growth gurus huddled around the statement, "We are going smaller, in order to go bigger." It was the rise of small groups replacing Sunday School, giving credence to the mega-church movement. "Yes," they said, "We are going to reach, gather, and build more, by doing it in little home groups." It was a fantastic slogan, and the ploy of highlighting discipleship while elevating numbers was underway. For some reasons to be explored elsewhere, the cell group, home group, small group, family group, or whatever you want to refer to it as, didn't succeed as expected. The experts and specialists from the old Sunday School system had bigger expectations and when small groups didn't measure up, they were just pushed to the side. If you ask about them in a church you are visiting today, the most likely response is, "Yes, we have small groups." And under their breath, they will say something like they will get back to you on them as they quickly forget. Very few churches in America do the small group ministry well.

The Great Go Mission

But the concept, bigger by going smaller, is a valid one... especially in the area of mission work. It could be, if employed, that the red-headed stepchild may be allowed to come back to the table. Mission work doesn't make any money for the pastoral staff or the church, it costs! Missions will always cost you something. There is no money to be made from it. I know many churches that have said "no" to missions because of the price tag. So they have either forgotten to do it, quit doing it, or refuse to do it. Maybe they don't do mission work because they have deemed it too costly.

Larger churches are able to absorb the cost, because of their astronomical budget, while receiving the praise of the people for their involvement. It's a status symbol these days for some churches to have their own mission staff position. All too often, however, they direct the little short-term projects by advertising them to the congregation then those with vacation time on their hands, a little extra cash, and maybe some guilty feelings, sign up with the desire to do something good.

My desire is not to be more critical, but to offer a plan for revival and reform in the midst of modern missions. It's comparable to going bigger by going smaller. It requires becoming significant and true to the Great Commission by corralling the churches. For decades, the idea of giant associations, conferences, and conventions were the norm. The truth is they are shrinking and splitting rapidly while many of the leaders are in denial and trying to hold on to the past. Instead of continuing to think complexly, we should go simple. Maybe the cooperating idea should be tied to relationships rather than resources. Here's the idea:

Simple Partnerships – Two or three churches joining together forms a strong cooperating team. When your strategy is to enlist as many churches as possible into your union or association, without proper oversight, you invite disaster. There is more accountability with just a few churches. There is also the personal side of things in relationships that is massive to successful mission work. Partner with a like church, with like core values and like theology, and plan the action of evangelism and discipleship. Pray about an area of town, somewhere in your region or country, or maybe in the world. Develop a long-range goal suiting to the two or three congregations, and go!

Simple Projects – Jesus said, "Truly, I say to you, unless you turn and become like children, you will never enter the kingdom of heaven" (Matt. 18:3). If our Lord is saying we need to be receptive and as trusting as a child to the Gospel, then it is incumbent upon us to simply state the Truth of Christ. Without guile, without ulterior motives, and without eroding the heart of the Gospel, our sharing of Jesus must be pure and with a pure heart. 'Jesus crucified, buried, and raised again' needs to be at the front, center, and back of our projects. Preaching the supremacy of Christ is the reason we do mission work. Scale back the focus on the logistics and concentrate the efforts mainly on the message. The project is secondary to the mission. The strategy is subordinate to the message.

Simple Projections – Throughout both the Old Testament and the New, and the last five thousand years of recorded history, God has used people to accomplish His purpose. Then, when the specific mission was/is over, the missionary, prophet, preacher, and/or servant either enters glory or moves on to another project. Perpetuating a project beyond God's timing and usefulness is not only beating a dead horse but wasting God's time. Hudson Taylor's work in China is historic and colossal in meaning to mission work but I've been to the exact spot where he was, and it's gone. Is it time for some denominations to likewise regroup? They need to beware that their predecessors shaped their vision simply by obeying the Gospel and not by adhering to the social agenda of the day. Set a reachable goal in mission work. Accomplish it and ask God, "Where do you want me to go now?"

Simple People - If we continue to look to hire the superstars, thinking that they are the ones who need to do the work, we are as good as gone. Training the whole church, discipling them to true mission work, is needed now more than ever. Enlisting and developing a strategic, yet bold, team for the mission work of the future is what is needed in every church. Gather a group of 8-10, pour the truth of mission work into them, challenge them, lead them by accompanying them, and watch the fire of revival start. The craziest thing we just can't seem to reconcile in our modern business-style brains is how the Lord Jesus trusted the message of forgiveness, mercy, and truth to twelve normal and simple men. Think about it.

A SIMPLE MISSIONARY

Wiley Glass was a missionary to China from 1903 - 1949, until he was expelled by the Communists during the 1949 takeover led by Mao Zedong. He lived to be an old man in his nineties, returning to his home state of Texas where he taught missions at Southwestern Baptist Theological Seminary until his death in 1967. To read his biography is to be moved by his boldness for Jesus and his commitment to the Gospel.

One day, after leading a class dealing with missions in China, Dr. Glass was walking across the campus of Southwestern. One of his students, a young man, stopped him and asked, "Dr. Glass, it must be hard to see all your work in China destroyed." Dr. Glass stopped, pulled himself up to his full six feet, four inches, and said, "Young man, I'll have you know when Jesus went to China he went to stay." His grave marker in a Fort Worth, Texas cemetery, simply reads,

> **Glass**
> **Wiley B. & Jessie P.**
> **Over 40 years as Southern Baptist**
> **Missionaries in North China**

For far too long, we've extended ministries beyond God's intentions. The church has flourished for two thousand years despite the enemy's efforts to destroy her. Still God calls out people for specific jobs, and then we should move on to the next assignment and calling. Moses did his job—he led the Israelites out of captivity. Then Joshua's story starts and in the first chapter, second verse of Joshua it says, "Moses my servant is dead. Now therefore..." (Josh. 1:2). God then worked in Joshua's life to accomplish His purpose. When God decides to end something, we need to move on.

Chapter Six
HOMOGENEITY MISSION

"The biblical corpus (however) leans toward the idea that missions itself should be defined by having an evangelistic or discipling orientation."
-George Robinson

"For I am the least of the apostles, unworthy to be called an apostle, because I persecuted the church of God. But by the grace of God I am what I am, and his grace toward me was not in vain." -1 Corinthians 15:9-10

PAY CLOSE ATTENTION TO THE following paragraph: Mission pluralism is skewing the way forward for the Gospel. Having multiple, insignificant goals, rather than totally adhering to the truth of the Great Commission, is causing massive setbacks undetected by casual observers. Not every endeavor titled "Mission" is Christ-centered. Many mission activities are viable, worthwhile efforts at alleviating pain and suffering. They help the down-and-out while giving them hope with renewed opportunities for the future. Needed supplies for essential living are being provided by the loads. Yet that doesn't mean we can categorize them all under God's hand, directive, or approval. Defining the true mission as it inherently relates to Jesus' command is vital to determining true mission work.

In Acts 9, Saul (a.k.a. Paul) was on a mission from God... or so he thought. Before Christ got a hold on his life, he was zealous for God's Laws. He was as religious and sanctimonious as you could get in the first century. He was a Pharisee, a priest, and in today's vernacular we would describe him as holier-than-thou. Wiping out the insurrectionists to Jehovah God was his burning passion. He believed Jesus to be a heretic, a phony, and a spiritual marauder of the true God. In Saul's time, you could receive no higher calling than to rid the world of false prophets. The truth is, Saul was not on God's mission. Mission? What is the meaning of mission here? We've looked at it and attempted to define it from several different angles so far. Think about this: Jesus is Lord, and Jesus is the Savior... making Him known is our mission.

God used a bolt of stunning, glaring light from heaven to knock Saul to his knees. God blinded Saul, who was blind to the Gospel (isn't that irony?), to allow him to see the Truth. Jesus is the Truth of our mission. True mission causes are those that first and foremost preach the Gospel of Jesus Christ in word and in deed. Francis of Assisi is attributed to saying, humorously but poignantly, "Preach the Gospel at all times and if you have to, use words." It was a cool sounding proverb 800 years ago, but in our Twitter and social media world, it has become the norm to just *do stuff* instead of vocally proclaiming Jesus is Lord. Many organizations and churches have skipped the preaching of the Gospel, gone straight to accomplishing good deeds for those far from God, and never shared the truth of 1 Corinthians 15:

> Now I would remind you, brothers, of the gospel I preached to you, which you received, in which you stand, and by which you are being saved, if you hold fast to the word I preached to you—unless you believed in vain. For I delivered to you as of first importance what I also received: that Christ died for our sins in accordance with the Scriptures, that he was buried, that he was raised on the third day in accordance with the Scriptures... (1 Corinthians 15:1-4).

You and I are not permitted to add anything to this Gospel or take anything away. Let me reiterate: Jesus died, was buried, and rose again. Paul reminds us in his opening statement of his epistle to the Romans that he was "set apart for the gospel of God" (Rom. 1:1). It's God's Gospel. The revelation of the New Testament is that God has given us the privilege of sharing the message of salvation in Christ and our duty is obedience. While performing good deeds is necessary and is surely Scriptural— for the Lord Jesus himself ordains it in the story of the sheep and the goats in Matthew 25:31-46— the Kingdom of God is propagated by the sharing of the Good

News. The book of James also tells us "So also faith by itself, if it does not have works, is dead" (James 2:17). However, that doesn't mean that works supersedes faith. Martin Luther and the Reformers separated from the Catholic church on the doctrine of faith. Luther said we are rescued in Christ by faith alone, but not by a faith that is alone. Let me clarify: Mere words don't justify you. If Christ is Lord and King of your life then you desire to please Him by showing His love for you through giving to others. We've reduced Christian service to feeding and clothing those in need and often think that is enough. It is not enough.

Preaching the Gospel is tantamount to success in real mission work. When Paul heard the "Macedonian man" call out to him in a vision to "Come over to Macedonia and help us" in Acts 16:9b, the help God meant for Paul to see was not a humanitarian effort. Feeding people in Jesus' name is a fantastic thing... when you feed them in Jesus' name. If you give someone food and water and never let them know the reason why, and what real satisfaction in Christ is all about, then what is the difference between you and the United States government? Or, the United Way? Or, the food kitchen down off Main Street? How does that equate to preaching the Good News of Christ? Human beings have figured out that we must extend a hand every now and then to help each other get by in difficult times. We Christ-followers, however, must systematically plan to share the story of Christ with everyone we minister to in His name. Tragically, for the last three or four decades many of the "mission trips," especially those connected to the local church, have morphed into a distorted view of the biblical mission.

PREACHING THE GOSPEL IS TANTAMOUNT TO SUCCESS IN REAL MISSION WORK.

The forensics of Scripture will show that many efforts today are D.O.A. How do we determine what is a true biblical mission? What does the text say? Remember directional theology? What you believe is taking you somewhere. Study the Book of Acts and you will see Paul's missionary journeys and the results. Observe Luke 9 & 10 and you will see Jesus equipping the twelve and the mysterious "72."[1] Jesus was essentially modeling what has become a modern-day leadership principle. John Maxwell outlines it like this under "Equipping" in his *Three E's of Leadership Development*:

> **Say it:** explain the task.
> **Show it:** demonstrate how to perform the task.
> **Assign it:** let the other person attempt the task.
> **Study it:** observe how the person performed the task.
> **Assess it:** offer feedback based on the person's performance

Don't get me wrong. I believe churches, small groups, and mission organizations have purpose in doing short-term projects and mission work these days, but maybe it's just that they have forgotten the real goal. Maybe they have never learned about the Great Commission. Perhaps our zeal for God has been hijacked by the enemy so as to make us feel good about our good deeds. The Barna research group offered new statistics on the Great Commission in 2018. The question is asked of churchgoers: What is the Great Commission?

> 51% Have never heard of the Great Commission
> 25% Have heard of it but don't know the meaning
> 17% Know it and know what it means
> 6% Not sure

Add it all up and you have 81% of churchgoers that can't even begin to relate to missions. How many times have you heard the uninformed ask, "Why are you spending all of this money going to another city when we have poor people in our own town?" I love it when I am asked that question because I am always ready to respond their foolish question. Here's my response: "Good question! But what are *you* doing right now in our community, town, or city to help the poor?" In sad summary, when mission work becomes just a rote activity for the local congregation, it's no wonder

---

[1] Some translations have the number 70. Who the 70 or 72 are is debated among the scholars. The best Greek texts translate the number Jesus sends out in Luke 10 to be 72.

The Great Go Mission

there is lack of participation and gross neglect of duty. We've taken the *mission* out of the mission and turned it into a simplistic motion.

STP/STM TYPES

Don't confuse Short-Term Projects (or Short-Term Missions) with taking shortcuts to get there. Let me take the rest of this chapter to attempt to define current mission activities and put them to the test to see if they are of God, and determine how much of our time and resources we need to give them. The following categorizations of projects are my own characterizations and classifications of mission work being done in the world today. They definitely overlap, but you will begin to distinguish between them to get the theological picture in order to see what is related to the Great Commission and what is not.

THE SECULAR/NONSPIRITUAL STM

My wife recently bought me a new pair of athletic socks that I like. They are called Bombas. These socks are very comfortable and give me great cushion while I am running. I highly recommend the socks for comfort, and the colors are cool. Besides, I like to support a company that strives to give back to the world. This new company points to socks as being the most requested clothing need by homeless shelters today. Bombas also explains they started the company to make an impact on our communities here in the United States. For every pair you buy, they will donate a pair to someone in need. *Impact* is a very general term and can mean almost anything. However, Bombas has a whole web page (bombas.com) devoted to explaining their mission, and how they work with numerous nonprofits and other organizations to provide aid to the homeless and at-risk. They then list several ways for you and me to get involved.

Blake Mycoskie, founder of TOMS shoes, began his company with the simple premise of giving a pair of shoes to someone in need for every pair purchased. This one-for-one philosophy is certainly not a Christian principle but it's a great idea for helping the underprivileged of the world. And it has expanded further beyond that idea. TOMS, in a move similar to Bombas, now demonstrates a like goal. They provide not only shoes, but other needs to the underprivileged as well, such as eyecare, clean water, and bullying prevention. It's incredible to peruse their website, toms.com, and see how they are making an impact all over the world— and they started by simply saying they would match your purchase with a gift of shoes to others in need. Interestingly, one word is missing from the websites of Bombas and TOMS: mission. This is a mission activity isn't it? Sort of. I would call it ministry. It is the service or function of ministers. You have to understand they probably want to keep away from the confusion of identifying with a church or a Christian organization. Regardless, they do mission/ministry work (secular) better than most churches. Yes, most.

Do companies like Bombas and TOMS really make an impact? Of course! Sadly, they are doing the stuff that the church should have been doing a long time ago. Churches aren't being creative enough these days to do short-term missions. Satan's assault on missions should force the church to get creative in mission work, and that means we must pray and seek Him. Many times the secular world is outdoing the local church at the church's job. So, what can we learn from generous, ingenious organizations like these?

- As they say, think outside the box.
- Risk. If these companies risk for money or a job, why can't we risk more for God?
- Change our mindset from taking to giving. Tragically, many modern-day churches will not get involved in mission work unless there is a payoff of some kind.
- Start small and allow the Holy Spirit to direct the growth. If you study the business plan of Bombas and TOMS, you will see that they started with a giving concept that was very simple.

Just like *missions* is missing from the websites of Bombas and TOMS, so is the Gospel from many of the STM trips that our evangelical churches are taking. My point in this illustration is that unless you are intentionally sharing the Gospel by preaching and teaching, exhorting, or sharing, then what is the difference between your organization and Bombas or TOMS? What is the difference between your church and the Red Cross, UNICEF, or the United Way? John's letter says, "The reason why the world does not know us is that it did not know him" (1 John 3:1b). A secular STM looks like they are doing godly things, and maybe they are, but they are not *of* God.

The Great Go Mission

GOOD SAMARITAN OR "IN JESUS' NAME" STM

Our church regularly gives money to a mission organization in Zimbabwe for the drilling of wells for fresh water. We, probably just like your church, give to several mission outposts that are grounded in the Bible and have a passion for carrying out the Great Commission in ways that most of us never even entertain cognitively. Mission connectivity happens when someone in the church has linked themselves to these ministries. Mission organizations need the financial support of congregations all over the world in order to live up to their purpose.

Yet there are crooks disguised as ministries, wolves in sheep's clothing, Jesus says. In my state, the secretary of state issues a "naughty and nice" list toward the end of each year at Christmas. The secretary's office does this in case you are feeling generous and have substituted the worship of King Jesus with giving $50 to a local charity in order to feel authentic in the "season of giving" (yes, that was meant to be sarcastic). The list examines the spending percentages weighed against the gifts received. Many state-registered, self-proclaimed "do-good" organizations with *Christian* tied to their name and their vision give only pennies on the dollar. It's a very common thing for charities to have an overhead of 85% and give only 15%, or less, toward their advertised cause. This is criminal, or naughty as the secretary of state likes to put it.

You should know the parable Jesus taught about the Good Samaritan in Luke 10. Here's the digest of it:

> A man is traveling alone on the Jericho road. Everybody knew not to travel the Jericho road alone because it was notorious for crime. Of course, this man is robbed and beaten and left for dead on the side of the road, and as the man lay trying to recover, bloodied and swollen in the face, he cracks an eye open and sees a preacher (priest) coming down the road, "Oh glory day! My help has arrived!" Jesus says the preacher crosses the road so he doesn't have to do anything. Then through his tears and agony he sees a fraternity brother (Levite) coming, surely this is the answer...nope, he crosses on the other side too! Here comes his enemy, uh-oh, this is the end...Jesus says the guy's enemy picks him up, gives him

113

water, checks him into a hotel, gets him medical help, pays the bill, and then says, "I'll be back to check on you." And Jesus asks the incorrigible religious people the undeniable question, "Okay, which one is the good guy?" The religious people had to say it was the bad guy...there was no other answer.

Layer after layer you can peel back this story, but the gist is there. Love conquers bad feelings, bad emotions, and bad actions. As Christians we should do loving things, perform loving acts, and go the distance to display our love for Jesus by giving to others. In other words, we should be Good Samaritans not only at Christmas but every day. John, in his first epistle, spends the better part of five chapters talking about loving our "brothers."

Having short-term mission partners with long-term missionaries is a good thing if expectations are obvious and the STM knows their role. Short-termers need to actually go, if possible, and do the work. We need to be obedient in supporting our LTM brothers and sisters who are on the fringes of societies, who have given up the coveted American Dream in exchange for going. The Gospel dictates that our motivation needs to be genuine in that our hope is for spiritual transformation of lives.

It is a fantastic thing to do things in Jesus' name and for His glory. Seek out opportunities for yourself and your church but make sure the purpose is Great Commission centered. Watch out for the naughty charities and ministries that masquerade as ministers of light when actually they are closer to darkness. Hint: if a ministry cannot define their goal in a simple sentence or statement, then beware. Not every so-called mission organization is ambiguous, because some are slick with their advertising for money. Just do what every person should do when you give: check them out thoroughly. The Apostle Paul speaks clearly about giving in just one sentence: "Each one must give as he has decided in his heart, not reluctantly or under compulsion, for God loves a cheerful giver" (2 Corinthians 9:8).

FEEL-GOOD STM

I referred to this earlier as *Christian Tourism*. This has got to stop. Not only is it costing ghastly amounts of money, but the negative effects on long-term missionaries is devastating. Feel-good projects and short-term missions are rampant. Hear me. It's is a fantastic theory to send small teams via the

The Great Go Mission

glocal concept (I'm all in), but many times it does not materialize in a productive way. It starts out as a Christian task force yet quickly mutates into a leisurely walk while mumbling and mentioning God for a few days. The middleman, a.k.a. the conference, the convention, the fellowship, or the association, does their job to help the local congregation get involved in mission work. Again, let me stop and ask: Why have we demoted missions to an exercise left to a handful of people in the church? Isn't the mission given to us by Christ, as the Great Commission, the reason we exist as churches? Shouldn't we make Jesus' command in Matthew 28:19,20 a foundational stone in our churches? Missions has to be elevated to a place of priority and primary ministry once again in order to understand the greatness about our God-given mission. To continue to push it around, offering it to a few so-called spiritual elites in the church or to those who have the means to travel and go, only contributes to its erosion.

Anyway, in order to stage productivity, the middleman provides funds, many times financing cost-effective trips for interested parties from local congregations to go where church planters are or where long-term missionaries are operating. The excursion's purported purpose is for the participants to scout out the territory, investigating the blueprints of the LTM, and then, hopefully, they will come alongside of the LTM. The outcome is a promise for some help.

DWYSYAGTD

The key word in my last sentence was *promise*. Somewhere along the line of your education you have learned the acronym DWYSYAGTD— Do What You Say You Are Going To Do. I have talked to many pastors about this problem: The church planter/LTM gets excited because he has been told a team of people from a certain state is coming to visit. They are told the representatives/taskforce are on a fact-finding trip for their respected congregations and to be ready to present their vision for the area. The church planter/LTM gets cleaned up, puts on a tie, and offers his best presentation. His hope is a rescue— a financial rescue— like they do on

115

reality TV by rescuing bars, restaurants, etc. After several drive-by tourist-like scenes, and many meals over the course of two to three days, the team captain shakes the hand of the church planter/LTM and says, "We are going to help you! I promise." And as the representatives are piling in the car to catch their flight home, wiping away the tears of compassion, they call out, "We'll be praying for you!"

I don't like to sound so condescending in my portrait of this but in my estimation, and based on my observations and experience, there are more church planters/LTMs who are disappointed and dejected by empty promises than there are those who are actually helped. I know, I've talked to them. Here's why Feel Good STM are missing the mark: The visitors determine their support by how they feel about the mission or the LTM. They look around as if they need to be impressed with the planter's efforts before they will give. This is wrong. In looking for a goose bump connection, by sharing a meal or getting to know the church planter and/or LTM, they make a judgment call. Wouldn't it be 50/50 at best?

First of all the mission, whether it is short-term or long, is not for you and it doesn't always produce sweet feelings of excitement. As a matter of fact, every time I have ever gone on a STM trip, I get physically sick! It takes weeks after I get home to readjust to an eating pattern and a sleeping pattern, and to reclaim a work and workout routine. It just throws off my rhythm. We shouldn't feel good about going to another culture and seeing the spiraling plight of man lived out in front of our eyes, among godless people. You are not going to have a jolly feeling about brothers and sisters being forced to comply with draconian governments when you leave to return home. We should be reminded of our own blessings yet be moved by the Holy Spirit that we are blessed for the purpose of being "already gone" to do missions.

Gospel-Lite STM

Okay, this is my last rant, I promise. Face painting, giving out snow cones, renting bounce houses, and mundane, monotonous prayer walking has got to stop. I'm sort of joking, but then again, I'm not. It's just been done so much in my community of believers and churches that they have carved it into an everlasting liturgy for church planting and the mission.

It is so commonplace these days that it has become boring. Selfishly, I suppose I'm tired of it. However, having a block party and inviting the neighbors over for hotdogs and hamburgers while letting the kids run and play in the cul-de-sac is a tremendous idea for outreach. But let's make sure our planning, execution, and intention is for sharing the Gospel. If it is, then short-term missions are truly functioning on a high level, and those engaged in block parties are those engaged in real ministry. If it is, then going to the other side of the world doesn't outrank this mission activity.

> **WE REACH OUT WITH LIGHT HEARTS, WE PRESENT A LIGHT SAVIOR, AND WE GET FLUFFY RESULTS.**

But heed this warning: To hold a block party without boldly sharing the Gospel is missing a huge opportunity. I call it Gospel-Lite STM because we've gotten too predictable about mission work. Proverbs tells us that our ways seem right, but God weighs the heart. It's become too packaged and too staged. There is no weight to our mission outreach anymore. We reach out with light hearts, we present a light Savior, and we get fluffy results. It's a way for church people who want to get involved to do so, but too often it doesn't go anywhere.

Many evangelical movements are struggling in America today largely because of a Gospel-Lite approach. You know what I mean don't you? When we realize we are tipping the scales too much and we talk ourselves into attempting to lose weight we will settle for the path of least resistance. Sure, we go for the low sodium, sugar-free, no gluten, lectin free diets, only to gobble up more calories with diet food while being frustrated with little to no results. Gospel-Lite STM look like they are doing a lot for the Kingdom, but they're not really. They are just doing *stuff*, packing on the activities. More and more movement doesn't equal the successful execution of a mission. It does not accomplish Kingdom work. If anything, the Gospel is power-packed, but we have over-packed it with fluff. The presentation of the Gospel on mission needs to throw a punch or two these days. To think we need to ease into a presentation of the Gospel by giving away trinkets is often just watering it down.

MISSION SUPPORT STM

Alin Patularu is a church planter in Windsor, Ontario, Canada. I met him when I was invited to be part of one of those Christian taskforce teams. After presenting the opportunity to our church, praying about it, being led by the Holy Spirit, and knowing that a STP/STM centers around giving, we gave to Alin's church, Life-Giver Church. God had blessed my church with an extra Bose Sound System, and it was exactly what Alin needed as he was starting the public worship service phase of the church plant. We also took up an offering one Sunday and presented it to Alin. Upon our team delivering the sound system and the offering and gathering in a circle to pray for Alin, he said, "Everyone promised, but you were the only ones that showed up."

Yes, I'm proud of our church and praised them for their obedience. It's a victory to help and to be called to stand with a long-term missionary as he stands tall for the Lord. Growing up in the early 1970's, one of my favorite sitcoms (before they were called sitcoms) was *Hogan's Heroes*. The threat from Colonel Klink, the commandant of the Nazi POW camp, to the clumsy and bungling Sergeant Shultz, was that if he messed up he would be sent to the "Russian Front." I had no clue what the Russian Front was until history class later on in high school. The Russian Front, a.k.a. the Eastern Front, was where you went to die. The Nazis were progressing towards and invading Russia and, in other words, the front was the frontline of battle where the bullets were flying, the bombs were exploding, and the tanks were rolling. God puts His best men and women on the front lines. Sometimes they die physically, but *everyone* who goes has to die spiritually.

Alin Patularu is on the frontline of what should be known as the Eastern Front of North American Christianity. He has died to sin and Christ has rebirthed him. He is in godless territory in Canada, just over the border from Michigan. He can't operate without the power of the Holy Spirit, and he can't be sustained with empty prayers. Is that what we are missing in the mission as we carry out the Great Commission? It seems we do not understand the gravity of the situation. People are lost, without Christ, and facing a Godless eternity– and that is called hell, my friends.

The Great Go Mission

The best we can do— and the very least we can do— in our churches is support just one other church in the world with our prayers, with going, and hopefully with some financial help.

Mission Support STM is just like going. You may not get to go for reasons of your health, your job, your family, or your call, but you can go with those LTM/church planter types by offering up your prayer support. The Psalter cried out to God repeatedly, asking God to intervene. So, if you cannot go— if you cannot physically go somewhere and proclaim the Gospel on mission, then ask God to point you in the direction of someone that is doing it and lean your support their way. For many believers it may be the same as going.

CSI-STM

In qualifying authentic short-term mission projects, maybe we should give them a new code name representing authenticity. I recommend the phrase "Christ Sent Initiatives," or CSI. While my heart warms and my face smiles in hearing of the multitudes of teenage short-term mission projects, and churches that organize them to go all over the country and world each summer, the necessary and defining question is, "What is your purpose?" If you cannot state the purpose in a concise short sentence then you are probably missing the real reason for going. If a desire to bring glory to God is not the intention, then maybe it's time to rethink your reason for going.

Christ-sent initiatives are harkening to and acquiescing to Christ's command in the Great Commission - Go and make disciples. Regardless, the modern-day church continues to add to, and subtract from, the mission.

Clearly stated goals, leading to the transformation of lives to look like Jesus, should be at the core of every mission initiative. No one turns down money, and no one rejects the STP/STM that wants to do construction or perform prayer walks. But the mass of all the parts to a successful mission trip should add up to church starts, aiding pastors and leaders in evangelism, and making disciples. Christ has sent us to do the stuff. What stuff? Examining how He was training the 72 in their STM in Luke 10, you can summarize His appointment to them with this alliteration:

>   (There is a) **Plentiful** harvest
>   **Pray** for workers for the harvest
>   **Pronounce** peace
>   **Pray** for & heal the sick
>   **Preach** the Kingdom of God
>   **Pronounce** judgment to the rejectors (yep)

That sounds like a pretty well outlined STM to me, what about to you? The exciting part of the short-term project account in Luke 10 is when the 72 return, and there is a debriefing. The consensus is meant to be very encouraging to us: "The seventy-two returned with joy, saying, "Lord, even the demons are subject to us in your name!" (Luke 10:17)

Wow! The debriefing part of all short-term mission projects is massively important. It is an opportunity to quickly respond and critique the mission while it is fresh on the mind. I've been a part of great mission trips and I've been a part of terrible ones. Here are the questions that need to be asked and answered honestly:

> → Was there a spirit of joy and oneness?
> → Did we do what we intended to do? Did we accomplish our mission?
> → Were the people responsive to the mission? What did they say?
> → Was the Gospel clearly communicated and preached with boldness?
> → What was the resistance to the mission? Did you detect an enemy response?
> → What did we fail to do? Was the plan viable? What were the problems?
> → Was the team prepared and adequately trained for the mission?

The Great Go Mission

→ Is there still more work to be done in this area?
→ Would you go again? How can you pray for them from here on out?
→ What would you do differently if you go again?

Jesus did not send the twelve or the 72 out on some religious expedition as part of the church calendar. Rather He was training them for real life, and for real ministry. Could that be one of the most misleading things about the modern mission movement? Have we not gone deep enough and been abundantly thorough in preparing individuals and teams for the job? I don't spend too much time praying for safety when I go on mission trips these days. If Christ sent me, and He knows I'm going, and I'm going on His mission for His purpose, then if He wants to take me from this planet during this short-term trek that's His business. We would probably have a lot less people going on short-term mission projects if we advertised it like this:

> **• NEEDED •**
> Christ-followers who are adventurous and want to do God's work on distant shores for a few days only, all expenses paid for, you will see things that most of the rest of the world will never see, eat delicious things you have never heard of, and experience things that are once in a lifetime... however, there is a slight risk that you may never return home.

If Christ has sent us on one of these initiatives that we label as short-term projects, then safety needs to be secondary to the primary reason of the Gospel.

HOMOGENEOUS

If your church wants to get started or continue to do mission work, then it is necessary to realize the Great Commission was spoken from the actual lips of our Lord. It means we should all be alike on mission. Making disciples while proclaiming Jesus has to be the undisputed aim of all Christian mission work. Being involved in construction, digging wells, and providing food and clothing, are all commendable efforts but only the Gospel brings us together. Taking the nations and communities to the Cross of Christ, lifting our Savior up and being obedient as He draws His people to Him, is the glue.

Not only do the multiple definitions divide us on our mission, but so do the innerworkings of churches and missionaries. Those who are trained and educated in mission work, usually the LTM, don't like it when the STM rush in without a plan and rightly so.

In his book *Striking the Match*, missiologist and professor George Robinson says that it would be rare to be able to get a missiologist to agree to the fact that strategic STM exists. Apprehension on the part of LTM leads to their suspicion of the small STM teams who are visiting on a quick basis. This divide in missiology in the twenty-first century between STM and LTM may be rooted in jealousy, but both should be joyful about the opportunities it brings to the local church. LTM question what the STM can significantly contribute to the long-term work of those who have been on the field for extended periods of time, which proves my hypothesis for this book: if we are not training and equipping *every* saint with the ability to lead others to transformation in Christ, spiritual formation, and church planting, then what gospel are we listening to?

Robinson dedicates an entire chapter in his book to this question. Entitled *Every Disciple a Church Planter* it states that every Christian should be involved in cross-cultural missions. He says the concluding clause in the Great Commission: "...teaching them to observe all that I have commanded you" (Matt. 28:20) directly addresses you and me, saying, "I take that to mean that every Christ-follower is to be engaged in the completion of the Great Commission, including making disciples cross-culturally." He further states that if the STM is not doing the job of planting a church or making disciples then he prefers to call it exactly what it is: a work trip. If you recall, I labeled them as *In Jesus' Name* STM but they could also easily fall into the category of *Feel-Good* STM. We raise the money, get the church pumped up to go, send out the team, put up some dry wall, build a ramp for the wheelchair bound, wash some cars in Jesus' name, and come back to the church feeling good about ourselves. Please hear me and don't try to misquote me— I believe these good deeds are valid and needed and I lead teams to participate in them, too, for the purpose of fully carrying out the Great Commission. Sadly, this busy-ness is what much, if not most of ministry has become and it has all been dumped into the same vat and branded "mission work."

Robinson nails the true focus of mission work:

> Over the last few centuries the focus of missions has broadened in scope to include activities such as education, healthcare, and social work. A cursory look at any sending agency website will show that one can engage in just about any type of activity under the banner of missions. The biblical corpus, however, leans toward the idea that missions itself should be defined by having an evangelistic or discipling orientation. Those other ministries should flow naturally from new believers being properly discipled in the context of a local church. This is not to say that contributions to education, healthcare, and social ministries are not valuable parts of living the Christ life.

Maybe you will disagree here, claiming your church is already obeying God and the leaders He put before you. Or, you feel that helping people "get along" in life is your calling. Perhaps you believe I am putting down good efforts all in the "name of Jesus," and maybe I am, but you have to take inventory of your ministry because a mere effort is not good enough. God wants us to obey the Great Commission. I firmly believe the New Testament delineates how we are to do STM work. Study how Jesus did it. Review Paul's missionary journeys.

In your persistence, you scream, "But Pastor GD, doesn't Jesus clearly tell us we are to feed the sick and clothe the naked and visit the inmate in Matthew 25 in the story of the Sheep and the Goats?" Yes, He does. But that is your life ministry, not the specific aim of a mission team. Jesus is talking about your personal behavior, not laying out a mission strategy. Believe me, I am not calling for a halt to churches that are doing "good" ministry projects but don't start churches or evangelize/disciple others. I simply want our pastors, STP/STM mission leaders, and churches, to focus more on the call of the Great Commission as a whole rather than just going on a trip merely to go. I'm calling our churches, associations, state conventions and conferences, pastors, lay leaders, and bishops to make the mission the Great Commission again. Let's get on the same page, and make sure we understand why we should have already gone. If you don't know why you are going and if your "going" does not match the words of the Lord Jesus, then it may be time to change the way you do mission work.

UNIQUE MISSION

I just hung up the phone with a Christian brother, David Miller, who serves as Director of Missions for his denominational association of churches in Alabama. I was inquiring about a ministry he oversees, in which a group of carpenters and builders give a week of their vacation time to go to different areas of the country, and even travel internationally, using their skills to construct ministry or church buildings. They are also involved in disaster relief efforts. This is a fantastic ministry, but is it missions? My inquiry was selfishly motivated. Our church was constructing our first building and we needed to cut corners due to the rising cost of lumber. I pressed on with David and I found out more incredible things.

This ministry is utterly amazing. The men and women camp out, sleeping on cots or pallets on the floor. They work long days, many times in the hot sun without air-conditioning. They are away from their families, the work makes them tired, and most of these brothers and sisters in Christ are older. Each participant pays over $100 for food and board, to go and spend their free time sweating and laboring for the Kingdom. It's all done pro-bono. It's a gift to the community or the church, and it's all Gospel-centered. Is it Christian ministry, or are they servants and missionaries of the Great Commission? Both.

To my great relief and encouragement, Reverend Miller explained that while a great many of their team are involved in the physical labor of erecting a building or doing the finish out, they always have an evangelism team simultaneously going door to door, sharing the Gospel. Wow. Our "sold out to the Lord" brother said he will not go, nor will he take his team, if they cannot go door-to-door witnessing and hold Vacation Bible School for the children in the neighborhood. Double wow. What I absolutely love about David Miller is that he does the work of an evangelist, a pastor, a ministry leader, and a missionary without forsaking his duty on account of bureaucratic jibber-jabber. The Great Commission never changes, it will always be about going.

AT LEAST BE THE LEAST

My early misunderstanding of missions was grounded in a faulty archetypal model... ancient if you will. Long before jet travel, the space shuttle, Wal-Mart, Starbucks, the mobile device, and even before FDR's New Deal, the modern Christian world had settled into a way of "doing" church and missions. Most of them have "missions" set off to the side, usually with some made-up activities so they don't look lame. The majority just tag some mission organization that they like, or they piggy-back on a ministry someone else is actually doing. Is their support legitimate? Who knows? Here's my point: missions is not something we select and isolate by making it an event... no, according to Jesus, it's a lifestyle of obedience where we count the cost, die to ourselves, and take up our cross. Jesus adds that if you don't hate your mother, brother, family and friends more than you love Him then you are not qualified for the mission. In short, the mission is very costly.

Are you the one of the least? Yes, you are. Start shifting to humility and, as one of the least, begin allowing Him to work through you. Discover the grace in which God wants to move in your life by sharing your story of God's grace in your life, and you will be far ahead of most of the STM I have ever heard about. Your giftedness is from above, you are what you are. But what He wants you to be is yet to be seen.

ARE YOU THE ONE OF THE LEAST? YES, YOU ARE.

Chapter Seven
STR

"*The Great Commission has experienced a great reversal.*"   -Alvin Reid

"*But Jonah rose to flee to Tarshish from the presence of the Lord.*"
-Jonah 1:3

THE DAY BEFORE ONE OF my recent short-term projects I began showing the symptoms of STR. Have you ever had it? I stared intently at my face in the mirror, recognizing the signs. It's a brutal disease caused by inner inquisitive interrogations. Doubt is the key symptom. If left undiagnosed, you will become emotionally sick and spiritually confused.

I was talking to a friend via phone 24 hours before I was to board a plane for eighteen hours and he asked me, "Greg, do you ever get traveler's remorse?" What? Honestly, I had never thought about it in those terms, but there were plenty of times in the past when I questioned myself and wondered, "What am I doing 9,000 miles from home? Am I making a difference? I sure don't like getting an upset stomach and having to take medicine. Jetlag gets very real when you cross the international dateline. I wonder if my wife misses me. Could this money be better spent? Am I really a missionary or am I just acting like one? Why don't I save the money for my travels and just send cash for more Bibles and organize a special prayer time for my brothers and sisters in that far off country? Why don't my friends see that it is cool to eat fried cicadas and scorpion on a stick?" I now call it Spiritual Traveler's Remorse – STR.

Packing up, leaving my wife, trusting my church responsibilities to others, seeing the sad eyes of my precious two Boston Terriers, I hurriedly exit the house and dash toward the airport. Making my mental checklist,

Why doesn't everybody in the church care enough to reach those without Christ in other parts of the world?

my obsessive-compulsiveness kicks in and I check my passport... is it is up to date? Is my visa good? I check my passport again, and I ask myself, "did I pack a toothbrush? What about my Bible, did I pack my Bible?!" STR is a burdensome and tiring mental maze to crawl through, but I know many that contract it, agonize through it, yet they continue to go.

Do mission trips, the short-term projects, really make a difference? Or have we oversaturated the market with just good deeds and made our message no different from the Buddhist monks, the Mormons (LDS), or the Red Cross?

What stands out about your mission? What are the distinguishing marks of God's mission? Like the bullseye, the Great Commission, and not just good activities, should be the central target of the Gospel message you are taking to others. I believe STR has negatively affected the mission world of STM and LTM. As I have stated numerous times up to this point, many have lost sight of the purpose. Maybe we have thought about it too much?

Why doesn't everybody in the church care enough to reach those without Christ in other parts of the world? How has the desire for fifteen-million-dollar contemporary worship centers eclipsed our concern for those who have never heard of Jesus? The popular missionary term used for the "lost" in the world is "unreached people groups" (UPG). Unreached people groups, in Christianity, are ethnic group without an indigenous, self-propagating Christian church movement. The current approximate population of the planet hovers above seven billion. Sociologists have identified 16,591 people groups and, according to statistics close to the latest world census, 6,741 of these are UPGs. That is a total population of UPGs of over three billion. The annual income of evangelicals is seven trillion dollars and we give $45 billion to mission work, or about the same amount America spends on dieting each year. Why don't we care? The simple answer: we are a self-absorbed people and have not heeded the call of our Almighty God. The more complex answer is that most churches cannot define mission work.

If we wanted, evangelical Christians could provide all of the money needed to plant a church among each of the 6,741 unreached people groups with only 0.03% of their income. Our Churches have approximately three thousand times the money, and nine thousand times the people, needed to finish the Great Commission. If every believer gave ten percent of their income to missions, we could easily support two million new missionaries. Let's put it into terms we all understand: Americans will spend close to $10 billion on Halloween candy and costumes this year.

Is spiritual travelers remorse an epidemic? Maybe the problem is with "going?" Remember, Jesus' Great Commission statement in Matthew 28 assumes we are already going. And even though it is not the imperative in that truth-telling passage of Scripture, it just may be the sticking point for many Christ-followers. I have encountered many believers who not only don't bother with thinking about others world-wide without Christ, they think it's none of their business. Furthermore, they go to extremes to avoid even talking about it. Again, it's selfishness. It's a flagrant misunderstanding of the Gospel. It's avoidance. Call it whatever you want. We have sold out to an American gospel that asks first and foremost, "What's in it for me?"

MORE STR THOUGHTS

Last year I read a biography of the Englishman, George Whitefield. Although thought of as an intenerate preacher of yesteryear, Whitefield was not considered a missionary by our definitions. We would call him an evangelist. Yet he did remarkable evangelistic mission work along the Eastern seaboard of the United States, from Savannah to Boston, three hundred years ago. You can summarize Whitefield's work as that of a long-term missionary in short-term missionary movements. If you read about him, you cannot help but feel the palpable intensity of someone who understands the call of a servant of God carrying out the mission. If he suffered STR he sure didn't show it, and we don't know about it.

Whitefield landed in Georgia in 1738 and, upon inspecting the leftover ministry of John Wesley, built an orphanage. That is surely mission work. But Whitefield was committed to preaching the Gospel and bringing revival. It is said he sometimes preached three times a day, every day of the week. The estimate is a total of 18,000+ sermons in his lifetime. London's famed Reverend Charles Spurgeon, considered by many the greatest pulpiteer of all time, said this of Whitefield, "Other men seem to be only half-alive, but Whitefield was all life, fire, wing, force. My own model, if I may have such a thing in due subordination to my Lord, is George Whitefield. With unequal footsteps must I follow his glorious track." Half-alive? That is a robust statement coming from Spurgeon. Research Whitefield and you will find a called servant of God, with the zealousness for the Great Commission, as is needed for missionary work today.

Nevertheless, I wonder, did Whitefield have STR? You bet he did. No one involved in God's work is without doubts. He lost his wife unexpectedly, he was sick a lot, and you can just imagine how fatigued and wearied one can become of logging all those miles up and down the East coast of what would one day be the United States. Think about it: no roads (long before I-95), no cars, no GPS, no planes, no five-star hotels, no fast-food restaurants. Your voice was the only amplification system you had—and it was long before the creation of cough drops! This was the life of an itinerate preacher? C'mon on now. It's been reported that John Wesley would sleep through his traveling, riding horseback while someone else led him. Can you imagine the backache? What job in the world was more difficult emotionally and physically? Six times Whitefield made the voyage by sea to the American colonies from England to preach. He literally preached himself to death, dying at age fifty-five. Wait...that's younger than me!

Did Whitefield die of STR? I don't think so. He had it, but I don't imagine he died from it. He knew his call was to go, and he went until God took him. His distinctive response was, 'I would sooner wear out, than rust out.' Whitefield was tireless! Even up to his closing days and preaching his final sermons, it is said he would look up to the heavens and say something like, "Lord Jesus, I am weary in Thy work, but not of Thy work." Exhausted, Whitefield finished the race.

Spiritual traveler's remorse is a common emotional feeling among Christ-followers, especially those who go great distances from home. The emotional health of Christian workers has been overlooked for far too long. Being encouraged, and reminded of a strength that only comes from God, is very important to short-term and long-term missionaries. Make sure you have a friend or group of friends that you can go to and pour out your heart. STR is a common heart issue that has to be addressed by the only medicine able to cure it – Holy Scripture.

The Apostle Paul urges us to mark the conclusion of the race of our called lives. He tells Timothy that he has "...finished the course... kept the faith" (2 Tim. 4:7). If the Master calls you, you need to go— you must go— because it's part of His shaping of your life. Don't miss out on it and don't put Him off until tomorrow. Respond with delight that He has asked you to participate but know that your calling is unique and with it comes difficult questions and circumstances you will have to trust Him for. Spiritual traveler's remorse is sometimes contracted from poorly planned mission work, yet the vaccine is prayer...a lot of prayer. Make sure you go to our great doctor, Jesus, meet with the Father, and call on the Holy Spirit, to give you boldness and a sureness to go. More times than we like to admit, our STM results in STR.

A BAD SHORT-TERM PROJECT

One day my student minister came into a staff meeting and requested to take our students to Latin America on a mission trip. He claimed the international experience had the potential to be significant to the spiritual growth of our teenagers and adults who would accompany them.

First of all, all mission activity begins with a purpose to impact the people and region you are focused on reaching, not on personal discipleship and renewal. Often you will see and hear, from poorly trained mission leaders, how a mission trip can help the spiritual growth and formation of young people. Don't buy it! You are serving others, not serving yourself.

Second, a mission trip of any kind involves much prayer. This prospective short-term project had neither of these first two requirements. I knew better. I acquiesced, but I knew better. Third, when planning and praying about a mission trip with teenagers and a young student minister, you should get as much information as possible up front. Never trust someone who says "everything will work out fine."

Fourth, a simple one-sentence goal statement is worth thousands of dollars and perhaps thousands of lives. Finally, do the research and find the victories of past projects and trips of the organization or church in which you are partnering.

Since the trip was almost a year away, there was ample time to raise the money to go, and our teenagers started looking forward to it. Carwashes, yard sales, spaghetti suppers, and other fundraisers kicked in to supplement the $1k-plus cost per student for the week-long trip. Starting six months in advance, in our staff meetings, I would query my student leaders about the purpose of going to this Latin American paradise. Remember, a purpose in doing missions is literally worth thousands of dollars and it translates into the gravity of understanding the brevity of life. Again, I should have known. I was better trained, and I was wiser. But his desire to go, the excitement among the kids, and my desire to do something "big" got the better of me.

> **...before I knew it, twenty-five of our teenagers were flying the fifteen hundred nautical miles to Central America, and I still didn't know why.**

Looking back, I don't remember ever being satisfied with an answer to why we were going. But time got away from me and, before I knew it, twenty-five of our teenagers were flying the fifteen hundred nautical miles to Central America, and I still didn't know why. To make matters worse, my fourteen-year-old son was going, so my wife informed me that I was going, too! I had to go, if you know what I mean. Several other leaders in our church went also, and we were genuinely upbeat and anticipated a fantastic mission trip. Disappointment set in quickly, however, because it was anything but successful in my eyes.

The Great Go Mission

A week before we departed, I was given a handwritten agenda of our mission. It looked average on paper. Would it translate into a legitimate, Christ sent initiative (CSI)? We would see. My assistant pastor, Bob, said to me, "Pastor, this doesn't look good." The schedule called for village to village witnessing in the hill country, knocking on doors, giving out some Bibles, and inviting locals to a worship service where our student minister would preach an evangelistic message. Our students had also prepared a dramatic presentation that would add to our efforts. I responded, "I don't know Bob, it has some merit."

We touched down in Panama City with our entourage late in the evening and caught a bus to a motel. I distinctly remember getting off the bus in the wee hours of the morning and the shark disguised as a missionary asking for the cash. It didn't take long to figure out his game... this guy was a crook. Although he belonged to a certain denomination, he had found a way to circumvent the process and make some side money. And we fell for it. I won't digress anymore because it's pointless to continue to beat myself up about it. Let's just say the Panama mission trip opened my eyes to more than the ugliness of mission work. I saw the diabolical and insidious plot of Satan.

The enemy wants to divert our attention ever so slightly off of the Gospel grid and on to busy-ness. Going and doing just anything in the name of Jesus does not work and has never been part of the plan. After a while of following that seemingly insignificant sidetrack we are not just a little off center... we are running away from God. Looking back I hope our Panama mission trip was not in vain. We preached the Gospel, and the results are left up to God. Someone said, "God hits straight licks with crooked sticks." Although I have forgiven the dude, I sometimes want to hit him with a crooked stick. I am afraid we missed a fantastic chance to do something meaningful in Latin America, among thousands. I will forever have spiritual traveler's remorse over that trip.

JONAH

Jonah's flight from God was probably a bit worse than our trip to Panama. You do not have to go very far into Jonah's account before you discover he had STR in a major way. In the opening few sentences of the minor prophet's book we see Jonah doing the exact opposite of God's instructions to him. In the very first verse we deduce God's short-term missionary call upon Jonah as it begins, "Now the word of the Lord came to Jonah the son of Amittai, saying, "Arise, go to Nineveh, that great city, and call out against it, for their evil has come up before me" (Jonah 1:1-2). The verses that follow shape up to be symptoms of STR that one could not bear. It's safe to say that most of us have a rich history of telling God we have a better way of doing mission work. We inevitably tell God our travel plans, and our list of supplies far exceed His plans. Some of us even go as far as to say we are not going to participate at all.

Nineveh was directly across from the east side of the Tigris river, which is now modern-day Mosul. In 2014, ISIS had taken control of this second major city in Iraq. In October of 2016, the Iraqi government launched an initiative to take it back and called it "We are coming, Nineveh." In July of 2017, the Iraqi president announced victory and promised to rebuild, at the tune of fifty billion dollars and five years.

No wonder Jonah did not want to go to Nineveh. It's always been a troubled region. From the looks of it, it may always be a difficult place to do God's work. Christianpost.com ranks the area as the fourth most dangerous place to be a Christian on the planet, behind North Korea, Somalia, and Syria. Christianity Today, meanwhile, puts it at number eight in the most dangerous ranking with Pakistan, Eritrea, and Libya ahead of it. Yet, our Holy God calls people to these dangerous places. Do you want to do something great in the Kingdom of God today? Then pray today for those who are on the mission front lines in these countries. They need your prayer desperately.

Things began to unravel quickly for Jonah as he sailed away from God. He was surely experiencing spiritual traveler's remorse by disobeying God's command to go to Nineveh. The journey in the opposite direction turns around only after Jonah responds to the turmoil at sea. With the hurricane like winds bearing down on Jonah's cruise ship, and in desperation, Jonah fesses up. Was Jonah having STR or what?

How do you combat this emotional/spiritual malady? Do you forfeit mission trips? Do you leave it to someone else that you think is better suited? I know one thing: the staunch, Great Commission-living men and women in the last two thousand years, that I've read about, didn't let it stop them. You know they suffered. You know it was difficult. They endured. It may

The Great Go Mission

be a forgone conclusion that STR dominated their emotions. However, they ran the race. How many thorns in the flesh did they all have? The Apostle Paul gives us a hint:

> So to keep me from becoming conceited because of the surpassing greatness of the revelations, a thorn was given me in the flesh, a messenger of Satan to harass me, to keep me from becoming conceited. Three times I pleaded with the Lord about this, that it should leave me. But he said to me, "My grace is sufficient for you, for my power is made perfect in weakness." Therefore I will boast all the more gladly of my weaknesses, so that the power of Christ may rest upon me. For the sake of Christ, then, I am content with weaknesses, insults, hardships, persecutions, and calamities. For when I am weak, then I am strong" (2 Cor. 12:7-10).

The answer to your STR in STP/STM or LTM is to endure. He will give you His grace. Missional suffering is real, and nowhere does God say we are exempt from it. Whatever you are going through pack a lunch, because God wants you to walk through it. Regretful experiences, spiritual warfare, and attacks from the enemy amid continued encounters with self-centeredness, are to be expected. However, STR and a bad short-term project still equate to being missional minded. Jonah's STR, even though it was severely selfish, still resulted in God's purpose being accomplished. Be cool, God is going to glorify Himself in His mission that you have been allowed to join— no matter what. Just do it better the next time and get it right.

A BAD LONG-TERM MISSIONARY

Rewind to my first church as pastor, I had only been there a few months, and I was still secretly praying God would send me and my wife to become a missionary somewhere, anywhere. I was blind to the fact that God had graciously and purposefully placed me in one of the most impossible mission sites in the entire state. If you wanted to do something great for God and knew that the odds were against you, this was the place. Steeped in racism and poverty, this town was a challenge. Years later, after I was long gone and despite the challenges, another faithful pastor and servant of the Lord started a fantastic movement that grew into a church still thriving today.

Back at my country church there was a biennial mission event on a particular Sunday. A long-term missionary (LTM), who was somehow acquainted with our small fellowship, was scheduled to speak on a Sunday morning. I got up early, excited to be hearing about her work deep in the continent of Africa, anticipating being wowed by the adventures and risk of life and limb to share Jesus. Maybe this was to serve as the catalyst for calling me to the mission field! The missionary's table of African paraphernalia was set up in our fellowship hall. Color brochures depicting life in the jungle were handed out, and the "old" people of the church were greeting the missionary with long lost hugs.

She began to give her presentation, following my animated anticipation-building introduction, and after only a few moments... yawn... I was bored to tears. The exhibition of life presented for the modern African missionary was the doldrums compared to what I thought mission life would be like. No doubt she had done some good work for the kingdom of God, but I questioned how anyone could compare this to a mission. Lacking was a definition and goal of the missionary's labor. Where was the excitement of serving on God's team as His ambassador? I wanted to see the pictures of the people of Africa that once were lost and now they are found. Where was the speech about putting your life on the line? Where was the risk?

I thought, if you are on a mission then shouldn't you repeatedly state the goal of the mission? It seemed she had taken the world's most thrilling missive directive and dulled it to the point of my nodding off into sleep. My other questions were multiple. Has mission activity always been like this? Have I been duped all these years? Was Isaiah wrong? Have we gotten to the point where God's Word returns void? Should we retitle this effort of the modern church, the boring commission? Quick, someone pull the curtain on this sham!

While I was puzzled about why the people in our church were all so excited about this LTM, I pondered the situation. My conclusion was that they liked the idea of *someone else* going to do mission work. *As long as we can send a few dollars and don't have to go ourselves* is a very real mentality

The Great Go Mission

among churches. Admittedly, it wasn't all bad. The LTM had accomplished great things, or God had used her to do so. There was great energy in the building that day and it was all directed toward one of our own who was called to go to the wastelands of Africa. Some of the most unsung heroes of our faith in the twenty-first century are LTM. I know plenty of fantastic, successful, kingdom growing LTM, and I pray for them while respecting their unique call. And so should you.

ONE MISSION

I often correct people when they naively mutter, "Well, it says in the book of revelations...." No, it's just one Revelation! It is the Revelation given to John to write down, revealing the majestic throne room of God and the return of the Lord Jesus. I feel the same way about the word "missions." Even though forced to have used the word thus far, I want to make a clear distinction going forward.

Jesus gave us one mission that if correctly administered will risk some part of your health. Oh yes, if the Christian life is lived properly, then you will suffer for the cause of Christ. The mission of carrying out the Gospel may cost you your friends, family, job, health, fortune, popularity, excommunication, being blackballed, or even your life. It may cost you advancement, political seats, or nasty stares and confused looks. How have we turned it into a ho-hum, religious exercise that is only fueled when we beg for funds or borrow from the church treasury? "Missions" has become the red-headed stepchild of the church, the second-class citizen. Even though more and more churches are funding short-term projects and the number of trips is increasing, they are still looked upon with some skepticism by a great majority of Christians. The mission Christ commands at the end of the Gospel of Matthew is not a postscript tacked on to give Christians something to do. No, it begins way back in Genesis.

You see, God's nature has always been missional. It is ludicrous to believe that contemporary models using short-term missionaries is the latest find among emerging church cultures. His redemptive plan, Missio Dei (God's mission), culminating in a relationship, began with the command to Adam and Eve: "Be fruitful and multiply and fill the earth and subdue it" (Gen. 1:28). Things became amplified when God unveiled His character even more after the rebellion of Adam and Eve in the Garden (Gen. 3).

Immediately the theme of salvation is introduced in Genesis 3:15, the *proto-evangelium* for the Christian gospel. Then the covenant with Abraham (Gen. 12:1-3) follows and further ushers in salvation history as we know it.

As Christ-followers, we serve a missional God. All of life is a mission and we are to be with Him on the mission. Someone may ask, "but if it's God's mission, and God is going to accomplish it without me, then why do I need to join Him?" Because He asks you to. And further, He allows you to be a part of His glorious mission.

If you want to know who you are, to know the mission for your life, then you must know who He is. When you bow the knee to Him as King of your life you are sealed "in Him," as Paul says in the first chapter of Ephesians. Paul purportedly borrows a line from the Greek poet Epimenides when he illustrates that God is not playing children's games with us. He says in Acts 17:28, "In him we live and move and have our being." As the Holy Spirit lives in you, you follow as He leads. It is where you get life. Our duty is lived out on the front lines of this life. As churches, we are all to be on board with this mission assignment. The church is meant to plan it, pray for it, lead it, and fund it. It's not covert, and it's neither your path towards self-promotion nor self-destruction. But He promises that He will never abandon us.

MISSIONAL

As discussed in chapter three, *missional* is a superb term used frequently among the Christian brethren today. When applied, every believer becomes a missionary because being missional in sharing the Gospel of Jesus Christ becomes the duty of every believer. The believer thus takes the posture of a missionary and, as a result, the church becomes missional. I'm afraid we don't take it seriously enough, though. Our religion has become an empty façade of colloquial speech and popular sayings that we can Tweet to show others our spiritual side. Yes, life is this contested adventure and God calls for you and me to quit talking about it and prepare to do it. Jesus said, "Stay dressed for action and keep your lamps burning, and be like men who are waiting for their master to come home from the wedding feast, so that they may open the door to him at once when he comes and knocks" (Luke 12:35-36).

The Great Go Mission

My friend Gene Broome (gone to be with Jesus) taught me that if you are on time, then you are late! He illustrated to me how to be prompt with this story:

Gene was Lieutenant in the White House in the late 1950's, during the Eisenhower administration. His commanding officer demanded that Lt. Broome always be ready for action. Part of his duty was to stand at attention at certain doors. When he was informed that the President would be coming through that door at 1pm, Gene told me his hand was on the knob at 12:55 and he was ready and waiting because at precisely 1pm, Ike would come walking through the door. He never missed an assignment.

The church is not nearly as prepared for the Lord to return, and many of us are ill-prepared for Him to work in our lives. We've missed assignments. Like a toy train that keeps jumping the tracks, the church repeatedly jumps from one religious focus to another. In John Calvin's famous work, *Institutes of the Christian Religion*, he discussed the credibility of Scripture and pointed to the simplicity of our mission. He pointed out that Moses didn't introduce the people to a new God, but rather reminded them of the doctrine concerning the eternal God that they already knew. And Calvin asks this question: "For what else does he do than lead them back to the covenant which had been made with Abraham?" Ours is not a new assignment. The focus needs to be placed back onto missional thinking in a worldly climate of the total depravity of mankind, reminding pastors to prepare and equip the body for action.

EPILOGUE

A few years ago, I was sitting in a restaurant in downtown Columbia, South Carolina, with a long-time mission mentor and friend. As we have done many times before, we engaged in secretive conversation of mission work in the Far East. Our talk turned to one of our mission heroes, Hudson Taylor. My friend shared how Taylor did just about everything wrong in doing missional work as we would look at it today. Yet, Hudson Taylor is considered a hero of the faith today when looking back on what he was able to accomplish with so few resources. Even though it was almost two hundred years ago, some things are similar in missions today despite their being quite different according to today's standards. My friend related something to me about Hudson Taylor that he experienced during a recent surreptitious visit to the Far East:

He was in a rural area of China, preaching at a church deep in the woods, when the locals informed him of a makeshift museum they had established in honor of Hudson Taylor. Being pleasantly surprised, he immediately asked where it was located, assuming it was some distance away, and they replied, "Oh, it's only a few meters from here." My friend said he was puzzled. He had not seen any building resembling a museum on his way into the village. He indicated he would be honored if they took him there right away. The Chinese Church officials were happy to escort him to their shrine. The leaders led him down a little path, through the trees and jungle-like dirt trail that led to a shabby tent and, inside, the memorial consisted of a few black and white photos from the 1880's of Hudson Taylor's family, crinkled and torn, and a broken-off piece of concrete from his grave marker. Nothing else.

Reflect on the major players in the so-called *Missions Movement* over the last two or three hundred years, and there is no doubt that Hudson Taylor was one of the top five most influential. He is what George Washington was to the presidency, what Beethoven was to music, what the Beatles were to rock 'n roll, and what Michael Jordan was to basketball! Musing over what the nationwide memorial consisted of— a few pictures and a chunk of a tombstone— my friend said these words to me: "G.D., if they think that little of him, what do you think they will do to us?" His point was, if that's the extent of the shrine or monument shown to a man that changed the way the world goes and does mission work, then what could they ever say about us? In other words, our work may just be forgettable in a few years, but we have to be cognizant of the eternal impact for the glory of God, so don't do it for selfish glory.

That statement was a tremendous relief for me and a wonderful, life-transforming, freeing moment. Hudson Taylor was simply being obedient to God's mission. He was not thinking about making a living, writing a book, or creating a movement to get famous. Taylor didn't have time to think how this was going to shape his career or make him look in the press. No, he was too busy taking care of the business God appointed him to accomplish. He acted on God's call upon his life. He looked for opportunity to start churches, to preach Jesus, and make fully devoted followers of Christ among the Chinese.

Taylor got something right despite the spiritual traveler's remorse he may have experienced in his long-term missionary life: He went, period. He was already committed to going spiritually before he ever left the continent of Europe for Asia. In his mind and heart, he had already gone. I believe it is a pre-requisite for you and me if we are thinking about mission work of any kind. As we continue to move forward, knowing our call as laity, ministers of the Gospel, missionaries (LTM), and part-time missionaries globally (STM), please realize it is not about discovering the correct title, getting famous, or passing on a methodology, as much as it is to inhabit fully the time and place He has put you and me in, and to continue to work glocally.

JESUS TEACHES MISSION

In Matthew 14, Jesus feeds the five thousand on the seashore. He had been ministering to them all day long. Surely, He was worn out, but He was the Lord, He could do anything. The day had to have been a remarkable and joyous one. It had all the makings of the old "dinner on the grounds" church and revival meetings. Jesus was ministering to them and He healed those that were sick. Who wouldn't want to hang out there all day? As it begins to get near nightfall, the disciples rush to Jesus to ask Him to tell the crowd to disperse and go home to get something to eat. Jesus responded, saying "They need not go away; you give them something to eat" (Matt. 14:16b).

Once again, our Lord is teaching and leading us to minister during mission. Instead of avoiding responsibility and work, Jesus says, "you" give to "them." The something to eat was minimal and was not the point of the quick nourishment assignment. It's you and me that God has called to go to them. And the *them* are always there. As we are praying for God to send somebody to do mission work, and as we applaud from a distance those who belong to our churches that go, the Holy Spirit is still calling *you*.

What is our problem? We are preoccupied. It's modern-day child rearing: Just put something in front of the kids to occupy their time. Data results for the last twenty-five years show us that technology is raising our kids, and that is not a good thing. And just like we can surmise our Lord's will for our lives in one word, we can also assume in one word where many in the Christian world live regarding evangelism and missions. We have become a nation preoccupied, with wandering minds. The usual diagnosis is Attention Deficit Disorder (ADD) and the prescription is always drug related.

Here's a good analogy for our preoccupation: the mobile phone/device. Instead of our heads bowed to our great Jehovah God, they are bowed in search of the next text or Tweet. Instead of searching for God's answers to our questions about life, we are searching for the next deal on Amazon. What if we carried the Word of God with us everywhere we went? What if we turned back to get our Bible when we forgot it? What if we checked it constantly for messages like we check our phones? What if it were our go-to in case of emergencies? What if we spent an hour or more a day searching it? To be preoccupied with the things of this world is to ignore the Lord. Unfortunately, it's easy to become preoccupied with what's going on around us.

Post-Script

As I am rereading and finishing up this manuscript, the Coronavirus has broken out in China and now spread globally. It's terrible. Thousands have died. My next trip to Asia has been delayed. It's now called a pandemic of epic proportions. And we've become engrossed with the numbers and the news reports coming at us on a daily basis. But while we're preoccupied with the statistics, what other harm is being done?

The Chinese government commissioned a new hospital to be built in Wuhan to combat COVID, and they completed it in ten days, but at the same time they shuttered all the churches. Do you see what is happening? In order to help cure the physical disease, China has accelerated spiritual death. More and more will miss the transforming message of Jesus Christ now that the government moves more to tear down the "red crosses" on the outside of churches. This signifies the Communist Party's desire to wipe out Christianity. As I write about risking on mission with God, you can see that I am trying to figure out my next move.

A day or two ago, I was on the phone with a good friend who often travels to China for the Gospel. Talking about the contagious disease, I was erring on the side of caution. My friend was planning to leave in 48 hours for China. I warned, "But what about the virus?" And he said, "Greg, the spiritual virus is much worse than the Coronavirus." My friend knows deep down the cost of the Gospel, and he definitely knows how to take risks. This attitude turns the world upside-down or right side up, whatever analogy you choose to use.

THE SPIRITUAL VIRUS IS MUCH WORSE THAN THE CORONAVIRUS

Chapter Eight
MISSION PLANNING

"Eppur si muove!" (Yet it does move!) — Galileo Galilei

"And a vision appeared to Paul in the night; a man of Macedonia was standing there, urging him and saying, 'Come over to Macedonia and help us.'"
-Acts 16:9

CONTRARY TO THE MODERN SPHERICAL shape of the Earth, and the Galilean supported heliocentric concept, there comes the laughable wisdom of one the National Basketball Association's greats, Shaquille "Shaq" O'Neal. Numerous online sources reported that the NBA legend legitimately believes the Earth is flat. It sounds whacky, but Shaq has repeatedly made the same comments, and shockingly it seems to be a growing sentiment in the NBA! Please pray that Shaq is joking around. However...

Shaq joined three other NBA players in stating that the world is physically flat. The four-time world championship, seven-foot center from the colossal champion Los Angeles Lakers, and collegiate star at LSU, said, "I drive from Florida to California all the time, and it's flat to me. I do not go up and down at a 360-degree angle, and all that stuff about gravity. Have you looked outside Atlanta lately and seen all these buildings? You mean to tell me that China is under us? China is under us? It's not. The world is flat." People, it is ridiculous to believe the world is flat in the twenty-first century.

Yet the world *is* flat. What? That is an apt description from author Thomas Friedman in his secular book by the same title. He uses the book to neo-define the condition of the succumbing transformation of the world. He also advocates a pause to take inventory to realize the world's flattening and how the tech age has spawned the turning of everyone's content into a digitized system and structure. Friedman's conclusion is that we have ended up with what he calls a "genesis moment" that produces a "crude foundation of a whole new global platform." Now, we can collaborate in real-time, whereas before there was a gap in communication time.

I've mentioned the term *glocal* and will comment further on it in the next few chapters while attempting to define it even more. *Glocal* is a term used to describe the modern phenomenon of comprehensive connectedness between technology, travel, vocation, business, communication, and everything else pertaining to the world flattening out, or merging. The knowledge centers of the planet are connecting into a single global network. Cooperation, innovation, and creativity will converge into something amazing if politics and terrorism do not get in the way. Agencies, communities, individuals, and churches could be on the cusp of ushering in a glocal strategy, whether or not it is acknowledged as such. What does this mean?

Do you remember the leadership line used in strategy in the 1990's when the righteous rambunctious pastors were trying to lead their crusty members to change – *Our methods must change, but the Gospel message can never change?* Improved technology, travel, and communication have marshalled in the new age. You and I have to decide whether we are on board or not. The very heart of the Gospel, and everything Jesus teaches, is about our own transformation. If the world continues to revolve and go through changes, then why wouldn't we change the way we accomplish the mission? After years of contemplating it, maybe it's now time for you to go.

Go...Where?

Has God called you to go? Yes, He has, and please understand it's not just anywhere. If you are a Christ-follower, your name has come up specifically before the Father to go and make disciples. Specifically, He has shaped you into His man/woman in order to tell your story of how you were rescued in Christ. It's not just a story; it's *your* story of righteous rescue, and you need to share it.

The Great Go Mission

Zealous, missionary-minded people quickly point to the Great Commission when preaching to others about Jesus' command for us to go. They also zero in on Acts 1:8, "But you will receive power when the Holy Spirit has come upon you, and you will be my witnesses in Jerusalem and in all Judea and Samaria, and to the end of the earth" as the plan for beginning at home and then expanding to outer regions, then to the edges of the planet. There are two difficulties, questions to be answered, in the book of Acts that we need to understand with accuracy in order to be God's effective servants.

WHAT DOES IT MEAN TO "PREACH JESUS" IN THE BOOK OF ACTS?

The answer seems straightforward because some translations state, "preached Jesus." However, the word *preach* seems to evoke a specific definition in today's vernacular. There is a pertinent point of translation in Acts regarding the speaking of the Word as it relates to missions. Some scholars even say that many of the translations of the New Testament are inaccurate in stating, "preached Jesus," where the better interpretation would be "shared the good news." Yeah, it seems like many of the interpreters of the Book of Acts in the New Testament used the "preached Jesus" term in colloquial speech, and it may cause readers to think the work of a missionary is a specialized call among Christians which excludes others from doing mission work, even STP. We may hesitate by saying we don't have "preacher skills." Maybe your excuse is to say you cannot preach Jesus, but all Christ-followers are called to share their story of how yesterday you were lost and now, today, you are found. Beware of the reversal of the Great Commission! Preaching Jesus is recapturing a commitment to a hard-hitting, yet loving, missional campaign. The message of the Christian faith will be most effective when the laity grab hold by simply talking about Jesus in the marketplace.

WILL ANY MISSIONARY PLAN OR PATTERN WORK?

Understanding the Great Commission from Acts 1:8 is to understand that this verse is not necessarily a systematic diagram of how to do mission work, i.e., the verse isn't a verbal graph of concentric circles of order in which to pattern the Great Commission. For the church to think of it in terms of starting evangelism and discipleship at home, then progressing out of town and, eventually, into the far reaches of the earth, is an inaccurate interpretation. If this were the case then a majority of churches would never move on to global mission work, claiming their work at home wasn't finished.

> # GOD'S DISPOSITION IS TO USE REAL PEOPLE IN REAL TIME TO ACCOMPLISH HIS PURPOSE FOR HIS KINGDOM.

Scripture neither outlines nor calls for one specific design in which to do missions or missionary work. Nevertheless, there can be myriad of ways of doing missions correctly and incorrectly. Historically mission agencies led by godly men and women, some connected to the church and some not, have done spectacular work in bringing the lost to Christ, making disciples, and planting churches. Despite success on the LTM field, however, problems have arisen in the recent past concerning control, decisions, and money.

Perhaps the modern-day church is cutting out the middleman. We are seeing a shift away from the churches being just a money supply chain. No longer are local congregations just writing out the checks and submitting to the will of the associations and mission ministries. God's missional plan has always been for the church, and you are the church. It is not reserved for a select group that has been singled out to specialize in a Christian enterprise. God's mission is theologically outlined, abundantly conveyed, and to a certain degree detailed in the New Testament as well as introduced in the Old Testament. The local church— you and me— is the key to world missions. The church houses the personnel, resources, support, and prayer.

God's disposition is to use real people in real time to accomplish His purpose for His kingdom. It is unrealistic and poor theological exegesis to perceive God's mission and the whole of mission work as an earmarked, reserved, and elite spiritual exercise for the professional long-term missionary. Instead, missions is a viable work commissioned by God and expected from every redeemed person of Christ in every congregation of Christ-followers, the church.

MORE GLOCAL TALK

Long-term missions and short-term mission projects can and should co-exist in a glocal world. Together, the climax is the operating character of a missional God. It is a nature of deploying true, trusting followers to carry out His plan for redemption. To miss His nature and person is to partially misunderstand salvation history. A world-wide missional approach fails to become realized when the church refuses to grasp the theological implications not only of the Great Commission, but of the entire missional counsel and authority of God's Word. There is a lot of talk in the modern, contemporary church about being 'missional,' but the church is missing the point. Being truly missional requires building one's life and ministry on Christ while realizing that He is the heart, and the Holy Spirit is the bloodstream, of God's plan.

THE BEST WAY

Study the Acts of the Apostles because they learned how to do it from the Master. If we paid close attention to Luke's work, Acts, then missions would be the most white-knuckled, adrenaline-charged, spine-tingling, invigorating, breathtaking adventure ever described with ink to paper we have ever read. R.C. Sproul said we can better title it, *The History of Acts of the Holy Spirit*. Can anyone be more exciting than Holy Spirit?

The evocative narratives of the missionary journeys of Paul are vivid, while simultaneously planting a missional desire for the true seeker of God. Adventure after adventure displays the boldness of the servants of God as they look to further the Kingdom. From courageous stands for the Gospel resulting in beatings and prison, to the suspenseful weeks at sea ending in shipwreck, God's men and women could not keep silent. The book called Acts is not only part two of Luke's Gospel book, but it also gives you the reality of the power of God in the gutsy, fearless, staunch, steadfast followers of Jesus. We need to be like them.

True story, believe it or not (I was there): Several teams gathered in central Asia, the Far East, armed for the task of giving out Bibles to the poverty stricken. We bought the Bibles legally and had them shipped to a rendezvous location where we met to give out assignments. Right logistics and cost effectiveness mean everything in distributing Bibles to the poor and the poor in Spirit. The Bibles cost us thousands of dollars, so we knew exactly how many we had. We received our appointments, split up, and traveled hundreds of miles to our destinations only to gather back for a missional debriefing. The debriefing is designed to share the stories of God. I cannot emphasize the importance of this enough. To tell and share what happens on any short-term project is tantamount to success. You have to talk about and celebrate what God has done. It's biblical...see the Master's story of the 72 in Luke 10 and how they returned in joy.

We gathered around a huge table with a lazy Susan in the middle filled with Asian cuisine, and we started telling our stories. My friend stood up and he was visibly trembling, could hardly get the words out. Tears streamed down his face as he said, "We got to a village (he paused), and word had gotten out that we were coming. Crowds and crowds of people were pushing into the medium-sized building built to occupy only 500. We looked at the manifest and discovered we were allotted 1,000 Bibles for this stop in this rural town." Having heard scores of stories like this, I yawned because it was late, as I anticipated the agony and heartbreak from my friend about not having enough Bibles. But that was far from the end of the story. I sat up, my mouth soon agape as he related the rest of the story.

"We asked our host, the pastor, if he knew that all of these people were coming? He replied that he did not. We asked him to guess the size of the crowd. He estimated two or three thousand because people were spilling out in the streets by the hundreds. We knew we didn't have enough, but the people were hungry for the Word of God in this town. We asked the pastor to join us and for the people to be quiet, and we gathered around the boxes containing the Bibles at the front of the church near the pulpit...and we prayed. We admitted that we knew we only had a thousand Bibles and that there were at least twice that many people, if not three times. Yet, we laid hands on the boxes and we begged God to supply the demand to move mightily among the people of this village."

By now, everyone from the ten teams that had fanned out all over that nation were sitting at attention, on the edge of their seats, wanting to hear what happened next. Yes, it was exactly like Jesus feeding the 5,000.

There was not enough bread and fish, but after the prayer, Luke says the disciples kept handing out the food. My friend said, "When we finished giving out the Bibles, everyone, every single person in the village walked away with a Bible." Impossible.

WHY SHOULD YOU DO A SHORT-TERM PROJECT OR BE INVOLVED IN STM?

Obedience— God is a holy God and He demands obedience. This is not sprung on us during the Acts of the Apostles, nor is it a phenomenon that has popped up due to the glocal concept or expedited travel. God, in His wisdom in shaping modern mission work for you and me, shows us through Abraham, way back in Genesis, that our God is a God on the move. Often He calls you and me to move with Him. The writer of Hebrews says of Abraham, "By faith Abraham obeyed when he was called to go out to a place that he was to receive as an inheritance. And he went out, not knowing where he was going" (Heb. 11:8).

I love the stories I hear of modern-day short-term missionaries and their trips. Regularly I ask them why they are going, or why they went, and the answer is often, "I don't know. I just felt God calling me to go!" When someone returns from one of those trips and has shared the message of Christ, how can you argue with it? As much as I urge a plan of action for STM, if you are boldly and clearly sharing the Gospel, then everything else becomes secondary and/or insignificant.

Privilege— Someone asks, "If God is all-powerful and He knows everything, then why should I go and share the Gospel?" You mean to tell me that your response to our Almighty, Creator, Life-sustaining, Sovereign, omniscient and omnipotent God, who simply spoke this world into being, and in His creativity designed everything we see and comprehend and things we don't... you mean to tell me when He says to us to join Him on His mission to redeem mankind, in which we did not have to pay for our sins, but He sent His only Son to do the work on the Cross... you mean to tell me that when He will be pleased with our obedience, and give us credit, shining down on us His blessings... you mean to tell me that you hesitate or maybe want to take some time to think about it? Are you kidding?

It is a grand privilege to serve the Lord God with all of your heart, soul, mind, and body. Life is about relationships and chiefly about the one relationship with God through the Son, Jesus. On mission with God we are able to experience more and more relationships. In a world that hungers for true friendship, and one that battles against loneliness, God leads us to meaningful, significant connections when we realize the privilege He gives us to share the good news of Jesus Christ. If you want to know what a great definition of God's blessings are, then look no farther than the people He puts in your life.

De-programming— My mind is cluttered with American Dream trash. From Beyoncé to Lady Gaga, from Jimmy Kimmel to Jimmy Fallon, and from Facebook to Instagram to Twitter, I have to guard my heart. Every commercial on television, every pop-up window on my social media, and every billboard is a direct assault on the heart. The Puritan preacher of four hundred years ago, John Flavel, wrote a little book called *Keeping the Heart*. He poignantly said, "[t]he keeping and right management of the heart is every condition, is one great business of a Christian's life." Flavel says we have a regular exercise of taking care of the heart that preserves the "soul from sin and maintains the sweet free communion with God".

Comparison to others is the name of the game in our culture. We spend too much time comparing our jobs, income, hobbies, etc. to that of our peers. Then we feel dejected and defeated to find out they are farther along than we are. It happens in the Christian life, too. Like the farmer dangling the carrot in front of the horse to get him to follow, we follow the enemy's attack telling us we need more spirituality or more theological devices and apps to get us on the right track with God. STMs help me to deprogram my mind from what this world says I need for success. I don't go for this purpose, but I certainly return knowing God has refocused my attention to the things that are important as a Christ-follower. All I need is Him.

They need you (Macedonian Call) — In Acts 16, Paul picks up Timothy as a fellow traveler in his merry band of evangelists, disciple-makers, and church planters. Paul intended to go to Asia (known as Asia Minor) but, Scripture tells us, the Holy Spirit forbade it. After they arrived in Mysia, Paul had a vision of a man standing and waving for Paul to come over. "Come over to Macedonia and help us." He was yelling for help, but

The Great Go Mission

not just any old help. This story is forever known to the mission world as the Macedonian Call. In mission circles it means we should go because the people need us! What do they need from us? They need help, and real help is the Gospel.

After twenty STMs to international sites, and at least thirty STMs in and around the nation, I have never met anyone who said, "I wish you had not come." No, they are starving for you to come. Long-term missionaries need a break, inspiration, encouragement, and prayer. Usually, those LTM are worn-out from loneliness. The people love to see and know that there are Christ-followers out there who want to share with them. When we approach mission work by seriously and lovingly sharing the good news of Jesus Christ, someone will get saved... at some point. Believe me, the call to go and help people is real. Just make sure the presentation of "Jesus saves" is paramount on your agenda in short-term projects and short-term missions.

Real Joy— Luke 10 is Jesus' account of sending out the 72. Jesus gave them instructions on exactly what to do and how to do it: preach the Kingdom of God. He gave them a packing list: nothing. We conclude that this was, evidently, a STP/STM. They were not to be gone long with no change of clothing. The central part of the trip was the Gospel. After the successful trip they returned for a debriefing, a time to share with Jesus what had happened. And if you slow down a little in reading the account you will notice a fantastic characteristic of serving Jesus by going... "The seventy-two returned with joy...."

Can you believe it? Many never go to serve the Lord because they fear rejection or feelings of inadequacy, but when Jesus equips us and we go in His power, we return with joy. In my interviews with short-term missionaries I have found that an awe-inspiring majority of people want to return to the mission field after they have gone, because the joy they received was literally indescribable. It is fun to serve the Lord, but you will never know that joy until you go.

World View (change of perspective) — True, our view of what this world is about is jaded and skewed. It's not some big conspiracy. It's just how capitalism has played out in a multi-ethnic, free-market system. We tend to believe the rest of the world thinks like we do and has the same values. We couldn't be farther from the truth. Being with Christians in the

Far East, sneaking around the local government just so they can worship and read the Bible, does something to you. Knowing you are in a place on an island in the Pacific where the overwhelming power of the enemy is making himself manifest in people is daunting. Taking part with a people group along the mountain border of Myanmar as they hold hands and dance in worship will make you laugh and smile with delight over their community joy.

If you cannot go to these places and witness it firsthand then read the mission magazines that tell the stories. Befriend someone on Instagram and look at their pictures. Pray, asking God to give you a change in perspective of how people in other countries worship and serve King Jesus. A world view of the challenges faced when sharing the Gospel should no longer be heard second hand. You need to experience it. Because of glocalism, you don't have to travel very far to encounter it. You can usually do it within miles of your home. Do whatever you can to understand more about how the Gospel is carried around the world.

Recognition of need for various people groups— I mentioned previously that there are 6,000+ unreached people groups in this world. This means there are whole groups of people who have never heard the Gospel, nor do they have access to a Bible. If this is not the church's responsibility in obedience and privilege, then whose responsibility is it? Sitting back and hoping someone will do it for us will not make it happen. While there may be contention with LTM and STM about old-style missions versus the legitimacy of the new style, the way to do missions in the twenty-first century is clear. Glocalism, the ability to travel and share communication in a nanosecond, is upon us and our duty is to go.

The very least you can do is organize a once-a-month prayer group to pray for STM and LTM for thirty minutes after church on a Sunday morning. If you want to do more, then find a missionary that you can support financially. It doesn't cost that much. A one-hundred-dollar monthly commitment to an LTM cause can be huge for that missionary. Find a way to send Bibles to a Communist country or a Muslim-dominated area of the world. If you can't do that, then start a Bible study in your home with two friends and ask God to grow it. If you can't do that, then ask God to send someone to your house so that you can share the Gospel with them. If you can't do that, then ask someone to go to church with you. If you can't

The Great Go Mission

do any of this just drop, right where you are, and on your knees ask God to give His grace and strength to missionaries around the world. Please recognize that the people God has placed around you are people who need Jesus.

Your own spiritual growth — My aunt Lois owned a florist with a gift shop attached to it and she operated the two as a single business. The florist was called "For-get Me Not" and the gift shop was "Serendipity." My grandmother, Eunice (we called her Bunny), answered the phone for the business for years. The phone would ring and my grandmother, would answer, "For-get Me Not florist, Serendipity." And at least once a week someone would misunderstand and say, "Sarah, can you let me speak to Lois?" Serendipity is discovering that desired *something* by accident. Some would call it good luck. We call it God's divine providence.

To grow closer to God doing mission work is serendipitous. It's inevitable that you will grow spiritually, however, it's not the reason you go. If there are ten reasons why you should go on a short-term project, then your own spiritual growth should be number eleven. I am not discounting the importance, but the second you make it part of your goal, then that is when you lose sight of the purpose of the mission trip. Selfishness and pride always demand a larger stage and louder amplification than humility and obedience. Selfishness tends to lead us to think sacrifice, and that is the antithesis of obedience. If you board a plane for a short-term project and pack a little bottle of selfishness, you may as well leap out of the plane at 36,000 feet.

> **If there are ten reasons why you should go on a short-term project, then your own spiritual growth should be number eleven.**

I cannot warn you enough about this because the primary purpose of going on a mission endeavor is to give away the love of Jesus, not to fill your tanks. As a matter of fact, if you return from a STP and you are not spiritually, emotionally, and physically exhausted then you didn't give all you had. A modern-day sports analogy is "leaving it all on the court/field."

When you leave it all out there, then you have emptied yourself of all energy and competition. It would do us well to understand the enemy knows of our arrival on his court long before the airline issues our flight itinerary. He knows you are coming, and he is ready with his counterstrategy.

If you've included, anywhere on your agenda, your desire to get closer to God while you are away, then you have misunderstood the mission project.

WHAT IS THE FUTURE OF MISSION WORK?

Church, and the relationship to missions and missional agencies, is in transition for the good. A glocal strategy is one to be used only after a right understanding of God's mission is realized. In essence, it is reassembling the pieces of an outdated, fragmented approach to sharing the Gospel with a holistic boldness and by accurate hermeneutics. The world is flat-out rolling along, reclaiming God's territory, and it is there for the taking. The potential impact and revelation of the glocal phenomenon rests in exploration of the Truth of Christ. Theory and sociological development of mission work, in conjunction with the historical and some prevailing current models in the missional world, will give us contemporary meaning in *Missio Dei* (God's Mission). The catastrophe of the modern-day church is separating the way we do church from the way we do missions. Let me add to that by saying it gets even more tragic when we separate biblical theology from our missiology. In other words, folks, churches need to return to the Bible to get the instructions for mission projects and make mission work *the* work of the local church.

Today's church is shortsighted when it comes to understanding God's overall purpose for the church. If we don't see it through the lenses of the Kingdom, then I am afraid we miss it. We have formulated programs which have resulted in a fragmentation of God's mission. Ecclesiology has simply been divorced from missiology. Succinctly put, we have focused too much on the "go" part and left out the mission part. Therefore, as the church sends and teaches God's mission, it must include the community of missions to understand the mission. Going glocal for the church means that it is doing more than just sending.

For too long, especially in the West, the focus has been on individuals rather than on church. Let's finally come to an understanding that the church *is* the missionary, and it must be equipped as such if it is to transform lives. The church is in danger of losing opportunities to evangelize and start churches. Proof of doing it right in this glocal world is found when the church serves not to count numbers, but to show it realizes a radical rescue by Christ.

In comparison, the church at Antioch in Acts 11 somewhat supports this same concept. Since the word *missionary* is not found in Scripture, questions arise over who trained the first missionaries and how they knew what they were doing. Acts 11:19, 20 says "λαλοῦντες τὸν λόγον", or *speaking the word*. Conceivably, the first missionary church in history, perhaps majoring in church planting, did not start because of missionaries, or missional work. Rather it began as the result of believers going and speaking the word, the Gospel, and living out the Great Commission.

Maybe the future of mission work is to put it back in the local church and to sideline the professionals. This is not meant to broad-brush genuine evangelical mission organizations, but if the church is ever again going to be a mission-going and -sending organism, don't you believe it should not only come to a right theological conclusion, but also actually put it into play? I would be counted as one to sacrifice the large, corporate-like mission groups in an effort to put the mission back on the local level of the local church.

The church is bleeding out spiritually today because of professionalism. State structures all the way down to the associational level pose as authorities on church matters, and advertise their expertise, wanting to aid the local church. It sounds good in theory, but it is not working in a modern world. We are told that the world keeps revolving and we have to change our methods. Maybe. But just maybe the best thing to happen in the American church these days to wake us up to the real mission, God's mission, is the closing of some of the doors. His mission has always been the evangelism and discipleship of His people. Whenever we separate the two by departmentalizing them, there will be trouble. The trouble is a shrinking church. Pastors, preachers, church leaders, and people in the seats on Sunday morning need to wake up and see that the world is indeed flat! You can get to where God wants you to go... if you just go!

Conclusion

In the one hundred years after Luther's Reformation one would think giant reform would come in many areas, and we suppose it did, but not in proving the world was round, or at least a sphere. It was a strange time when the church and the government in Europe were somehow linked together in terms of justice and science. The famed Italian mathematician, physicist and philosopher Galileo Galilei (1564–1642), after standing up against a flat world view, was forced to recant in order to save his life. The church was frightened of such a claim and demanded Galileo take back his words. He did. But under his breath, in a silent attempt at getting back at the established church he said, "Albeit, it does move!" It doesn't matter what the church believed, thought, or taught, this planet is spherically shaped, and it does turn on the axis God set it on. The church can interpret church work, mission work, and even Gospel work however they want, but hear this flat out: God doesn't depend on our approval of Him to do His work. He keeps moving and going and sending even if you won't join Him.

Chapter Nine
STP

> "The age of technology and technique is the age of endless methods, formulas, recipes, seminars, how-to manuals, twelve step programs and the constant lure of efficiency."
> —Os Guinness, Fools Talk

> "Now Barnabas wanted to take with them John called Mark. But Paul thought best not to take with them one who had withdrawn from them in Pamphylia and had not gone with them to the work."
> —Acts 15:37,38

MISSIONARIES TO WEST AFRICA A hundred years ago just packed their belongings in a coffin, anticipating and expecting to return home in it. Back then, missionaries didn't have furloughs every few years, built in vacations, or retirement packages. They were in it for the long haul or the short ride, whichever came first. They sold all of their worldly possessions and kissed their families goodbye like it was the last time they would see each other. Many times, it *was* their last parting, though because of their security in Christ it was not to be their last meeting. Without the option of a short-term mission experience, or for going from local to global in a few hours, those long-term servants committed their lives in service to King Jesus.

William Carey, the father of modern missions, came home for the first time after thirty years on the mission field. Jim Elliot never really got to say goodbye to his wife because of the ambush. Wiley Glass buried two children and a wife a hundred years ago in China while on the mission field. One of my favorites, Lottie Moon, was a servant to China. She stood only 4'3," but she packed a walloping punch. During the Boxer Rebellion days in 1900, Miss Lottie quit eating so the starving Chinese children could have food. Emaciated, her little body weighed less than sixty-five pounds when they finally forced her to go home. She didn't make it back to Virginia but instead died on the boat, in a Japanese harbor, on Christmas Eve. Gone are the days when a missionary speaker would make an appeal from a church pulpit and their hearers would jump up and volunteer for 'the field.' These are new days — a new era that involves a glocal look and an accurate short-term model.

Every week I am evaluating mission work in my life, my church, my friend's lives, my town, my city, my state, your country, and our world. It is essential to inspect the validity of going on a short-term project in order to get the mission right. Just adding *mission* to a project doesn't make it God's mission work. Just because a church goes in the name of God doesn't make it a true mission work. I am very afraid the modern-day church continues to contribute to the attrition of biblical truth by sanctioning the travel plans to do good things. For every church or evangelical group making plans to carry out the Great Commission by going across town or across the world, let's adhere to a simple checklist to try and get it right.

CHECKLIST FOR TRUE & AUTHENTIC MISSION WORK:

- ☐ What and who have we prayed about specifically as we go?
- ☐ Write down specific goals & scrutinize the goals – are they aligned with the GGC (Great Go Mission)?
- ☐ Get proper training!
- ☐ Make assignments to carry out the main goal of sharing Jesus.
- ☐ Trust the Holy Spirit to lead you.
- ☐ Inspect the work while on the field and make adjustments if needed.
- ☐ Remember: always debrief ASAP by examining your work.

NEW MISSIONARIES

In my hometown I interviewed two teenagers, brother and sister, that had recently gone on youth mission trips. Their parents have raised them with a bold world view for Christ. The whole family is involved in feeding the homeless and ministering in an urban setting.

Brother and sister each took part in separate mission activities two summers ago that I would classify as "Missions 101." While the church prays for a renewed zeal for the Gospel to be taken around the world, acknowledging that the short-term project should be used and taken advantage of, we must remember that purpose and organization still need to be taught. Instilling the truth of the Gospel in young people is more important than teaching them to go. Theology trumps motivational speeches. God will call them to go and He will send them if only we teach truth.

Too many church growth experts are trying to tell us how to "close the back door" when we should concentrate on the precision of the Gospel in opening the front door. If our style is just to get people in and then worry later about how we are going to grow them up as mature disciples, we will undoubtedly fail. Understand, the Holy Spirit will take care of the going. The urge to get on a plane and travel in the name of Jesus, without realizing the cause, never works. If you are just wanting to do something, to go somewhere to satisfy some personal pilgrimage aspiration or to score points with God, then it will likely undermine the heart of the Great Commission in the long run, thus leading to a confused understanding of any mission call upon your life.

Cindy & Scott

Cindy is eighteen, planning for college and working full-time at a local fast-food joint. Outgoing and energetic, she joined some friends from a church on the other side of town for a "mission trip." For the low cost of $1,000 per person, the team traveled to the Dominican Republic for a week during the summer. Approximately twenty-five teenagers, accompanied by seven adults, went on a mission project to help do construction on a church building while staying with members of the church. Sounds familiar doesn't it? While the mission was successful in the leaders' eyes, Cindy said they did not have training prior to going, and the mention of the saving love of Jesus in an evangelical type of presentation was sparse. If the church is going to recapture mission work of any kind, we need to be careful about preparation.

My wife is an excellent cook and excels in baking. She knows every television program on cooking and, believe me, I know half of them because I watch them with her. She has preached to me over and over that the key to being a good cook or chef is the preparation. The culinary skills of cutting, shredding, precise measurements of spices, and choosing only the freshest and best ingredients, are essential to creating the perfect dish. Here's the twist to this illustration: I am a horrible cook. The reason is that I don't have the patience to prepare. I'm not a cook, I'm an eater. My philosophy is to let someone else to do the cooking and I will do the eating. Sadly, that same mentality goes for the church who doesn't see the necessity in preparation. If the church is just concerned about consuming the notoriety of missions, instead of planning for the harvest that Jesus talks about, then how is the church different from any secular charity group?

Cindy said that she doesn't recall the Gospel being shared or preached while in the D.R. Now that she has returned from the trip and after our conversation, she sees the great importance of being trained and prepared in advance to present the Gospel of Jesus Christ. Here's a good lesson from introductory-type mission activities: let's not dampen the enthusiasm of young people, but instead encourage them to listen to God about going and being involved. As churches, let's really get back to the Great Commission and see that there is a greater purpose to be achieved.

Let's not dampen the enthusiasm of young people, but instead encourage them to listen to God about going and being involved.

Painting walls, hanging sheetrock, pouring foundations for church buildings, and even digging wells for clean water are all very important, honorable, and needed. Let me state it again so that I am not misunderstood here: repair work to a dilapidated house, patching a roof with a hole in it for a widow, and offering a sandwich to the hungry are all altruistic and honorable, but there is a reason why you do those things. Unless the rationale of preaching Jesus is elevated to the number-one job of short-term projects and long-term missionaries, then we are completely missing the reason. Let's keep feeding the homeless and shoeing the shoeless with a renewed effort of training the short-term volunteer as an agent of

The Great Go Mission

Christ first while giving them the Truth of Christ.

Scott, Cindy's brother, went to the urban area of Kansas City, Missouri. Going with an inner-city mission organization from his hometown, they essentially took their mission on the road. Scott was able to pray with people on the street while walking the streets of Kansas City and observing the plight of the lost.

They did incredibly kind things in the name of Jesus. Scott said they set up showers for the homeless to bathe, using firetrucks to channel the water. They brought in barbers to cut hair, did yard work at halfway houses, and found people to feed. All of their activities reflected Jesus' words in Matthew 25:35-36, "For I was hungry and you gave me food, I was thirsty and you gave me drink, I was a stranger and you welcomed me, I was naked and you clothed me, I was sick and you visited me, I was in prison and you came to me." The work done by Scott's team was absolutely gracious and kind, good deeds. But if you are quoting the story of the Sheep & Goats from Matthew 25 make sure you understand that Jesus is not talking about short-term projects or even long-term missionary assignments. He is referring to your daily lifestyle. He is talking about 24/7 Christian living. He is surely stating the fact about reflecting God in your relationships. As we learn in the book of Acts, helping and serving and going in missions is a whole different approach.

It would be easy to be highly suspect and critical, and maybe you think that from reading my stance on mission work in this book. But I'm not interested in touting my own pessimism in modern day mission work. That doesn't help me or you. I simply want churches to learn from inattentive actions, half-hearted efforts, and the absence of evangelical proclamations of Jesus in order to give their all for Christ in complete obedience to the Great Commission. God, and God alone, is to be glorified. We are to go, and should have already been taught that. Scott is a fifteen-year-old impressionable young man so let the church, and Christian mission groups, be responsible for impressing upon him a courageous and correct Christian and biblical philosophy of mission. A passionate Great Commission strategy for short-term projects remains the key to dynamic mission activity.

I contend that Cindy and Scott took part in introductory-level mission work during their short-term projects. It was Missions 101. They both came back excited and joyful about their experiences, desiring to go again. As a Christian community we capitalize on this eagerness and mission zeal. We pray to produce potential life-long missionaries and ambassadors for Christ. Jesus says, "Let the children come to me, and do not hinder them, for to such belongs the kingdom of God" (Luke 18:16). I see even more: if we will lead our children to Christ, discipling them by the Holy Word of God while pointing them to the dynamics of the Great Commission, then they will go all out for Christ. Anyone who hears and believes the Gospel, must live and share the Gospel.

Giving water to someone in the name of Jesus and praying for their relief is being obedient according the Scriptures. But Jesus didn't come as a benevolent crusader to heal social issues. The Gospel goes much deeper than that... it goes to the heart! So, let's teach our children that it's about more than just doing nice things for the poor disadvantaged and providing them with the fair essentials for life. Basic, entry-level mission work is a good place of embarkation for children and teenagers into a lifestyle of long-term mission projects, if we have the goal of leading them to salvation found only in Christ.

ONLY BY TAKING PART IN SERVING THE LORD JESUS WILL YOU FIND THE TRUE MEANING OF THE GOSPEL.

Beware: If we discredit altruistic efforts because they fall short of true evangelism, then it makes Christians look insensitive. But if we embrace them as the standard of Christian giving, then we undercut the Gospel. Learn to take the effort a step farther and completely obey the command of our Lord to make disciples. One helpful hint: Remember to hold the debriefing session with the team as quickly as possible after returning, to reveal what worked and what didn't.

Maybe the Holy Spirit is currently working in your life to get you involved in a mission activity in your church. If He is, then I say, "Go!" Buckle up, pray hard, and get ready for the experience of your life. Only by taking part in serving the Lord Jesus will you find the true meaning of the Gospel. You may experience some bumps and bruises but learn from them.

The Great Go Mission

Go and make Jesus the holy hallmark of your STP. The modern church has so packaged mission work that you can customize your weekly devotional delivery via feelings. But don't you think it's time for you to contribute to the cause of Christ in truth? You see, we had a built-in excuse a few decades ago. We could easily avoid our service and mission for God by saying we couldn't leave home. There were children to raise, the family came first, and our jobs wouldn't allow for us to take off for long periods of time in order to go. However, with the rise of the glocal knowhow, coupled with short-term project philosophy, your pretexts for participating have vanished.

You can now go. And there are others who God is calling to start mission projects, works, and ministries. Maybe that is you? I'm not saying it is emotionally or spiritually easy because of our technological advances, because there is still the issue of spiritual traveler's remorse among other factors. Rather, I'm saying you don't have an excuse anymore for not doing something in the name of Jesus as it pertains to missions. No one has a defense any longer to say they can't go to the prisons, the streets, the cul-de-sacs, or even to the other side of the world. In reality, there was no excuse even before the invention of the automobile, the jet plane, the Internet, and advanced communication. God has always been calling you to the work. He waits and waits while you try to justify not going. Maybe He has kicked the props from underneath you so that you will stand for Him? When will you answer?

How do I start mission work?

Prayer & Passion

The origin of mission work— planting a church, doing evangelism, discipling believers, and being part of a team— has not changed in two thousand years. Prayer is the ultimate key to our mission activities. In Acts 13, the church in Antioch was worshipping and fasting. Does this mean they were praying too? You better believe it! The passage starts out by telling us that Barnabas, Simeon, Lucius, and Herod the tetrarch's lifelong friend (strange coincidence don't you think?), Manaen, as well as Paul were there at the church gathering. We can refer to it as the genesis of modern mission work: "...the Holy Spirit said, 'Set apart for me Barnabas and Saul for the work to which I have called them.' Then after fasting and praying they laid their hands on them and sent them off" (Acts 13:2b).

Think with me for a moment, does mission work fail or do all mission activities succeed in some way? Sounds simple, but it's a deeper question than it looks. Failure to meet intended goals may lead to future success. Improper planning, refusing to put in the work to understand the need of the host-recipient, the financial burdens that mount up, and spiritual traveler's remorse are just a few of the possible obstructions that can cause a mission miscarriage. Why do these things happen when churches and organizations are trying to do good works? You should not even broach the talk of mission work without spending a considerable amount of time seeking God's face, looking to understand how the Holy Spirit would send you out on mission. Don't let my flippant, one-word answer - *prayer* — to the question of how to get started, lead you to minimize the colossal component needed to begin your mission work. A lot of people sidestep prayer thinking it's a given while I believe it's the most important, most ignored, part of our mission work. And don't turn "GO" into a motivational chant forsaking preparation.

If the Holy Spirit leads you to go to the Far East to minister in the name of Jesus, you need to pray first. Why? You need His infinite omnipotence. If He calls you to visit the local prisons in your area, please pray before you go. If God lays upon your heart to go downtown to feed the homeless, then you need to pray — the enemy usually lives downtown because the downtown scene welcomes him into their fold. Maybe you think God is leading you to do something nice for the down and out, but I promise you the enemy has a well thought out insidious scheme in mind for those hurting people. He doesn't want you there. He will do what he can to rid you from his hip scene. Paul tells us, "we don't wrestle against flesh and blood, but against the rulers, against the authorities, against the cosmic powers over this present darkness, against the spiritual forces of evil in the heavenly places" (Eph. 4:12). So, you are going to tell me that you are going to waltz into his dark den and steal his sheep? No chance... unless you are what the old preachers often referred to as "prayed up."

My good friend, Jan Mathias, was in the US Army until she flipped a dump truck and broke nearly every bone in her body, as well as causing all kinds of other internal problems she has had to live with for years. The doctors told her she would never walk again. She walks okay today. She has fought off six different cancers, and as I write this she is in the hospital for another MRI for yet another cancer. She experimented with the gay lifestyle and she will tell you straight up that God delivered her from it. She prayed about how she could serve more effectively. She has given financially to mission causes for years, but her prayer was one of how she could "do" something. Her fingers are gnarled from all the surgeries, but she took up knitting a few years ago. Now, a few times a year as winter nears, Jan loads up her scooter on the back of her car and heads downtown to Main Street where she ties a dozen or more knitted scarves to one of the decorative trees that line the streets of Columbia, South Carolina. Jan will tell you her mission is due to her prayer life and not just some idea she had for helping the homeless on cold nights.

WAIT, BUT DON'T WAIT

Timing is crucial in mission work, so you pray and wait. And when God calls, don't delay – Go. It was time for the second missionary journey of Paul as recorded in Acts 15:36: "And after some days Paul said to Barnabas, 'Let us return and visit the brothers in every city where we proclaimed the word of the Lord, and see how they are.'" Little did Paul know he was modeling short-term and long-term projects simultaneously. They had gone on their first missionary journey, they came home, they rested, they refueled by spending time with the other disciples, and the Holy Spirit led them to leave again and go. Wait on God to deliver the supplies you need, whatever they are, and then get ready to go.

What else do you do in the waiting period? I know so many who have missed this opportunity to train and gather more knowledge for short-term projects. It happened to me again while in China... I thought I knew more than my interpreter. We had gathered with what was a small congregation in China, about five thousand, and we celebrated God's Word with them. As they received Bibles, one asked me to sign her Bible in the front. As Americans we believe it is cool to reference our favorite verse on the inside cover and give a quick autograph. My interpreter said, "Pastor Greg, don't do that... say, 'No!'" I quipped back, "It's no problem Autumn!" But it quickly became a huge problem. Because when you sign for one, the rest want their Bible signed too! Wild hysteria broke out as I finished signing that first Bible. I know what the Beatles felt like in 1963 – the British Invasion – when they arrived in America. I was mobbed with nowhere to turn! I frantically just kept signing the Bibles. My once legible signature had now become just a scribble because of the cramping of my hand, and a rush to get them out of my personal space. After 45 minutes, Autumn made it through the crowd to rescue me. Dragging me through the chaotic mass, we escaped to the van.

The moral? During the waiting time absorb as much information as possible. Learn about the culture, study the history of mission work in the area, know what to do and what not do, and by all means *always* listen to your interpreter – they know better.

PLAN = PURPOSE

Do I really need to go over it again? Get a plan. Work the plan. Don't take shortcuts. Don't neglect prayer. Map out a strategy, and by all means seek out Godly advice from pastors, missionaries (LTM & STM), and fellow believers and followers of the Lord. Make sure that a crystallized vision and purpose results from all your prayer. Be able to state your purpose in a single statement. Make the Great Commission your focus!

Make a simple plan and go. It's a Go-mission.

Twenty years ago, I had an idea to do an egg hunt the Saturday before Easter for our community. It was a mission outreach concept to reach the children and families that didn't have a church to attend on Easter Sunday morning. We did it for five years. My wife, who is a marketing guru, set it up and managed it. We presented the Gospel with moving parts (our church carpenters constructed a tomb with a roll-away stone), our band performed songs before, during, and after the hunt, and we gave away prizes. It was mammoth. Each year we grew larger and larger. By the fourth year we had 50,000 plastic eggs stuffed with candy and Scripture verses! To give you some semblance of how big our egg hunt was, the annual White House Egg Roll in 2017 only had 18,000 eggs.

The Great Go Mission

Year five of the Great Irmo Egg Hunt was totally out of control! We had 80,000 eggs, scores of volunteers, and 3500 people showed up congesting the traffic for miles on the little two-lane road. My wife, Missie's, planning was not, as they say, rocket science. She had a simple game plan. The children picked up eggs, we gave out a few prizes, shared the Gospel, invited people to church, and went home. Even though we planned and worked all year long, the whole thing was over with in less than 90 minutes. When urged by other well-meaning friends to set up bouncy houses, invite food trucks, serve ice cream, hand out cotton candy, and bob for apples, among a thousand other ideas, Missie's answer was always no. Why? She simply said, "Do one thing and do it with excellence for God." Her point was that it was an egg hunt, children come to find eggs... period. The goal was not to have a big party, but to excite children, starting them on a road to really understanding Easter.

I find that many are missing the goal of the Great Commission because they want to present a fancy, promotion-slick deal to the community. Jesus calls us to go and make disciples, and the two-thousand-year-old call on our lives doesn't depend on you hiring a company to do your graphics. Make a simple plan and go. It's a Go-mission. Make sure it leads from the Great Commission, and the Holy Spirit will lead you to the people and the mission. The end goal for the Christ-follower must have the preeminence of the Gospel, stated and faithfully observed. To put any facades above sharing Jesus is to turn it into a charade of God. That's idolatry.

LOCK IN SUPPORT

Your friends are waiting for you to ask them to participate in God's work. People want to be a part of something bigger than themselves. They want to know that they have been a part of something that has made a difference. Why?

- → It reminds them of the true, great God they serve.
- → It gives them a story to tell as they relate the goodness and mercy of God to others.
- → It draws them to more ministry.
- → It spurs on their prayer life.
- → It improves their walk with the Lord.

→ They truly want to give, because they are givers at heart.
→ It brings them joy.

What is support? Support can be by prayer, money, use of a spiritual gift to help, encouragement, and admonition, among many other things. The problem? We become myopic when we fall short of receiving the best things for our mission work. Too many times we are quick to dismiss someone if they are not ponying up cash. Online pleas for support are mostly wrought with insincere petitions and unclear motives. Most of the requests I see for support leave me wondering. Understand that God pays for what He orders. If He has called you to go, then He will provide the way. I didn't say it would be easy. Raising the financial support to go may be the most difficult thing you have ever done. But don't miss the other support the Holy Spirit wants you to have.

Look forward, get ready to go, but still have an ear for God. In other words, pray for caution and admonition from fellow believers. If all you ever want to hear is good stuff, then where will you be when the reality sets in on your mission or STM? For the most part I have been healthy while going and doing mission work. A little stomach problem here and there, but nothing serious. Recently, my friend Joe cautioned me about some shots I should think about getting. Joe's wife, Chris, was infected with hepatitis C years ago and had to struggle and fight against it for almost a dozen years before being cured. I've never really been sick on a short-term mission trip before, so why worry? Because I learned something valuable a long time ago. Just because you've never had it doesn't mean you won't get it. We are not naturally immune to hepatitis. So, I'm going to get the shot. Listen to caution and weigh it out with the guidance of the Holy Spirit.

Some are called to give you the financial support you need. Let's admit it... raising money is very difficult these days. I am the worst at asking for money, yet I do it. Never has God called me to a short-term project that He did not provide for. Never. I've been to the other side of the world no less than twenty times, and God has been faithful every time. Here's a suggestion: Just as you would send notes of appreciation to those who support you monetarily, also take the time to thank those who offer you prayer support and words of wisdom.

The Great Go Mission

POWER & PRAYER

I like reading the old guys. I'm not talking about the dudes that wrote in the 60's and 70's, no, I mean the ones from the 1600's and 1700's. Those men wrote about chasing the heart of God while guarding your own heart. I've noticed that the deep, deep Christ-followers of three or four hundred years ago never talked about leadership principles or the next great plan to grow a church the way we do in this ever-emerging post-Christian culture. Guys like John Flavel, the English Puritan preacher who was pastor and confidant to Oliver Cromwell, wrote about the importance of making sure you know the Holy Spirit's job is to illuminate the Word of God, and that you can't separate the two. Flavel hinted at this power source when preaching the guarding of the heart. He said, "The greatest difficulty in conversion is to win the heart to God; and the greatest difficulty after conversion is to keep the heart with God."

Another "bad to the bone" guy who no one really remembers was Richard Sibbes, the Puritan who wrote begging Christ-followers to hold on to the security of God's covenant in times of political turmoil and religious upheaval. Your heart in Christ, guarded by the Holy Spirit, given to intercessory prayer with the Father, is going to be your power. All mission work done in the book of Acts is done in the power of the Holy Spirit. It wasn't that they were in the right place at the right time. They were in constant danger and always on Satan's home turf. Listen, if you are going to go, be aware that not only is Christ resisted and rejected these days, but also His followers are ridiculed and scorned. Jail was the norm for the Apostle Paul. If you plan to do short-term projects or mission work of any kind, please do not attempt to do it without the power of the Holy Spirit. You will die one way or another.

Emotionally, you will be eaten alive by the enemy if you go without "bathing" your work in prayer. Spiritual burnout will attack you and get the best of you if you neglect meeting with God over the journey that lies ahead of you. Physically, the enemy will attack, and prayer is the only way to be prepared. Flavel lays it out for us here: "Another season, wherein the heart must be kept with all diligence, is when suffering for [Christ] is laid upon us. Blessed is the man who in such a season is not offended in Christ."

I have to pray every day and ask others to pray for me beginning six months in advance of one of my other-side-of-the- world mission trips. Yes,

I'm begging you to go and to be on mission but at the same time I am begging you to pray for God's strength as you go.

FALLING INTO THE TRAP

Christmas is coming and my happy baker wife will surely add to her cookie-cutter collection. The shape of the cookie doesn't determine my desire to eat her cookies, though. Rather it's the delectable, sweet, sugary taste in my mouth. Yet, this is another example of the contemporary Christian life. Following a cookie-cutter system, technique, or formula continues to be the popular way to do the work of those called by God. Canned approaches to evangelism, discipleship and church planting are the rage of the age.

Our goal is not just to do something. If we settle for doing just anything, then we will fall for anything, and we will end up accomplishing nothing worthwhile. Failure to understand the goal of the Great Commission or the carrying out of the Gospel of Jesus Christ produces quitters. The path of least resistance is to believe that doing anything to help the poor is God's ultimate business. The easy route is to purchase a kit to teach people about God. But you are not called to teach people about God. You are called to teach them to *come to know* our Almighty God.

We cannot simply juxtapose short-term and long-term missions, weighing the positives and negatives. It's imperative we recognize the glocal perspective of travel and technology and take advantage of it, utilizing its strengths. Going across the street and going to the other side of the world have gotten easier for us. Forget trying to uncover another formula that will take us another one hundred years into the future. Let's learn that short-term missions coupled with glocal enterprise gives the church a dependable, steady, and almost endless supply of volunteers wherever we are. In other words, we are taking mission work back to the local church rather than leaving it up to the professionals at the big organizations. So let's equip the church-level volunteers by teaching them how to effectively do the work of missionaries.

In the scope of all missional work, short-term missions is relatively new. And according to many missiologists, STM is an option our Western generation needs to heavily consider alongside long-term missions. Millennials are less compelled to support the lifer missionary financially,

The Great Go Mission

because they do not understand supporting an operation that is not recognizably tangible. On top of that, too often we find that mission agencies just want our money and for us to get out of the way. We've grown up in a fluid, glocal culture that gives us instant access to pictures of people in need of the Gospel. This generation does not need to be world travelers to witness the atrocities of governments and the poverty of nations. We can see it easily on the smart phone screen in the palm of our hand.

Instead of teaching the heart of the Gospel, many are still trying to pull at people's heartstrings to get them involved. Continuing to prop up the old paradigm of supporting someone else, on a continent somewhere else, sending our money to who knows where, and doing something we don't understand, is fruitless in the modern age. People are not going for that plan anymore. The proof is in the shrinking pocketbooks of mission institutions and senders. Undoubtedly, this all leads us to the question: Why spend thousands of dollars moving a family to the other side of the world, have them spend years learning another language and hope they make a difference when, for less money, a STM can be quickly assembled, trained, and deployed to possibly achieve and accomplish more?

Don't forget there are thrilling, poignant, and proactive accounts of the gospel in the Book of Acts. But there was also contention among those early church planters and missionaries, if you will. A working out of a different way... a better way was in the works. Isn't that what happens these days? Paul announced the follow-up second journey and was ready to go when Barnabas said, "Yes, and let's take John Mark with us again." Paul's jerky, quick response of an emphatic "no" leads us to believe there was something afoot.

In the rock 'n roll age we would liken it to the split of the Beatles. The outcome of the breakup was that Barnabas took John Mark and Paul took Silas, and they went their separate ways leaving us with questions of what could have been had Paul and Barnabas remained a team. There have been tons of speculation on the reasons as to why Paul was so adamantly opposed to John Mark accompanying him again. I think it's simple... Paul didn't like quitters. John Mark quit the missionary journey. What was the reason? We don't know. Then again, Barnabas was always up for the challenge of making great leaders out of so-called losers.

THE TAKEAWAY

What's the takeaway? You can learn about people, their commitment, and your chemistry with them while traveling, yet the most important characteristic is their understanding of the truth. Paul knew it wasn't going to work for him. Barnabas was just itching for an opportunity. Accomplishing the goal was more important to Paul than just going on the missionary journey, and he somehow knew it would be impossible with the same exact team as before. Missions, ministry, and the work of the church is not a one-size-fits-all approach. We hope Barnabas and John Mark found success going the other way, but we are not told. We do find out that in the end God wasn't finished with Mark... yet as a team on mission, they are not heard from again.

As early as the double digits on the first century calendar the mission was beginning to take shape as churches were planted and the Great Commission remained mobile. The geographical strategy of the apostles never outweighed, congested, or got in the way of the continual movement of the message. The local nature of the stage where the Great Commission was introduced does not imply that the gospel never, in fifteen hundred years, went beyond the Holy Land region of Jerusalem and Samaria. It simply means travel was treacherous, life expectancy was short, and resources were sparse and insufficient. Learning a second language meant a lifetime commitment and would limit the rapid expanse of the gospel. Paul and many others were called to go beyond the traditional limits of travel, but most mission-minded Christians could not move with ease from nation to nation for Gospel purposes.

The world has changed. It is important these days for the church to weigh the benefits of short-term projects as an alternative missional plan to the traditional long term. Go ahead, look into it and you will find opportunity after opportunity to go and to make a difference. The reality is that servants from the local church can be involved in missional work and return home quickly. You don't have to go to die like those that have been martyrs and missionaries before us. However, unless you die to yourself to live for God, you cannot go *successfully* for the glory of God.

Chapter Ten
BUCKING THE SYSTEM

"We must wake ourselves up! Or somebody else will take our place, and bear our cross, and thereby rob us of our crown." - William Booth

"Do not be slothful in zeal, be fervent in spirit, serve the Lord. Rejoice in hope, be patient in tribulation, be constant in prayer." -Romans 12:11,12

BETH GREER GREW UP ON the mission field in Brazil. Her parents were long-term missionaries, making Beth a MK — a missionary's kid. Through God's grace, and the spiritual transfusion of bowing to God (repentance), Jesus' righteous blood is on her and in her. Naturally, because of her parents' calling, mission work is in her blood too. By day, this busy wife and mother works a 20+ hour a week job as a teacher, while in her "spare time" she is a short-term missionary (STM). Here's a paradox: Beth takes several international trips each year to share the Gospel and carry out the Great Commission. She ministers evangelically with two other women who are sold out to God. They regularly travel to both domestic and foreign places to minister in churches through singing and teaching. Beth is active in her home church's choir and also teaches a Bible Study. How can you get more full-time in ministry than that? However, I say Beth is a STM. It's axiomatic to say that Beth and her kind are Missional Superheroes!

One summer, not too long ago, Beth went with e3 Partners to Kome, a little island off the coast of Tanzania. Their purpose in visiting that occultist sliver of African earth was to share the Gospel message, to disciple new believers, and to plant churches. Fifteen women and one man traveled there to evangelize as many as possible. Slow down and try to picture it: all those God-fearing, praying, Christian women, equipped with the Word of

God and empowered by the Holy Spirit... the enemy really didn't have a chance, did he?

Training and preparation were a must. e3 makes it mandatory that participants get acquainted with what the culture looks like and how to share the Gospel with island occupants. One training session all its own was dedicated to such logistics as living in a tent, having no running water, and eating the barely digestible island food. To skip this knowledge would have resulted in the worst sort of culture shock. To be without communication of any kind (no phones, no Internet), sleeping outside in complete darkness with no electricity, and bathing in a river, is really mission work on the edge. It's reminiscent of the mission work that was done four hundred years ago. Most Americans, accustomed to comfortable living, cannot sustain this type of sacrificial life even if only for a few days, and even if promised a prize at the end.

In my interview with Beth, I asked, "What one thing sticks in your mind from the short-term project?" Beth related the story about how a witchdoctor came to them and told them he saw in his spirit that they would be coming to the village. He received instructions to stop them and to cast a spell on them, even if it meant death. He told them he showed up the first night at their camp to attack them as they slept but could not penetrate the ring of fire surrounding the campsite. The witchdoctor had proceeded to try to break through the fire for four hours but was unsuccessful, so he left. The next day, he came looking for the ring of fire and inquiring of the missionaries as to where it was. Beth and her team had no idea what he was talking about. The missionaries were dumbfounded at first and had no clue of the ring of fire. They never saw it, but the enemy did. Realizing the power of God and answered prayer, they told the witchdoctor that God protects them. They shared the Gospel with him. He laid his satanic worship aside and became a Christ-follower. They burned his idols. Wow.

I know we live in a fantasyland of motion picture heroes like Superman, Spider-man, Captain America, and the Black Panther, but these genuine teams of short-term missionaries are the real deal. We get all excited when a professional athlete comes to Christ or when we witness a wrestler from the WWE give his testimony, but they pale in comparison to people like Beth and her team who go out on the front line of battle for Christ. It's tragic but gone are the days when the local church related stories about the

The Great Go Mission

faithful men and women of the past who were bold heroes of the faith. Hollywood gets it, why don't we? Where have the days gone when churches talked about real heroes for God? These days our church time is spent on the pseudo-psychological mumbo-jumbo of how to get what you want, when you want it. Do you want to strengthen your faith? Read about the mission heroes of the faith.

BOXER REBELLION

I explicitly remember my 7th grade teacher mentioning the Boxer Rebellion that took place in China at the turn of the 20th century. But little did my 13-year-old mind comprehend the atrocities committed a hundred years prior against my fellow brothers and sisters in Christ.

The Society of Righteous and Harmonious Fists, called *Boxers* by Americans because of their martial arts training and preparation, hated Colonialists and Christ-followers. These young Chinese men were motivated by the Empress Dowager's tirade against foreign involvement. The rebellion started out as a secretive movement among the Chinese to completely eradicate Imperialism. Why? Go back to 1858, before the U.S Civil War, when the Treaty of Tientsin was signed and was counted by the Chinese among the so-called *unequal treaties*. It opened the Chinese ports to foreign trade permitting more foreign diplomats into the Chinese capital of Peking/Beijing, legalizing the import of opium, and allowing Christian missionary activity. Then, just as American policy was despised in China, so was our relationship with Christ that was brought with it.

The emerging church in America knows very little of the commitment and sacrifice of those who have gone before us. In the summer of 1900, there were 239 missionaries— 189 Protestant and 40 Catholic— killed by the Boxers. The two mission societies with the greatest toll of deaths were the China Inland Mission, who lost 79, and The Christian and Missionary Alliance, who lost 36. Besides the missionaries killed, a number of Chinese pastors, and over 32,000 Chinese Christians, lost their lives.

These numbers don't take into account all of those who were attacked, knifed, raped, and robbed. How do you count or describe the thousands of sexual assaults or machete attacks that severed limbs? It was horrific. Yet, here's the point: Wherever God calls you to go... you go. For two thousand years people have responded to the call of Christ to go and to give their lives, if necessary, for the Gospel. The Boxer Rebellion is only one example of hundreds of thousands of the enemy's oppositions to Jesus.

WHEREVER GOD CALLS YOU TO GO… YOU GO.

What I admire about friends and colleagues like Beth Greer is that outside of her circle of friends and ministry she is not famous. She is self-described as a "lipstick-wearing girl" called to go to a desolate place where there isn't even a mirror to guide you to put on makeup! She is a humble servant that gives all of the glory to God. She doesn't complain about how difficult her mission work is, nor does she get involved in humble brag on social media about all she does for the Lord. She just goes. Maybe my favorite thing she says about her recent going to Kome was this: "…and it's not one of those mission trips where you have a shopping day at the end before you come home!" Ha! For those that do modern short-term projects, you get it. For those who don't, an enticement to go on a STP is the promise to see the sites and do some discounted shopping in a foreign country, maybe snagging a bargain on a knock-off pair of Christian Louboutin shoes, a Louis Vuitton purse, or a tailor-made suit. Yes, I've done it.

We've even made going, which should be total obedience, into a game. Denominational and mission organizations have resorted to using alluring advertisements that promise exotic voyages for Christ. These tantalizing opportunities are made to sound like the adventures of Indiana Jones. The only truth in the advertising is that it could be your last crusade.

How does Beth decide where and when to go? She prays. She really prays and has her friends and family pray for her too. The Holy Spirit guides her in going. Is it really that simple? Yes. It is for someone who walks with the Lord. She doesn't make it into a big deal, she just goes. She decidedly nailed down that foundational part of a mission long ago. It's for the Gospel.

Maybe God wants you to go. Guess what? Yes, He does. It is never a question of whether He wants you to go and share Jesus. He does! Just make

The Great Go Mission

sure you go in the name of Jesus. You should be going anyway, that's the nucleus of Matthew 28:19. It is what you signed up for when you became a Christ-follower. I can scarcely believe that old-timers like the saints who gave their lives in the Boxer Rebellion would have stayed on the mission field, subjecting their children to terror, if they didn't know beyond a shadow of doubt that God had called them there. As Christ-followers, we go anyway.

JUST STARTING OUT

About the same time as *Mission: Impossible* debuted on American TV, I was introduced to the word "mission." I was three years old. My parents made sure I was going to be a giver of God's mission. They started me out with my nickel offering stuffed in my offering envelope as I took off as a toddler to Sunday School. I grew up giving to both local and international missional causes. Constantly, there was the influence of men and women in history who risked their lives for the Gospel. Our small congregation at Jackson Creek Baptist Church in Columbia, South Carolina was steeped in mission heritage, supporting missionaries by praying for them, learning about their respective assignments, and giving "above and beyond the tithe" to the missional cause. I heard the valiant names of my Christian denomination: Annie Armstrong, Bertha Smith, and William Carey were frequently called out in our "Sunbeams" preschool missionary program in the 1960's.

By college I had absorbed the biographies of Jim Elliot, Rees Howells, and Bruce Olsen. I then moved on to the accounts of Wang Mingdao and Richard Wurmbrand. Reading about all these heroic people of God have inspired me. Their Captain Marvel-like faith and ability to "go," despite the odds and the risk of death, fired me up. I was then introduced to Scottish runner Eric Liddle in the epic movie *Chariots of Fire*. I saw the film three times in the theater and have recently read the details of Liddle's life in Duncan Hamilton's biography, *For the Glory*.

While Hollywood was enamored with the Oscar possibilities, I was captivated by the commitment to God which kept Liddle from running on the Sabbath during the 1924 Summer Olympics in Paris. Shortly afterwards, Liddle returned to China to serve as a missionary for the rest of his life, even serving during the Japanese occupation and through the massacre of three thousand Chinese in Nanking in 1937; he was a martyr for Christ. My heart palpitated missions and my hope, too, was built on nothing less than Jesus' love and righteousness... all other ground was sinking sand. These guys were changing the world. I wanted to be a missionary!

WHAT IS A MISSIONARY?

Someone who goes on a mission. And let me add... God's mission... it is someone who goes on God's mission for the Gospel of Jesus Christ. In terms of the New Testament church and a New Testament missionary we can begin with the Apostle Paul. Paul's focus was his commitment to preaching the Gospel. He told the church at Corinth in his first letter to them, "For I decided to know nothing among you except Jesus Christ and Him crucified" (1 Corinthians 2:2). For Paul, it wasn't rock-paper-scissors to choose among other selections in Christian ministry. No! He was called to preach Christ. He was called and he knew he could do nothing else.

There is a dramatic difference in that impossible 1960's TV show and our own seemingly impossible mission: God is with us. The Holy Spirit never leaves the believer. If you and I could understand the power we possess by the Spirit, we would approach our own lives as superheroes for the cause of Christ! What is a missionary? A missionary goes for God, and God equips the missionary as he goes.

The mission to which God calls us is one of power. You see, this is about your calling to radically live a Great Commission life as outlined by the Lord Jesus. Maybe there is something missing in your walk with God and you are pursuing meaning. I believe that meaning is found in our mission from God, and for God's glory. It is due to our interaction with the action of the Gospel. The Christian life is complicated in some respects, but ultimately you are to be a spokesperson for God. You are an ambassador whether you are staying home and supporting missions or participating short-term or full-time. In any example, God expects your involvement with the message of Jesus Christ.

In short, you need to join up for missions in your church. Stop right here. Not Missions, but a *mission*. Perhaps nothing is more misunderstood these days than what it means to live out the Christian life as the mission Christ gave the church. It's staggering to conceive, but it is likely that the majority of Christ-followers are not living out God's mission for their lives.

The Great Go Mission

Read it in Matthew 28:19,20... isn't it simple enough? Missing in our comprehension of God's mission for us is the intensity and excitement God desires for us to experience. Here's another weird thing: The Great Commission is not called the Great Commission in the Bible. I read somewhere that we have missionary Hudson Taylor to thank for first referring to God's mission as *great* and that it was given to us by God to share.

The mission and missionaries have received a bum rap. Modern movements have sought to bring about a resurgence by terming church activities as missional events. I'm not wrong in this: Being a missionary *is* the call upon the church and your life. I want to say again, to be missional is my passion and zeal for life, but those are just words that often get lost in what religious people do. Let me sum it up in a twenty-first century vernacular: It's my passion. I've decided it will be where I pour my money, my ministry, my travels, my study, my efforts, and my entire life until retirement... if I retire. Living a normal life expectancy, I have less than three decades, but maybe far less... and maybe that's the case for you. When it comes to living out our lives for the Great Commission, we as Christ-followers should give it all.

> **When it comes to living out our lives for the Great Commission, we as Christ-followers should give it all.**

I have a missionary friend who has risked it all for God's mission, and he refers to it as his hobby. I love that terminology because hobbies are those things where we want to spend our free time, and we freely throw our money into them. What if Christ-followers considered their service for the King as a pastime or interest according to the American definition of hobby? We are so bought into hobbies and extracurricular activities that massive stores are built to accommodate our interests. What if...?

There is nothing more exciting than being on God's team, to accomplish His great plan of redemption and restoration. Get this: The Almighty has selected you and given you carefully selected gifts and talents to express the Truth of God, His righteousness, justice, and then His mercy in His Son, Jesus Christ. It may take you across the world. It may simply give you the opportunity to converse over your fence with your neighbor. But either way it's a massive assignment. It's thrilling! Why would anyone refuse to put all of their training, attention, and money somewhere else? Jesus says, "Do not lay up for yourselves treasures on earth, where moth and rust destroy and where thieves break in and steal, but lay up for yourselves treasures in heaven, where neither moth nor rust destroys and where thieves do not break in and steal. For where your treasure is, there your heart will be also" (Matt. 6:19-21). Put your livelihood in God's mission for your life and you cannot go wrong.

Not only has God given us a manual on how to do it but has also given us Luke's inspiring account of the Apostles in gripping action, harrowing stories of life and death escapes, potent images of men and women encountering the Almighty, and emboldening accounts of the early days of the church and how it exploded in growth while led by the Holy Spirit. The mission is simple, but the results are multifaceted pictures of a Savior that gave His love to rescue His kidnapped children! You should do anything you can to take up this "hobby."

Even More Glocal

Long-term missionary work is, and has been, viable and productive. To even contemplate doing away with it altogether would be a huge mistake. The entire structure of foreign missions was built on long-term missionaries for denominations such as the Southern Baptists and the Methodists, as well as other longstanding sending agencies. The LTM structure remained up and relatively strong until as recently as 2001. As you know, things began to change in our world. First came the invention of the combustible engine and automobile, then the jet-age. The change was easy to overlook at first, but when combining modern transportation with contemporary communication, something changed. Short-term missions (STM) became a reality. Looking back, it literally exploded on the scene. The globe is no

The Great Go Mission

longer inaccessible, local has come closer, and I suppose you can say we are now living in glocal times.

Here's another view of the glocal phenomenon: it means you can sleep in your bed, get up in the morning, board a Dreamliner to Asia, rocketing at close to 600mph, seven miles above the planet, breeze through customs with your fast-pass, sightsee, eat indigenous cuisine, swim a few laps, and then turn in for the night in a luxury hotel... all in one day. It means you can hire an interpreter, then plan several ministry meetings where you will give out Bibles, commentaries, and Gospel literature for children without worrying about the language barrier. It also means that in one email, several texts, or by video conference from the comfort of your plush bed while multi-tasking in between several other work-related conversations, you can manage an entire project. Glocalization is to modern day mission work as the transporter platform was to the USS Enterprise. You can go from local to global... almost instantly.

Glocalization is a joining of local and global works, brought about by the rapid advances in technology. From a practical standpoint, the church should "go" glocal. Although not a coined "church growth" word, the glocal concept has tremendous bearing on the missional efforts of the modern church. The local church can implement a glocal missions strategy with relatively practical ease. Gene Wood, in his break-through work entitled *Going Glocal*, examines how cultural changes relate to the mission of the church: "No longer does it really matter where we are on the planet. We are connected to the world. The Internet allows us to manage, supervise, encourage, and chastise from almost anywhere. Better yet, we don't need to wait until the recipient is home or in the office. We can write our messages and send them 24 hours a day, seven days a week, 365 days a year. The world has gone completely glocal."

The world has drastically changed since long-term missionaries were singled out and called by the church to be envoys for their denomination on the mission field. The past practices of LTM may well be outmoded. Travel has improved, cultures have shifted, and production of any kind has been streamlined so that companies are more financially sound. Applying this transformation to the local church can, over the course of time, make a massive impact on another church and another people in another culture.

CHOOSING A MISSIONARY DIET

Buffet eating is not good for me. I get way too involved. In the backwoods of South Carolina, in the combined towns of Batesburg-Leesville, there is a country place called Shealy's BBQ. It's incredible, comforting food for the soul. People line up around the building every single week, waiting in line to experience the food. The Shealys, the Christian family who own and operate the restaurant, offer all-you-can-eat for one low price. They are of course closed on Sundays, and they are also closed on Wednesday nights so Mrs. Shealy, the whole Shealy clan, and their staff, can go to church. A plethora of Southern cuisine fills their buffet bar: BBQ, vegetables, rice and hash, livers and gizzards, cornbread, and potato salad. There is also a loaded salad bar, that I've never visited, not to mention another bar loaded with desserts like apple cobbler and banana pudding that I've made selections from many times. Oh, and dare I mention the self-serve soft-serve ice cream machines... again a part of the all-you-can-eat price. I love Shealy's, I hate Shealy's. You can hurt yourself by going back to get all you want time after time.

> **Churches have spread themselves so thin and become so diverse that they really don't make any long-term or significant impact for the Gospel.**

However, there is an insider secret to eating at Shealy's that is only known to the regulars. If you're from the South you know what a pulley bone is, and at Shealy's you have to ask for them. Not on any menu, yet temporarily plentiful in the kitchen, are the coveted pulley bones. It's the heart of the white meat at the core, between the wishbone, in the chicken breast. They trim all of the excess bones off, and before chicken tenders came along, the pulley bone was the treasured part of fried chicken. Yes, fried chicken is on the Shealy's food bar, but not the pulley bones.

When you sit down with your plate, the ladies (the elderly women that have been working at Shealy's for years) ask you what you want to drink. At this point, slyly and discreetly you interrupt her like it's a guarded fraternity secret, and ask, "Can you bring me some pulley bones?" And

The Great Go Mission

then, she will discreetly ask you how many. Why? They do not like to waste the pulley bones at Shealy's. They are precious, delicious, and coveted. They will bring you all you want, but there is no to-go bag. Please don't tell the folks at Shealy's I told you this secret.

The mission ministry in the church has become too much like an all-you-can-eat buffet with a surreptitious goal. We pay one price of joining a church and we are invited by the pastor to find our place of ministry. Hidden, tucked away, only to be talked about when asked about, is the real ministry of the church – making disciples. Included in the church's "menu" of ministry are discipleship options. Many churches today have so many options on their ministry buffet that some people try to sample everything, thereby never really enjoying anything. You could say we miss the meat of the ministry by going to the sidebars of dessert and salad and never understanding what is at the heart of the meal. Churches, even whole denominations, spread themselves so thin and become so diverse that they really don't make any long-term or significant impact for the Gospel.

The problem has been the assumption that everything is the mission. I believe that everything is missions (plural) like digging wells for water, medical excursions, providing food and clothing and needed supplies, and things like urban renewal, development and education. However, *the mission* is still the mission. As Hudson Taylor put it, it is the "Great Co-mission." I call it the great Go-mission.

Here's a solution to the superfluous modern mission movements. Get rid of the buffet items, put the pulley-bone on as the main course, and offer nothing else. Churches need to repossess missions, plural, and quit allowing it to be sublet to other organizations while reclaiming the mission, singular. Let's take the short-term thinking, which includes glocal philosophy. Instead of sending one or two from our congregations for long-term projects, let's send many short-term missionaries, on many short-term projects, over the course of a long time. Yeah! That's it! Each church should find a long-term project (or several long-term projects) with short-term goals. Instead of using a metric of the number of participants and the amount of money it costs to go, measure the mission program by the numbers of disciples made and churches started. Over the course of years, in cumulative accounting, then and only then will you be able to measure the success of your unique mission activity.

Here's another scenario from the buffet analogy: Organizations, especially churches, want to go to many places and do many things. Maybe, just maybe, they have the resources. If you are in a megachurch then you probably do. But for the most part churches do not. What I'm saying is that maybe your church needs to focus on one mission project, with short-termers, over a generational period. *Be in it to win it*, was the implied message of coach Dabo Swinney when he inspired the Clemson Tigers to win the college football championship, and to become a dominant force, with just two words: *all in*. Are you all in when it comes to the Great Commission?

My long-term focus is to get Bibles into the hands of the people of Asia by supporting the pastors and church leaders there. I cannot single-handedly win all Asians to Christ, but I can be a part of a local team of people who make global long-term commitments by doing short-term projects. If we supply them with the Word of God to read, study, and grow in the Lord, then I promise you the Holy Spirit will make the demand on their lives to live righteously. Being pragmatic about missions points us toward responding glocally. The church can play an active part in doing missional work on the other side of the planet without being relegated to sideline supporter. When a church becomes glocal in their thinking, perhaps by taking ownership in a project, they will give more – and give more of themselves. With 4.5 billion people in Asia, it's ludicrous to dream of having enough money for that many Bibles. If I singlehandedly gave out a million bibles a week for the next 40 years, I would still only be halfway there. But one day soon, your Master will ask you and me if we did what we could to share the Gospel in East Asia, and all over the world. May your answer be, "Yes, Sir." The expectation will be from Him that it was a job well done.

GOING GLOCAL

My friend Gene Wood, a glocal thinker, predicts substantial change will result from missionary work going glocal. Too many churches think of themselves as isolated and unable to make a significant impact on the world for Christ. Gene claims people in the local church will become excited about missional work. They will then begin to attract big-thinking people and will discover financial resources they never knew existed. In short, returning the core of missions to the local church mobilizes the church into

The Great Go Mission

engaging in the true fulfillment of the Great Commission. Does your life study of God's Word reflect a plan of engagement?

R.C. Sproul was one of the greatest theologian-preachers of the last one hundred years. He was asked in a forum about his "life verse." It seems that a life verse is a Scripture verse claimed by many well-meaning Christ-followers, having adopted their favorite verse from the Bible as their own. They have written it in the front of their Bibles or share it often on social media. Sproul, when asked the question, seemed a little dumbfounded, which in turn dumbfounded the person asking the question. Have you ever thought about having a life verse? The guy asking the question thought everyone had one. Sproul admitted that he had never considered singling out a single passage of Scripture to claim.

Sproul gathered his thoughts and said that he didn't have one, but if pinned down on one, he would have to choose Romans 12:12. It says, "Do not be slothful in zeal, be fervent in spirit, serve the Lord. Rejoice in hope, be patient in tribulation, be constant in prayer (he added verse 11)." It was one of those times that I said to myself, "Self, I wish I had claimed that verse, too." The two verses makeup a fantastic description of a missionary.

WHY IS IT THAT MOST CHURCHES HAVE THIS BLURRED APPROACH TO MISSIONS? THE GREAT COMMISSION SEEMS STRAIGHTFORWARD ENOUGH.

If you wanted to paint a picture of someone going on a mission for God, then you don't have to look much farther than these verses, do you? Compressed into these twenty-four words is a portrait of exactly what God wants one of His missionaries, long-term or short-term, to look like.

Paul, as a minister of the Gospel, was a missionary on a mission. He begins this letter to the church at Rome, "Paul, a servant of Christ Jesus, called to be an apostle, set apart for the gospel of God..." (Rom. 1:1). Whose gospel? God's gospel. God's gospel is one of merciful redemption delivered to us from a just God. You see, our gospel errs too much on grace or truth. As someone said, "Too much truth is brutal, and too much grace is hypocritical." Paul stated upfront who he was, what his calling was, how he was called, and for what purpose. There is no confusion nor collusion. Only a direct statement of purpose.

Why is it that most churches have this blurred approach to missions? The Great Commission seems straightforward enough: "Go therefore and make disciples of all nations, baptizing them in the name of the Father and the of the Son and of the Holy Spirit, teaching them to observe all that I have commanded you" (Matt. 28:19-20). How does the church mess this up?

We've been guilty of a lackluster performance for Jesus. Is there zeal in your service for Him? Being fervent means a showing of intensity and enthusiasm! Smile about the hope you have every day and, by all means, build into your Christian life a habit of waiting on God. Expect the wait. Get in line with God by getting in line with His commands. Notice that Paul doesn't leave off the single most vital discipline of power in serving God on the mission – prayer.

How many people do you know today that are longing to live the life of their dreams? They go to the cinema or to the game and cheer and scream for their heroes, yet their lives are filled with boring decisions that lead to their making no significant differences in this old world. Your job is to lead them to do exciting things like my friend Beth. Just one trip, just one service of love with others in your church, just one mission endeavor in your neighborhood, gives you enough fuel to energize your life for a long time. Don't let the imaginary characters of stage and screen steal away your life of risking for God.

The real superheroes are not made by standing on the street corner waiting for a tornado so you can leap into action by changing your costume in a phone booth! Some will ask, "What's a phone booth?" No, you start by volunteering for a mission from your church. I promise you if you do, God will promote you to the front lines of adventure quicker than zigzag lightning. He wants you there. He will put you there. God wants His best men and women on the front lines.

BANQUET TALK

For twenty-five years I played basketball at the downtown YMCA with the same group of guys every Monday, Wednesday, and Friday, at 3:30pm... sharp. A bunch of grown-up men, we called it the *Inflated Spherical*

The Great Go Mission

Society of Columbia, ISSC for short. Our leader and president, RC, would call everyone each week to guarantee our punctual arrival. It never worked.

On gathering we would shoot around, get loose, and shoot the breeze about life until finally, my friend Adam called us to order. Adam, growing impatient and aggravated, would shout playfully, "All right guys, we can talk at the banquet!" It was the time-endured, euphemistic line that told us to *stop all the useless chit-chat, and let's do what we came here to do – play basketball.* We were old guys who once had a flare for the game but were now reduced to slow-motion replays of our glory years. Adam would continue in his shouting attempt to corral us: "we are all grown men, with wives and families, jobs, and responsibilities... let's just play basketball!" Interestingly, I've applied this "talking at the banquet" concept elsewhere—it speaks loudly to the modern church and how we take up the mission of God.

Meetings, seminars, and conferences rule the twenty-first century as the fix, or rescue, for our Gospel-spreading problems. Mind you, I am not referring to all the information we receive at these gatherings. I am talking about the phenomenon of just attending the meeting and hoping for spiritual osmosis to occur. I am talking about us assuming everything we do related to church or charity is deemed *missions* by God. It is not. Some of the things we do are just good things we do, and sometimes planning meetings are necessary. But more often Churches will jump on any old bandwagon because it gives the appearance that something is happening... besides, most think that is what they are getting paid for.

Pastors are searching frantically for the answer to their lack-of-growth woes. The banquet has become the game, the awards ceremony is now the arena. The church growth conferences, along with the church consultants, combine to create the spectacular events we live for. We are adults, with callings upon our lives by the Everlasting God, and yet we just want to talk about how to do it. No longer is there a systematic approach to our ecclesiology, nor our theology, never mind our inept understanding of soteriology. Our sin problems are amplified in this advanced technology age and are seemingly getting worse. And the answer seems to be to "dialogue" about it. Folks, we can talk at the banquet, it's time to go.

The Gospel Bus

A dynamic approach has everything to do with the mission and carrying out the Great Commission. The first missionary journey recorded in Acts comes to a close in chapter fifteen when scripture says that after "some days" the Apostle Paul suggests to Barnabas they do it all over again! That first missionary journey was exhilarating and gratifying. Paul wanted to see the progress of their efforts. He was interested in the headway made by the churches that were started: "Let us return and visit the brothers in every city where we proclaimed the word of the Lord and see how they are."

Paul is making his pitch for a second missionary experience/journey. He wants to go back to every place where they had ministered before and to see the growth. What kind of growth? I think this language lends to the construction of a strong case for Paul's priority of discipleship. In a modern church culture where we are great in calling for the decision for Christ, it's rare that churches have a follow-up or metric for spiritual growth. Besides, we don't see a great amount of time elapsing, either, before Paul's desire to return to each church. It seems that there was little to no down time between the tours.

Paul's methodology to the mission is apparent throughout his plea for the second go-around. He recognizes the necessity in going/returning, feels strongly about the purpose, and is aware that the right team is a must. Jim Collins' instant classic leadership book, *Good to Great*, can be summed up in a sentence: In order for the business to succeed, not only do you have to get the right people on the bus, but you also have to get the people into the right seats. Paul had this same philosophy in place two thousand years ago.

The scene that unfolds at the conclusion of Acts 15 is all about getting the right people onto the bus and into the right seat of leadership. After only a few days, which probably consisted of purchasing or making a new pair of sandals, taking an extra nap or two, and eating at their favorite falafel spot, Paul floats it out there: "Let's do it again! Let's now go back and check on each place we went and make sure they are growing in the Lord." As we saw previously, immediately out of Barnabas' mouth comes, "Great, I'll let John Mark know so he can plan accordingly, I really see potential in him." Paul responds, "What? Are you serious? No way...it'll be over my dead body before he goes back with me. He deserted us before!"

The Great Go Mission

It may seem disconcerting at first to look at the strife between two brothers in the Lord but not only was this significant, it was imperative to shaping the growth of the church. Also, I believe it was God's will, imposed over our remorse of "hurt feelings." What was John Mark's problem? We don't know for sure, but for some reason — maybe homesickness or maybe someone hurt his feelings — John Mark abandoned the first tour. Barnabas was forgiving and believed John Mark deserved another chance on the Paul/Barnabas bus, but Paul thought otherwise. Paul saw the importance of this second trip. And as verse 39 records, "And there arose a sharp disagreement, so that they separated from each other." The Greek word here is "παροξυσμός" and means an explosion or incitement that provokes someone while leading to or demanding a response. Barnabas makes an immediate decision to take Mark and go on their own. Many don't like the initial implications of this passage of Scripture. They think Paul's words sound like discord or bullying. But the leadership outcome is colossal to our approach to missions and ministry work.

Paul was adamant about having the right people in the right seats on the Gospel bus. Barnabas was fiercely loyal to John Mark. The big picture was the preaching, teaching, and spreading of the Gospel of Jesus Christ across the earth. God is glorified in it all. With two teams, the outcome is twice as effective. As Barnabas continued to cheer for John Mark, the result was the indispensable Gospel of Mark written by a freshly charged, once wayward disciple. For us, it is the essential pointing to preparedness and the correct approach that is necessary for successful ministry.

Chapter Eleven
DIRECTION

"It is not simply to be taken for granted that the Christian has the privilege of living among other Christians."   -Dietrich Bonhoeffer

"O Timothy, guard the deposit entrusted to you. Avoid the irreverent babble and contradictions of what is falsely called "knowledge," for by professing it some have swerved from the faith."   -1 Timothy 6:20,21

MY GOAL IS TO CALL you back to the centrality of the Great Commission. The Gospel mission does not splinter into a thousand different directions of "good works" performed for the disadvantaged, hoping that people will come around one day to put their trust in Christ for their salvation simply because we were nice to them. Jesus says, "I am the vine; you are the branches" (John 15:5). We branch out and go with the message of "Jesus saves" to the world; we don't branch off into kind deeds to beef up the message of Christ's salvation. The Gospel is one message and it's God's message of rescuing love, to bring the lost and wandering, home.

Ministry is frequently difficult and disappointing. It's often that my wife, Missie and I remind ourselves of the following story by just reciting the last line of it to each other when we find ourselves frustrated with people with regard to missional living. It's a great old missionary story, perhaps you've heard it,

> An old missionary couple had been working in Africa for years, and they were returning to New York City to retire. They had no pension; their health was broken; they were defeated, discouraged, and afraid. They

discovered they were booked on the same ship as President Teddy Roosevelt, who was returning from one of his big-game hunting expeditions.

No one paid much attention to them. They watched the fanfare that accompanied the President's entourage, with passengers trying to catch a glimpse of the great man.

As the ship moved across the ocean, the old missionary said to his wife, "Something is wrong. Why should we have given our lives in faithful service for God in Africa all these many years and have no one care a thing about us? Here this man comes back from a hunting trip and everybody makes much over him, but nobody gives two hoots about us."

"Dear, you shouldn't feel that way," his wife said.

"I can't help it; it doesn't seem right."

When the ship docked in New York, a band was waiting to greet the President. The mayor and other dignitaries were there. The papers were full of the President's arrival, but no one noticed this missionary couple. They slipped off the ship and found a cheap flat on the East side, hoping the next day to see what they could do to make a living in the city.

That night, the man's spirit broke. He said to his wife, "I can't take this; God is not treating us fairly."

His wife replied, "Why don't you go into the bedroom and tell that to the Lord?"

A short time later he came out from the bedroom, but now his face was completely different. His wife asked, "Dear, what happened?"

"The Lord settled it with me," he said. "I told him how bitter I was that the President should receive this tremendous homecoming, when no one met us as we returned home. And when I finished, it seemed as though the Lord put his hand on my shoulder and simply said, 'But you're not home yet!'

The Great Go Mission

IT'S A DIFFICULT MISSION

In twenty plus STP's to East Asia I have seen God's work repeatedly and continually and I am fascinated with how the Light of the world moves among the darkness. Don't fret about news stories saying that Christianity will be stomped out, the church kicked out, and the Christians stamped out. It's not going to happen. Reportedly, hell's gates are high in America and in Asia but are not able to withstand the consuming and prevailing power of the Righteous One, as Jesus affirms to His disciples in Matthew 16. The enemy, first and always, attacks via hype, morphing into hysteria on every front. Negative news headlines drown out the good news of the Good News being shared. It's massively important to ground yourself in the truth of your missional activities and ministry. You should particularly and decisively determine what you believe and why you believe it before you set out on your mission.

Understand this despondent tenet of missional going and returning: Generally, people really don't care to hear about your mission or your stories. **Yes, they will...**

...**listen** to you about your mission trip...for about five to ten minutes.

...**look** at your pictures as you swipe through them on your phone...but only about 4-5 and then they become disinterested or have to go.

...**give** you a nice offering for your initial short-term project...but don't expect much ongoing support.

...**smile** at you as your face brightens when you talk about God's calling in your life to go...but most are condescendingly thinking, "that's wonderful you have found your niche."

...**make** small talk about the condition and shape of the world, but they really don't care about lost people, communities, or tribes on the other side of the world.

...**nod** their heads in agreement as you talk about the plight of suffering humanity in need of our merciful and loving God, yet they are looking over your shoulder or looking to change the subject as soon as possible.

...**tell** you to call them and let them know how they can help, but secretly they hope you forget or lose their phone number.

...tell you they will pray for you... but you already know how that goes.

It's just not that uncommon to return after a mission trip where you have given your heart and soul— mentally, emotionally, and spiritually exhausted— only to be met with a lack of interest. Usually, it's not intentional. The truth is, even the masses of true believers do not understand the extent of the Great Commission. Is it because of decades of relegating and promoting it to a select few? Or, is it because our apathy towards sharing the Gospel has been exposed? The questions are surely endless here, but the answer is... most have simply decided to put their search and effort into other areas. Here's a reminder of what Paul wrote to the Philippians, "But our citizenship is in heaven, and from it we await a Savior, the Lord Jesus Christ, who will transform our lowly body to be like his glorious body..." (Phil. 3:20,21). Missional living, of any kind, first denies selfish desires.

With apprehension and trepidation, I will tell you that not many will cheer you on as you decide to go on your call. Go anyway. Initially, friends and family will wish you well. Your expectations of maximum support, applause, and accolades will fade after disappointment. Keep praying and keep going. The more you seek Him, the more you realize it is for His glory. You will find He is faithful, but you may not realize the full impact of your work until you are home, my friend.

BREAKOUT

The summer of 2018 may one day be observed as a breakout season for mission work among short-termers and the church. Several stories of STPs made the evening news. In one instance, a church group of fifteen teenagers and five adults doing mission work in Haiti had their travel home to Delaware delayed after being caught on the island during a local riot. A team from South Carolina was also stranded in Haiti due to those same clashes with local government. On another occasion a youth mission group from Kentucky headed to Mexico for a week of STP and had difficulty leaving the U.S. because the national airline could not handle the logistics of big group travel speedily enough. Does this mean we should re-examine the STP, curb our efforts, and consider scrapping it? No! It means the church is doing the right thing. The enemy hates the return to the heart of sharing the Gospel glocally and the fresh, new methodology by the local church. He will go to great lengths to stifle, squelch, and cause us to question our efforts. We must not be deterred, nor should we listen to Satan and his minions as they attack us from hell. It is necessary to see it as positive reinforcement to keep marching, and to keep going, in the name of Jesus.

Mission work is difficult. Paul writes his letter to the church in Rome for the purpose of keeping the relationship solid. At that point Paul would have been about halfway through his missionary career and his work would have pushed him through the Eastern Mediterranean, or modern-day Serbia. Equally, in the Western region of the Mediterranean was Rome — darkness — with only the church as the solitary point of light. Paul is very careful about choosing his words as he prepares to develop the church at Rome to have a missionary strategy.

Maybe the glocal stratagem isn't new after all. Maybe we can find it in the first century! The strategy of the first century church was both missional and glocal, and not isolated as an item of selection from a long list of ministries the church "offers" on their website. In other words, most are doing things glocally without even realizing it!

When the church is directed to go glocal, it operates and acts as the connector between the believers and the environment of the local society. In the first century, then, the first job of the church was to function as a connective center for training the body of Christ to reach and make disciples, in turn making more disciples. It then focused on training Christ-followers who became motivated to go and tell. Applying that strategy, whatever one's vocation, they were able to intersect and connect with their sphere and spread the Gospel to the end of the earth. That shows us that the local congregation needs the mobile team. The church was the mobile team then, and for the future of missional work the church must be mobilized as a glocal team today.

THE NEED FOR YET MORE GLOCAL

In further defining the glocal strategy and the global impact of short-term mission work, we must realize that how we do missions will be tested, contested, and determined in just a few short years. Nevertheless, it is a bygone conclusion the world has become glocal regardless of whether the word makes the etymological transition into the next urban dictionary. It doesn't matter because, again, people are doing it despite a formal recognition. In short, glocal initiatives can connect anyone, anywhere, at any time. Short-term projects are a feasible option considering travel, time, finances, and impact. Moreover, don't forget that the short-termers need the long-termers like a child needs a parent. STM can be beneficial in this glocal world, but it cannot arbitrarily assume an emerging philosophy that LTM was ancient missional history only to be discounted, discarded or pushed out. Looking to the future of a symbiotic effect of STM and LTM, glocal-guru Gene Wood, in his book *Going Glocal*, offers ten premises that the church, missions, ministers, missionaries, laity, senders, and goers need to agree upon:

- → We live in a much smaller world that we did a decade ago.
- → The shrinking world demands new and appropriate changes in how we **do** our missions.
- → The glocal world offers unprecedented opportunities for local churches to live out Acts 1:8.
- → It is time to explore new vocabulary to reflect our new reality.
- → The relationship between local churches and mission agencies needs continuing evaluation.
- → Career "missionaries" may be wise to considering a glocal partnership with local churches.
- → Reciprocity and accountability will reach new levels in a relationship between overseas groups and state-side churches.
- → Local churches will never again be content to view themselves solely as "donors."
- → The term "glocal" is not designed to create or **make** anything happen. The term summarizes/acknowledges what **is** happening.
- → Fulfilling Acts 1:8 is not an option, it is a mandate.

If short-term projects are anything, they are a movement calling the church back to God's Great Commission. The church desperately needs to recover a biblical understanding of God and its role so that it can expect and attempt great things from God again while guarding against the "amateurization" of Christian mission. There are also ramifications of getting involved in a radical independent missionary force. Do we really know their hearts? You see, Jesus died for the church, and I believe everything in Jesus' name should be done through the local church.

Also, reinventing the wheel, or what we can call *mission failure due to lack of training*, is on the rise. Yes, short-term missionary projects are flourishing like never before, but the solution is to avoid a convoluted, chaotic showdown between STM and LTM by returning to the genuine call of the Great Commission. It is simple: connection and transformation are not going to be determined by the length of time of missionary service, but rather by the depth of training respectively invested in preparation. Jesus did it.

CRITICAL ANALYSIS AND CONSIDERATIONS IN STM

Short-term missions has become a widespread phenomenon in the last two decades. A myriad of churches jumped on the proverbial bandwagon and sent out STM teams in order to circumvent traditional approaches to missional work, i.e. LTM. Unfortunately, the management and leadership are left to inexperienced youth leaders that are pressured to produce short-term projects to the satisfaction of parents who want their children involved in ministry. This is creating an administrative nightmare as well as a bureaucratic system steeped in potential failure. The reason is because leaders have very little, if any, experience in cross-cultural settings and are ill-prepared for the clashes in cultural values.

While some short-term projects have been successful, many have failed to produce the intended results. A less than serious approach produces religious neophytes. Churches, in their zeal to do missional work and report results back home to the local church, have introduced amateurs onto the mission field and subsequently created great problems for the real "called" missionary. Some short-term activities, certainly amateurish in their work, have produced grave results for the life-long called missionary. However, on the other end of the spectrum are some who have made missions and ministry a spiritual exercise reserved for the professionals. This inevitably leads to pride and spiritual bigotry.

The proposed solution is to define both missional work and the missionary. Some argue for defining the church as the missionary and others argue for better leadership. Just understand that a universal call for missionary volunteers in the New Testament does not exist. Christians are called to be witnesses, but it is not true that all are called to be missionaries any more than all are called to be pastors, teachers, or evangelists. As I have said, the word *missionary* does not exist in Scripture, but there is a precedence for some kind of calling for the missionary that results in something more than an amateur but less than the attitude of a position reserved for a professional.

> A MISSIONARY IS NOT JUST SOMEONE WHO GOES, BUT SOMEONE WHO IS SENT.

Mission leaders need to be developed primarily by helping people to think bigger, broadening the limits, deepening preparation, and stretching the goer. In the New Testament they are identified with the apostle. The English word comes from the Latin word meaning "send" (mitto), which, in turn, is a translation of the Greek word for "send," apostelló. Actually, two words are used for "send" in the New Testament: pempó occurs eighty times and apostelló one hundred thirty-five times. Pempó is the more general verb and refers to the act of sending. Apostelló is the more technical term. Originally it may have been used to mean a ship sent out with a cargo of grain to be delivered to a given port. But by the time the New Testament was written, apostelló referred to sending someone with authority to deliver a message, or to accomplish some stated mission, much as an ambassador or envoy might be sent to a foreign country. The New Testament word for *missionary*, then, is the noun form of this more technical idea: apostolos or *apostle*. The critical idea is *sentness*. A missionary is not just someone who goes, but someone who is sent. As sent by the Father, Christ is the "prototype" missionary, the "apostle and high priest of our profession" (Heb. 3:1).

MAKING THE SHIFT

The discovery of America, the embedment of Imperialism, and the establishment of trade routes shrunk the globe from large to medium-sized. Trade became truly global. Companies competing for foreign markets and labor make it even smaller today. Because of this shift our churches became world players in ministry outreach. This is where the long-term mission work flourished, and our churches pushed untold amounts of money into it.

Gene Wood explains that this golden era of missional work reached unmeasurable amounts of people as thousands of Christians were able to have meaningful local, national, and international ministry. He says it created a complex system that required missionary agencies to move people from nation to nation. For the purpose of understanding how missions have operated for the last two hundred years, Wood lists several assumptions usually agreed upon during the global era:

- → To make a significant impact, one should look at overseas missions as a career decision and required a professional degree from a Bible college.
- → This type of work required a clear call from God to a particular location. Many felt to leave this field of calling meant failure at least to some degree.
- → No one should attempt such an endeavor without working under the direction of an agency and its international professionals.
- → People who follow these assumptions earn the title "missionary."

The global era brought radical change in a brief period of time, considering the centuries of operating in an uncontested method and arrangement. Wood indicates that in addition to the assumptions above, churches were essentially informed and taught a framework of missions. It is what we know of as LTM – long-term mission. This framework developed into a paradigm of normal operation and assumptions regarding mission work. Wood concludes for us that the church has unfortunately learned these imbedded lessons that must be unlearned for glocalization to take place. He lists some of the norms in our long-held beliefs on mission work that must be undone. Here is a sampling of Wood's suggestions:

→ A "missionary" is a professionally trained and divinely called person.
→ A "missionary" will probably stay on the field of calling for a lifetime unless there are extenuating circumstances like medical challenges, children/family challenges, etc.
→ It is best for the "missionary" to stay on the field of service because the ability to have an impact in a distant location requires many years of living in that location.
→ Local churches are encouraged to know and pray for their "missionaries" but should not attempt to evaluate their effectiveness. The agency professionals do this best because they are equipped to comprehend the cultural complexities of each field.
→ Each "missionary" should come home and give a report to his or her supporting churches every so many years so the church stays connected to the "missionary" and has a better understanding of how to pray for him or her.
→ "Missionaries" need a large, professionally trained supporting agency staff that uses approximately 10%-30% of their funds.
→ Missionaries work for their agency but should report to their supporters. This is necessary because only trained professionals can comprehend the issues of a foreign ministry. Two implications which derive from this are: (a) Missionaries should not discuss problems on the field with their supporting churches. (b) Churches should not interfere by challenging or questioning the work of the "missionaries."

Somehow, spreading the Gospel and starting churches during the first few hundred years transmuted into an archaic structure for doing missional work for the next several hundred years. The *Golden Years*, let's call them, were shaped into a system that is now struggling to survive, gasping for air in the twenty-first century. These assumptions and lessons have led to observing, considering, and transforming a new glocal effort involving short-term mission projects. This glocal phenomenon is happening whether LTM organizations embrace it or not. The further shrinking of the world occurs daily and it is not a new occurrence, nor is STM. One missionary of the Evangelical Foreign Missions Association wrote as far back as 1987, "Christians need to see that a giant for the cause of Christ is striding among us. It's called the short-term missionary movement."

As recently as 2016, mission boards made the difficult decision of laying off many long-term workers in foreign countries. One organization made mission headlines when it announced the proposed cut of between six hundred and eight hundred LTM and staff. The call for voluntary retirement led to a startling loss of 1,132 workers, almost twice as many as expected. Christianity Today reported 983 of those were missionaries, as opposed to office staff. Although the cuts, made because of budget restraints, may look like a retreat or regression, it forces them to seek the Holy Spirit in guidance and renewal in mission work. It's time for a new strategy.

This incident does not negate long-term missionary efforts, but it does make a bold statement for short-termers, especially in a glocal society. It was the boldness of men like William Carey, who devoted themselves to going and living with indigenous people groups, that laid the groundwork for modern missions or, in this case, STP. What is going to be our response to this movement? Can't you see it happening? If you are a member of an evangelical church with a heart for missions, you cannot help but seeing and feeling a shift occur in strategy. While pundits are weighing the positives and negatives, one thing is certain: with so many engaging in STM, something is going to happen.

COMING BACK FROM BEYOND

A missional movement that totally adheres to the Great Commission is perplexing to a self-centered American church, particularly when coupled with and measured from an American social ethos. Anything beyond counting the usual numbers on a typical Sunday morning— worship attendance, visitors, and the offering— is as foreign as the Mandarin language is to the average English-speaking church. Recognizing the significance of Jesus' command to make disciples is sadly, yet surreptitiously, laughable among those ignorant to the Great Commission. Is the church today just uninformed? Misinformed?

Advocating STP, along with the glocal concept, for the missions program of your church is not enough to ignite a movement toward putting the Gospel at the forefront. The theory of glocal missions must go deeper, and way beyond the practical philosophies of the church these first two millennia. Comprehensive responses from churches regarding STM are mandatory if disciples are going to be made and true transformation is going to take place.

Some of today's church leaders have mistakenly assumed that people in the church seats are excited about missions, but they are not. As we survey the mission history, one can conclude that for 200 years the church was just trying to connect with a religious reaction. Glocalization allows for a purely organic response rather than forced or mundane activity.

For decades it was America that influenced other cultures with its work ethic, fashion, style, technology, and flair for freedom. In the meantime, the world shrank exponentially and more rapidly than the globe could comprehend. The world is changing rapidly and dramatically. Gene Wood weighs back into this glocal phenomenon saying "[w]e are increasingly becoming a monoculture. Other places do not seem so peculiar any longer because they are not!" This change has more of an influence than most can fathom on the way the church operates and thinks today.

WHAT IS HAPPENING IN THE WORLD?

Missiologists are quick to state that goals have been met, but they question whether the Great Commission has been completed. You can go back fifty years and see the brazen objectives set by wonderful Holy Spirit-driven servants of the Lord, and you can quickly calculate the poor achievement of those goals. Translation of scripture, availability of Bibles, evangelism, and church planting are all factors in the measurement of success toward the fulfillment of God's Mission.

Scripture, in the form of 371 complete Bibles, is available in 2,233 of the world's approximate 6,800 languages. Eighty percent of the world's people have access to the Bible in a language they can understand. On the other hand, there are 4,300 people groups who do not have any portion of

The Great Go Mission

Scripture in their language. Illiteracy is another problem. Even if they have Bibles, two billion people cannot read them. This problem has been addressed by organizations such as the World by Radio initiative, which is making headway but realizes the need has not yet been met.

Evangelism and church planting have made great strides but have further work to do before reaching their goals. Both have seen focus on a "saturation" method for spreading the gospel. Church planting organizations have been working to populate small communities worldwide with evangelizing churches in areas where there previously were none. At the same time, evangelizing initiatives such as the distribution of the *Jesus* film resulted in reaching approximately three billion people worldwide but, although it was an effective tool for planting the gospel, it excludes the all-important human element. Friends, understand the power is in the righteous acts of the called, not in the plan. The solution to reaching the world will continue to be *people*, and the strength must be returned to the local church. That will take all of us.

Here's another angle on what has brought about the quick rise of STM: Christian baby boomers took seriously the need to seek their spiritual giftedness. They had a desire for revival, or reformation, to come to our churches, and that has propelled STM. Our bigger problem was we were not prepared for the thousands of churches that have been started in the last three decades. So ministry and leadership organizations, as well as mission agencies, were launched to accommodate them.

According to Wycliffe Global Alliance, as of November 2015 there were a reported 1,778 languages without a Bible translation. That adds up to 165 million people with no Bible in their native language.

Then those same baby boomers who sought to see reformation began to see world missions in the same way they saw the other ministries in the church. This in turn led to them saying, "We can do this ourselves."

Yet another sign of a glocal shift: The world is connected instantaneously, and the church has the means to jump in and connect with it. It is beneficial to the church to participate, and to utilize the advancements to transform the world for Christ. Our job is to connect and produce disciples that are not just sweet, kind, moral people, but fully devoted, obedient, men and women of God. This connection center is a church that is going glocal in order to return to kingdom work. The church must continually redefine its mindset toward fostering people rather than incessantly searching for fastidious evangelism projects that bloat into a goliath, quasi-spiritual, corporate-minded body of believers.

Bearing this in mind, the church cannot afford to push "missions" to the side, or to give only a small token percentage of offerings, as their answer to sharing the Gospel everywhere. Instead, churches must exceed the glocal approach. The church has to actually *become* the missionary. Perhaps the reason the term 'missionary' does not appear in Scripture is because God intended not for people to become missionaries, but for the church to do the work collectively. The commission was given to the church so that every Christ-follower had a missional responsibility. It must be said over and over and preached repeatedly to every believer lest we forget our duty to go.

Expecting to discover an effective new prototype of evangelism and church growth but continuing down the same path will be fruitless. Yes, the church is awakening somewhat to the need of a glocal response, but "old" missions will not do it. Missional work was thriving just forty to fifty years ago, but the ability to adjust quickly enough to swift global changes may have hampered Great Commission efforts. STP, then, could be the revival the local church needs to be true to the Great Commission, and to make true disciples, in this glocal age. While the church finds itself somehow unable to project and make adjustments for future growth, the secular world seemingly has better vision than the church.

Cancer is easier to cure if caught early, but it is more difficult to detect. A business or corporation that has been around a long time is able to move things around and can look healthy on the outside, but maybe it is on the edge of disaster because of inward decay. If this is indicative of the church and the state of missions today, then the focal point must shift. Instead of reflecting on what could have been, the key concern should be over what today's servants are doing with the Gospel and how they are living the Great Commission now.

ONE LAST THING...

Perhaps you missed the star in the opening story in chapter one. It wasn't Phan Li, her mother, Greg Allman, the two dudes from the Midwest,

The Great Go Mission

or me. It was Autumn. Autumn flies under the censoring communist radar that searches for dissentients. She lives in a country that tolerates Christianity as long as it conforms and doesn't step over the party line of nationalistic patronage. Here's her story, a beautiful one, and it's all too common in Asian culture:

Autumn's mom, Betty, was a poor farm girl married to a peasant wannabe holistic doctor. His dream was the exact opposite of Oliver Douglas of Green Acres fame. When he fled the farm for city living, he left a pregnant wife with a two-year-old son, lots of bills, and one-less farm hand. Betty and her children were left to live with her husband's parents. Every day, Autumn's grandfather verbally abused his daughter-in-law, often hitting her while blaming her for his son's departure and desertion. One day it went too far, and the old man beat Betty, kicking her in the stomach, putting the pregnancy in danger. Somehow— yes, we know how... it was God's provision and protection— Autumn escaped harm and was born healthy.

The family were not Christians— far from it. They worshiped like so many Chinese: they adhered to the state religion of Taoism. What do they believe? There are some figurines involved, burning of incense... get the picture? They really don't know, and so it's difficult to even put into words; it's polytheism, it just looks like a bunch of Chinese symbols, with a Buddha thrown in there somewhere.

One day, the little group of Christian women in the village invited Betty to a Bible study. She didn't know what a Bible study was, nor did she own a Bible, nor could she afford one. But because of the love of a group of people in the United States who are committed to sharing God's Word worldwide, she was given a Bible. Not too long after that, Betty became a believer and follower of Jesus Christ.

Years later, Autumn was home on spring break from college, relaxing from the intense study schedule and visiting her mom and brother. My friend Tony, a short-term missionary doing long-term work, was on a short-term project to give Bibles to the multitudes of people in the same village. It was during a Chinese festival and, due to an emergency, his translator was called away. In the middle of the town square, Tony was pressed at every side by a mob of people who were crying for a Bible and asking questions he could not answer because he didn't speak the language. Tony yelled above the crowd, "Is there anyone who can speak English?" Autumn happened to be walking by at that exact right time. She had been studying English since she was a little girl and was now furthering her study in college. She replied to Tony, "What can I do for you?" Tony hired her on the spot to be his interpreter for the next few days. Those few days turned into a full-time job for Autumn. She has been secretly serving Jesus for the last ten years. Her job is so undercover it's like a Bond movie... not even her closest friends at church know what she does, and neither does her pastor.

Last fall, I met up with my friend Autumn on a planned trip with friends to the Holy Land. It's customary for many believers to be re-baptized in the same river as their Lord. As Tony baptized her in the Jordan River one day, he asked her if she had anything she wanted to say to her friends as they watched her be immersed. I got out my iPhone and videoed the baptism. I later transcribed the video, and this is what she said in her Chinese English,

> I know... that I can only be reborn once... after I know Jesus Christ, and I've already changed since the first baptism... and I, uh, want to renew my relationship with our God. And because I have all the grace from Him... and then I did nothing to get this. So... I... and it's like a dream, I still feel like I don't deserve this, I don't deserve all of this. So, I want to renew my, um, experience, how, I uh, I received this grace from Him. I want to, uh, present myself in front of Him, ...another new Autumn. I want to divulge my whole life to honor His name... thank you.

Autumn understands God's redeeming grace. Giving out the Word of God to people groups around the world is a good thing. It becomes the catalyst many times for the Holy Spirit to speak truth into lives. Autumn is one of the most special and precious souls God has ever created. Her tender heart has one goal in every situation – to seek God and be on mission with Him. I have reflected on that time when Phan Li's mother was dying. As I sat in the back of the van trying to escape into my own little getaway world,

The Great Go Mission

Autumn was still working and ministering. And the very first thought she had once she learned of that sick and dying woman, was to ask me to pray. The real foreign missionary that day wasn't me, it was a young woman who thought that her only job was to translate.

What mission has God called you to that you have pushed aside? Real revival in your life occurs when you honestly, humbly, and genuinely seek Him. Continued repentance for the maturing faithful in Christ is crucial, and prayer is essential and necessary as we wait upon God. A van carrying you on dirt roads in a distant country, or maybe just walking in the cul-de-sacs of your suburb and looking for opportunities to share Christ and invite to your church, may be the exact point of obedience God wants for you to turn this world upside-down. Don't dismiss the door that God opens for you to serve Him. Some of my greatest positions I've found myself in are when I go in obedience to God. Remember daily that He has called you to be on mission with Him, and it requires you to go... most of us should already be going before you are gone.

Bibliography

The Apocryphal New Testament. "The Acts of Peter." III. XIII. M. R. James trans. and notes. Oxford: Clarendon Press, 1924.

Barna Group. "51% of Churchgoers Don't Know of the Great Commission." Research Releases in Faith & Christianity." March 27, 2018. Barna.com/research/half-churchgoers-not-heard-great-commission.

Betz, Bradford. "Louisiana televangelist seeks donations for $54M private jet: report." Fox News online. Tuesday, May 29, 2018. Foxnews.com/us/Louisiana-televangelist-seeks-donations-for-54m-private-jet-report.

Calvin, John. *Institutes of the Christian Religion.* 6th Ed, revised. Trans. John Allen. Philadelphia: Presbyterian Board of Publication, 1813.

Flavel, John. *Keeping the Heart.* New York: American Tract Society, 1830?.

Gibson, Mel, Alan Ladd, Bruce Davey, Sophie Marceau, Patrick McGoohan, Catherine McCormack, James Horner, Steven Rosenblum, and Randall Wallace. *Braveheart.* Hollywood, CA: Paramount, 2000.

Guthrie, Stan. *Missions in the Third Millennium: 21 Key Trends for the 21st Century*, revised & expanded. Crownhill, Milton Keynes: Paternoster Press, 2004.

Hamilton, Duncan. *For the Glory: The Untold and Inspiring Story of Eric Liddell, Hero of Chariots of Fire.* New York: Penguin, 2017.

Hammond, Peter. *The Greatest Century of Missions.* Cape Town: Christian Liberty Books, 2002.

Hesselgrave, David. *Paradigms in Conflict: 10 Key Questions in Christian Missions Today.* Grand Rapids: Kregel, 2005.

"Killing of American Missionary Ignites Debate Over How to Evangelize." *All Things Considered.* NPR. November 27, 2018. npr.org/2018/11/27/671285330.

Lawson, Steven J. *The Evangelistic Zeal of George Whitefield.* Long Line of Godly Men Profile. Orlando: Reformation Trust Publishing, 2014.

Maxwell, John. "Three Es of Leadership Development." *How Leaders Develop.* The John Maxwell Company. May 20, 2012. Johnmaxwell.com/how-leaders-develop.

McArthur, John. *Good News: The Gospel of Jesus Christ.* Orlando: Reformation Trust Publishing, 2018.

Muller, George. *The Autobiography of George Muller: A Million and a Half in Answer to Prayer.* London: Pickering & Inglis, 1929.

New Greek-English Interlinear New Testament. Wheaton, IL: Tyndale House, 1990.

Owen, John. "The Mortification of Sin." *The Works of John Owen. Vol VI.* William H. Goold, ed. Carlisle, PA: Banner of Truth Trust, 1974.

Parsons, Burk. "The Acts of the Spirit & the Apostles." *Tabletalk Magazine.* March 1, 2010. Ligonier.org/learn/articles.acts-spirit-and-apostles.

Peterson, Roger P., et al. *Maximum Impact Short-Term Mission: The God-Commanded Repetitive Deployment of Swift, Temporary Non-Professional Missionaries.* Minneapolis: STEM Press, 2003.

Powell, Paul W. "The Church Today." Nashville: The Annuity Board of the Southern Baptist Convention, 1997.

Rainer, Thom S. *Breakout Churches*. Grand Rapids: Zondervan, 2010.

Robinson, George G. IV. "The ministry of e3 partners as a case study of strategic cross cultural short-term missions." Doctoral Dissertation. Western Seminary, 2007.

Robinson, George G. IV. *Striking the Match: How God is Using Ordinary people to Change the World Through Short-Term Missions*. Franklin: e3 Resources, 2008.

Rockne, Knute. "Recreation of a Pep Speech." University of Notre Dame Archives. archives.nd.edu.

Rosenberg, Adam. "Shaq is a flat-Earther too, apparently." Mashable. March 19, 2017. Mashable.com/2017/3/19/shaq-flat-earth-explanation.

Slater, Bryan A. "Short-term Missions: Biblical Considerations." EMQ Online. October 2000. www.emqonline.com/node/376.strategy?

Sproul, R.C. *Mark: An Expositional Commentary*. Orlando: Reformation Trust Publishing, 2019.

Stallone, Sylvester and Bill Conti. *Rocky III*, USA, 1982.

Vandagriff, Carlton. "Five Things That Make Missionaries Leave the Field." Church Planting. Blog. IMB. September 28, 2017. imb.org/2017/09/28/5-things-keep-people-off-mission-field/.

Willis, Dustin and Aaron Coe. *Life on Mission: Joining the Everyday Mission of God*. New Ed. Chicago: Moody, 2014.

"Woefully Misrepresented." Real Men Love Pink. Blog. March 19, 2010. awpink.wordpress.com.

GD Dowey

Wood, Gene. *Going Glocal: Networking Local Churches for Worldwide Impact.* St. Charles: ChurchSmart Resources 2006.

Wycliffe Global Alliance. www.wycliffe.net/statistics

ACKNOWLEDGEMENTS

I want to first thank my wife, Missie, for reading, proofing, and suggesting ideas for this work. However, she has done much more than that. Almost thirty years ago, I began traveling out of the country to do short-term mission projects and she never held me back. Rather, she always said, "Go." She is my partner in ministry and mission work. Her super-supportive attitude has been a massive encouragement for me and my writing. I have seen the world, but she has sacrificed by staying home and taking care of our son and our home. In addition, she started *Simple Ministries*, our mission to buy Bibles to give them out all over the world. She is the driving force, managing this endeavor while casting vision for our next project. Her heart is for the Great Commission (GC), and she goes to the Far East as God allows. Without her, I am half a man in this work...with her, we are a marvelous team for the glory of God. I love you honey.

For the past several years, my assistant, Karen Hulvey (a double English major), has read everything I have written, and has graciously corrected my grammar. I cannot thank her enough for her patience with me and for making needed changes to the manuscripts. She has tremendous insight in her editorial recommendations and layouts of my projects. Thanks Karen, you are valued!

My parents, Kenneth and Vivian, never knew the impact they were making by exposing me to the Savior at such an early age. I began learning about the GC and "going" because they took me to church at Jackson Creek Baptist Church as soon as I was born. They buy Bibles, and support the ministry. Thank you; I love you. Thank you also to my sisters, Cheryl and Laura, for also buying Bibles and going.

A huge thanks to my cheerleaders, Ben & Sandy Howell (my in-laws). They both lead the charge at their home church in Alabama to buy thousands of Bibles for people they will never meet. Yet, their love for the Gospel by giving and sharing is unmatched.

Thank you to Tom Fillinger for reading the manuscript for this book and for praying for me twice a day, and "every night as his head hits the pillow." Tom is the quintessential short-term missionary.

GD Dowey

Thank you to special friends, Arnie & Becky Cribb, and Joe & Chris Burns. They love Jesus with all their hearts modeling the GC for all to see.

Last, but important to my work and life, is Gene Wood. We've been together in the major cities of the world (Los Angeles, Chicago, Dallas, Washington D.C., Shanghai, Beijing, Tel-Aviv, etc.) doing and talking the GC. Gene challenges me to go and inspires me to think creatively. I cannot imagine doing what I do without him. He is a true friend in the Lord Jesus, and I love him. Thank you, Gene.

Then, there are three friends and partners in the ministry that I want to remember, but because of safety reasons, I cannot mention their names. I receive much credit for the work, but they are the true heroes because they risk their lives and their family's lives by taking me to places most people have never heard of or never will. They know who they are, and they know I love them fiercely.

Finally, I want to thank my son, Jack, for going with me many times. I'm directionally and technologically challenged, and Jackie always calms me by his remarkable and wise decisions in taking care of his dad. He is God's man. I love you son.

One last thank you – FRESH Church. They are givers and goers in the truest sense and continue to walk by faith, living out the GC. I wish I could list you all. Some have gone and some have given large amounts to buy Bibles, God knows who you are; He is pleased that you go!

ABOUT THE COVER PHOTO: In an undisclosed location on the other side of Planet Earth, my friend Autumn snapped this photograph of me with my brothers and sisters in Christ receiving the Word of God. It's a common scene in our Bible distributions to verify our work for our gracious donors back home. I literally have hundreds of these pictures in my files. They never get old... and I never tire of looking at them.

About the Author

Greg Dowey is the Founding Pastor at Fresh Church in Chapin, South Carolina (a suburb of Columbia). He is also a writer and missionary. His first book, Eight, a study in Romans 8, was also released this year (2020).

He holds a BA from the University of South Carolina, a MDIV from Southwestern Theological Seminary in Fort Worth, Texas, and has a DMIN from North Greenville University. He and his wife Missie live with their two old Boston Terriers, Racket and Miss Dixie. Their son, Jack, now lives in Indianapolis and works in the corporate world.

Visit Pastor Greg's website at gddowey.com.
For more information about Simple Ministries, visit provesimple.com.

OTHER BOOKS BY GD DOWEY

Eight: The Book About Just One Chapter
ISBN 978-1-7359876-0-6

A study of Romans 8, perhaps the greatest chapter in the Bible. Dr. Dowey reminds us of the freedom we have in Jesus Christ and shows us that walking with Jesus is a new beginning and that God is more interested in our transformation as believers than the political and geographical alteration of nations.

Available now from Amazon in Paperback and Kindle editions.

www.ingramcontent.com/pod-product-compliance
Lightning Source LLC
Chambersburg PA
CBHW032107090426
42743CB00007B/273